Trading Services in the Global Economy

Trading Services in the Global Economy

Edited by

Juan R. Cuadrado-Roura

Professor of Applied Economics, University of Alcalá and Director of the Services Industries Research Laboratory (Servilab), Spain

Luis Rubalcaba-Bermejo

Titular Professor of Economics, University of Alcalá and Secretary General of the Service Industries Research Laboratory (Servilab), Spain

J.R. Bryson

Senior Lecturer in Economic Geography, Service Sector Research Unit, School of Geography, University of Birmingham, UK

Edward Elgar
Cheltenham, UK • Northampton, MA, USA

Published by
Edward Elgar Publishing Limited
Glensanda House
Montpellier Parade
Cheltenham
Glos GL50 1UA
UK

Edward Elgar Publishing, Inc.
136 West Street
Suite 202
Northampton
Massachusetts 01060
USA

A catalogue record for this book
is available from the British Library

Library of Congress Cataloguing in Publication Data
Trading services in the global economy/edited by Juan R. Cuadrado Roura, Luis Rubalcaba Bermejo, J.R. Bryson.
    p. cm.
Selected papers presented at the 9th RESER Congress, held at University of Alcalá in October 1999.
Includes index.
1. Service industries – Congresses. 2. International trade – Congresses. 3. Globalization – Congresses. I. Cuadrado-Roura, Juan R. II. Rubalcaba-Bermejo, Luis. III. Bryson, J.R., 1963– IV. RESER Congress (9th: 1999: Universidad de Alcalá de Henares)
HD9980.5. T733 2002
382′.45—dc21
2001056912

ISBN 1 84064 610 1

Typeset by Cambrian Typesetters, Frimley, Surrey
Printed and bound in Great Britain by Biddles Ltd, *www.biddles.co.uk*

Contents

List of figures and tables		*vii*
List of contributors		*x*
Preface		*xii*
Acknowledgements		*xiv*

1. The relationship between services and globalisation   1
   *Juan R. Cuadrado-Roura, Luis Rubalcaba-Bermejo and
   John R. Bryson*

PART I   GLOBALISATION AND SERVICES: CONCEPTS AND
          TRENDS   25

2. Services in the age of globalisation: explanatory interrelations
   and dimensions   27
   Luis Rubalcaba-Bermejo and Juan R. Cuadrado-Roura
3. The globalisation of services in economic theory and economic
   practice: some conceptual issues   58
   Orio Giarini
4. A comparative approach to the internationalisation of service
   industries   78
   Luis Rubalcaba-Bermejo and Juan R. Cuadrado-Roura

PART II   GLOBAL TRADE, GLOBAL INVESTMENT AND
           GLOBAL MANAGEMENT   109

5. EU service trade, with particular reference to business and
   professional services   111
   Peter W. Daniels
6. Transaction modes and the internationalisation of business
   service firms in the Haute-Garonne   134
   Pierre-Yves Leo and Jean Philippe
7. Internationalisation of commercial activities: some recent
   theoretical contributions and empirical evidence   150
   Peter Sjøholt

8. 'Trading' business knowledge between countries: consultants and the diffusion of management knowledge 175
   John R. Bryson

PART III   THE LIBERALISATION OF SERVICE TRADE – THE GATS 191

9. Services trade and globalisation: governmental services and public policy concerns 193
   David Hartridge
10. The liberalisation of international trade in services: issues of competence and legitimacy for the GATS – and the impact of its rules on institutions 206
    Julian Arkell
11. GATS 2000: the issues at stake, an EC perspective 231
    Sergio Balibrea
12. An American policy perspective on service trade: the views of the Coalition of Service Industries on the United States Negotiating Objectives for Services at the Seattle WTO 251
    Robert Vastine
13. Developing countries and the GATS 2000 Round 257
    Pierre Sauvé
14. A real Single Market for services? 265
    Jean-Yves Muylle

Index *291*

Figures and tables

FIGURES

2.1 The four dimensions of service globalisation   43
3.1 The changing structure of the German economy, 1880–90   62
3.2 Service functions and the production system   64
4.1 Trends in service international trade, 1990–99
     (Annual growth rates)   86
4.2 Trends in EU Foreign Direct Investment, 1992–98
     (Absolute values)   88
4.3 Trends in world mergers and acquisitions in service
     sectors, 1987–99 (sales and purchases absolute values)   89
4.4 Main traders in services in the advanced countries
     (% sum EU, US and Japan, 1994–98)   95
4.5 Main dealers in service investments in the advanced
     countries (% sum EU, US and Japan, 1994–98)   96
4.6 Net exports and outflows of services in selected
     countries, 1985–98 (mio ECUs)   98
5.1 Services and goods BOP, EU9, 1996   115
5.2 Transportation, travel and other services BOP, EU9, 1996   117
5.3 Markets for service exports, major sub-categories, EU9, 1996   120
5.4 Exports of other services, EU9, all markets, 1996   121
5.5 Growth of all service exports, by market, EU15, 1992–96   124
5.6 Growth of service exports, all markets, E15, 1992–96   125
5.7a Change in exports of MBPTS, intra-EU15, EU7, 1992–96   128
5.7b Change in exports of MBPTS, extra-EU15, EU7, 1992–96   129
6.1 Adaptations of services to foreign markets according
     to the service provided   147
7.1 Worldwide location of IKEA stores as of 1999   166
14.1 Evolution of number of mergers involving EU firms
     1986–97, industry and services   271
14.2 Number of cross-border routes and breakdown per
     number of competitors   275
14.3 Interconnection rate for call termination in the EU15   288

TABLES

2.1   Relationships between services and globalisation: some
      examples   40
4.1   Stocks of EU investments in the world and the US, 1997   83
4.2   Service orientation of global trading: some key indicators   85
4.3   Service trading in the EU and the US: a comparative outlook   92
4.4   M&A in Europe and the US: annual growth rates and
      cumulative values, 1987–99   94
4.5   Net outward investment position in services   99
4.6   Net exports of services   99
4.7   Summary of service internationalisation indicators:
      sectorial distribution and annual growth rates of EU
      global exchanges in the world   102
4.8   Internationalisation index for services in the European
      Union, 1998   103
5.1   Top ten exporters and importers of commercial services, 1998   112
5.2   Trends in exports of commercial services, world regions,
      1980–99   114
5.3   Trends in balance of trade in commercial services, world
      regions, 1980–99   116
5.4   Value of exports to all markets and relationship with
      population and GDP per head, EU9, 1996   118
5.5   Exports of miscellaneous business, professional and
      technical services (%), by market, EU9, 1996   123
5.6   Trends in intra- and extra-EU exports of miscellaneous
      business, professional and technical services,
      EU7, 1992–96   127
6.1   Types of relationship with foreign customers depending
      on service sector   142
6.2   Types of network by the geographical location of the
      market   142
6.3   Quality control procedures depending on network type   143
6.4   Service activities provided abroad by delivery mode   146
7.1   World trade in services 1988–98   153
7.2   Motives behind the internationalisation of Norwegian
      companies   163
7.3   Positive factors identified by Norwegian companies for
      locating activities abroad   168
7.4   Factors that constrain the internationalisation of
      Norwegian companies   169
14.1 The importance of intra-EU services trade relative to GDP   268

14.2   The share of manufacturing and services in intra-EU
       FDI inflows, 1992–96   269
14.3   Evolution of M&A operations – share of the total   270
14.4   Intra-EU mergers and acquisitions – total number of
       operations   272
14.5   Mergers and acquisitions in the banking and insurance sectors 272
14.6   Share of services in GDP   277
14.7   Share of services in total employment   279
14.8   Ad-hoc state aid in manufacturing, financial services
       and air transport   285

Contributors

Julian Arkell, In private practice as a sole consultant specialising in international trade and services policy issues. He provides independent advice to private sector entities and to governmental and intergovernmental organisations.

Sergio Balibrea, Head of Sector, European Commission, Directorate-General for Trade.

John R. Bryson, Senior Lecturer in Economic Geography, School of Geography and Environmental Sciences, The University of Birmingham, UK, and Distinguished Research Fellow, Foundation for Research in Economics and Business Administration (SNF) Bergen, Norway.

Juan R. Cuadrado-Roura, Professor of Applied Economics at University of Alcalá and Director of the Service Industries Research Laboratory (Servilab), Spain.

Peter W. Daniels, Professor of Geography, Service Sector Research Unit, School of Geography and Environmental Sciences, The University of Birmingham, UK.

Orio Giarini, The Geneva Association, Geneva, Switzerland.

David Hartridge, Director, World Trade Organization.

Pierre-Yves Leo, Senior Research Fellow at the Aix-Marseille 3 University, France.

Jean-Yves Muylle, European Commission DG Single Market A/2.

Jean Philippe, Senior Research Fellow at the Aix-Marseille 3 University, France.

Luis Rubalcaba-Bermejo, Titular Professor of Applied Economics at University of Alcalá and Secretary General of the Service Industries Research Laboratory (Servilab), Spain.

Pierre Sauvé, Head of the Trade Policy Linkages Division at the Organisation for Economic Co-operation and Development (OECD), in Paris and non-resident fellow of the Center for Business and Government at Harvard University, USA.

Peter Sjøholt, Professor Dr Emeritus, Department of Geography, The Norwegian School of Economics and Business Administration and the University of Bergen, Norway.

Robert Vastine, President of the Coalition of Service Industries (CSI), USA.

Preface

The current process of economic globalisation is, undoubtedly, a complex phenomenon. Some recent reports and the recent growth in the academic literature on this subject have clearly shown that globalisation is central to current debates in nearly all social sciences. Additionally, it is a process that is not just about economics but also involves cultural, social and political factors, although economic factors and elements form its basis and constitute one of the key driving forces.

It is clear that there are important interrelationships between globalisation and services. Some service industries, for example transport, communications, advanced business services or banking and other financial activities, are clearly linked to the process of economic globalisation and directly influence its evolution. Other service activities remain heavily localised either due to their mode of delivery or because of cultural factors. Such services, for the time being, appear to be relatively unaffected by the forces of globalisation, for example personal services and some basic advanced business services. However, it is clearly the case that globalisation and services are strongly linked in such a way that, in many cases, the latter act as direct instruments of globalisation and contribute to the process of globalisation that is being experienced by most industrial and service sectors as well as economies. Globalisation and technological developments are clearly implicated in encouraging as well as forcing service companies, as well as service delivery modes, to change.

To explore these and related issues, for example factors that are influencing the liberalisation of services on an international scale, constitutes a task which cannot be covered in a single book. However, it is possible to raise questions and provide some answers or, at least, try to clarify problems and bring elements together that will enrich and deepen the debate. This is the primary aim of this collection. Our starting point for this debate was the opportunity to organise the IX RESER Congress that was held in October 1999 at the University of Alcalá, Madrid,[1] under the organisational responsibility of SERVI-LAB,[2] a research centre particularly focused on the analysis of service activities, their problems, prospects and policies.

Under the title 'Service Industries at the Eve of the XXIst Century: Growth, Globalisation and the EMU', over 150 experts from a wide range of universities, research institutions and firms explored the relationship between services and globalisation. The conference explored three related themes: the growth of services, globalisation of services, and services and European Monetary Union. The quality of the papers and the importance of these issues have led to this edited collection of some of the most significant papers presented at the conference on the issue of services, trade and globalisation.

The themes highlighted around the globalisation–trade–services nexus are developed through three parts and in fourteen chapters. The first chapter provides an introduction to the state of the current debate into services and globalisation. It also explains the structure of the book and introduces each of the chapters. Part I explores the current state of (interdisciplinary) thinking into the changing role of services and the globalisation of services.

Part II draws from and illustrates many of the issues examined in Part I providing theoretically informed case studies that reveal the growing complexity of service trade and foreign direct investment (FDI). Specifically, these chapters through their focus on modes or ways of globalisation explore trade, investment and services management from a global perspective. A key theme that underlies all these chapters is flows of knowledge (management models, modes of service delivery, and so on) between countries, and especially flows of both traded and untraded knowledge.

The focus changes in Part III to consider recent global trade negotiations involving services. The purpose of this section is to provide a valuable resource for academics and policy makers on the current round of trade negotiations. Some of the issues explored in Part I and II are revisited, but this time a policy focus is developed. These trade negotiations are on going, and the authors of these papers are some of the most important individuals involved either directly or indirectly in the negotiations.

NOTES

1. RESER (Reseau Services Espace) was founded in 1988 as The European Network of Research on Services and Space. RESER is an interdisciplinary network involving academics from all the major social sciences as well as representatives from the policy-making community. Its objectives include contributing to the progress of research into service activities, the evaluation of research undertaken into service activities, the development of new statistical methodologies to analyse the service sector and the development of models and theories to support political and business decision making. RESER is currently the sole European Research network exploring the relationships between service activities, the economy and space, and one of its main characteristics is to encourage multi-disciplinary and comparative approaches to the study of service industries, functions and occupations.

2. Service Industries Research Laboratory, founded in 1996 through an agreement between the University of Alcalá and the Chamber of Commerce and Industry of Madrid.

Acknowledgements

The range and quality of the papers included in this book give some indication not only of the importance of this field, but also the vigour with which economists, geographers and other professionals are contributing to the development of knowledge of services' role in the global economy. So, our first acknowledgement must go to the chapter authors. Most of those attending the Alcalá Congress have partially or completely rewritten their papers, whilst others have been commissioned to write specially for this collection. All the papers have been reviewed and the authors have accepted the comments and suggestions made by the reviewers. Julian Arkell deserves special thanks as he was instrumental in completing Part III and in persuading some very busy members of the policy community to contribute to an academic book.

We would also like to thank the participants of the RESER Conference held in Alcalá as many made important and interesting comments on the papers. We also need to thank the institutions and companies (particularly the University of Alcalá, the Chamber of Commerce and Industry of Madrid, UniCaja and Telefónica) that provided financial and logistic support for the Congress.

In a book that brings together academics based in seven countries and working through four languages we must thank the translators who have tried to revise the papers written by non-English authors to ensure that the original meaning is retained. In particular, we want to thank P.A. Lowe, who undertook a final revision of the manuscript under John Bryson's direction.

Finally, the publishers wish to thank Kluwer Law International for their kind permission to reprint 'Developing countries and the GATs 2000 round', Pierre Sauvé, *Journal of World Trade*, **34** (2), 2000, 85–92.

Juan R. Cuadrado-Roura, Luis Rubalcaba-Bermejo and John Bryson
April 2001

1. The relationship between globalisation and services

Juan R. Cuadrado-Roura, Luis Rubalcaba-Bermejo and John R. Bryson

The ongoing process of globalisation that has taken place over the last twenty years can not be attributed solely to economic factors but nevertheless the importance of economic factors should not be understated, for example increasing international trade, foreign investments and financial operations, business mergers and takeovers. The path that the global economy has travelled in recent years towards increasing 'globalisation' has left images of a shrinking world that are commonly held by the majority of people living in the advanced economies: the rapid development of new communications; faster and cheaper transport; mobile phones; the Internet; global commodity chains that span the world and link our supermarkets with most countries; the simultaneous worldwide availability of musical recordings, computer programmes and films; the rapid transmission of news, television channels that provide news coverage 24 hours a day; and, last but not least, the ever-increasing requirement for multilingual employees.

Hundreds of stories can be told that are all evidence of a single apparent reality: the world economy is now more interconnected than at any time in its history. Investment decisions, production processes, labour market regulations and even environmental legislation made by one country or company affect other economies, other companies and the lives of individuals. In fact, it is nearly impossible to think of a country that is not connected to the world economy in some form or another and it is no exaggeration to state that 'globalisation' is already an unassailable fact. The historical roots of this process are, undoubtedly, to be found in distant historic times; periods can be identified in the past during which parts of the world were strongly interrelated (Bryson and Henry, 2001: 343). There has, in fact, being a global production system for centuries, but the definition of 'global' should always be defined in relation to the time period under discussion. The difference between the global economy of the twenty-first century and other centuries is one of scale, complexity and speed of change. At the centre of this whirlwind of economic and social change are a set of economic processes and, importantly for the topic of this

1

book, service functions and activities. Many of the examples of global production identified so far are directly linked to service industries: transport,
communications, trade, computer and leisure services, education and training.
Some of the most obvious signs of globalisation are strongly associated with
the ongoing development (partly due to technological sophistication) of the
service economy.

Over the last ten years geographers and economists have begun to discuss
the processes and implications of what has been termed a shrinking world.
David Harvey even goes as far as developing the concept of 'time-space
compression' to describe the process by which there has been a 'speed-up in
the pace of life, while so overcoming spatial barriers that the world sometimes
seems to collapse inwards upon itself' (Harvey, 1989: 240). By this it is meant
that places are becoming closer together, trade is becoming easier and cheaper
and that an international economy is developing, as more and more places
become incorporated into the global economic system. Many of these statements are apparent truisms or even clichés. Nevertheless, most if not all social
scientists would agree that something is happening that is altering relationships between countries and even between people and that this something, call
it a process of globalisation, is complex and as the months and years pass this
complexity is increasing.

Globalisation is a seductive concept or what Axford terms 'a designer
concept of choice' (2000: 238). Like all such 'designer concepts' the term
globalisation needs to be used with care; it is used in different ways by different authors with varying degrees of precision. At worst it is used as a short-
hand descriptor for the dramatic changes that have been experienced by the
economic system, and at best it is used as a term to highlight the multi-dimen-
sional processes that are at work reshaping the global system. It is clear that
these processes involve the flow of objects (money, services, goods, information, capital) as well as subjects (people) (Lash and Urry, 1994) and the
creation of global or transnational institutions, but there is still considerable
debate over whether a single global culture or global identity is being
produced. Wrapped up in this debate is a much larger and even more controversial debate concerning the end of geography (O'Brien, 1992) and the
declining importance of the nation state. A common picture is of complex
'global' organisations that switch production and investment between countries in the twinkling of an eye and that economies are becoming placeless, or
unrooted in national or even regional economies. The nation state as a key
controller or regulator of national economies is being undermined by suppos-
edly 'placeless' or 'unrooted' transnational companies (TNCs). There are, of
course, real problems with this type of analysis in that there are few, if any,
'unrooted' TNCs. Economic activity is still nationally based with TNCs, on
average, retaining two-thirds of their assets in their home country (Amin,

1999: 41); TNCs are thus nationally bounded and are highly sensitive to national regulations and policies.

At its simplest the process of globalisation represents a deepening and extension of the operation of capitalism. This could be described as a simple quantitative change in the operation of capitalism, but there are also more important qualitative changes in the ways in which business is managed and organised. Geographically, capitalism operates via networks or linkages that tie people, companies and organisations together. Complexity enters the system as some places as well as companies are more linked than others and some places (and people) are even partially excluded from the system. There is, however, an important tension between the ongoing development of globalisation and the ways in which people experience the world. Whilst companies and economies are rapidly experiencing some of the ramifications of globalisation the majority of people live their lives locally, in particular places and bounded by specific cultural and even political and religious practices. This tension is reflected in Held's often cited definition of globalisation as a process that:

> can be taken to denote the stretching and deepening of social relations and institutions across space and time such that, on the one hand, day to day activities are increasingly influenced by events happening on the other side of the globe and, on the other hand, the practices and decisions of local groups can have significant global reverberations. (Held, 1995: 20)

There are a number of important myths concerning internationalization/globalization perpetrated by the media and economists (Bryson, et al. 1999: 23–33; Hirst and Thompson, 1992; 1996a; 1996b). First, that by its very nature it signals 'the end of geography' (O'Brien, 1992), and second that it is associated with cultural imperialism or the decline of local cultures. This type of argument can be summarised in debates that suggest that in this rapidly shrinking world distance and location no longer matter and space and geography are becoming increasingly irrelevant. This is a suspect and rather simplistic argument. Globalisation does not mean the homogenisation of social and economic relations. Rather, as Amin (1997) suggests globalisation highlights the pluralism of places and within places. Globalisation is not a one-way set of flows of goods, services and economic relationships. Rather it is a complex two-way process that links local and global processes together. Some geographers have labelled this process as 'glocalisation' (Swyngedouw, 1997). Maybe it is time to move beyond the simple dichotomy of global versus local and recognise that organisations are increasingly positioned in complex networks of economic and social relationships. It is via these networks that places become known and become incorporated into the capitalist economic system.

THE INTERRELATIONSHIPS BETWEEN
GLOBALISATION AND SERVICES

The 1999 the United Nations report on human development focused on the analysis of globalisation and highlighted the novelty of the current processes that are producing globalisation. The report notes that globalisation is not an absolutely new process and that the world was perhaps more integrated in relative terms during the nineteenth century. Twenty-three characteristics are identified that define what is truly 'new' in the current process, from the perspective of markets and participants, new rules and norms, and new communication technologies. The first characteristic emphasises the recent development of 'growing world markets of services: banking, insurance and transport'. Other points that are noted refer to 'new multilateral agreements – on services, intellectual property and communications – which are more binding for national governments than all previous agreements', 'internet and electronic communications, which simultaneously link many people together' and to 'increasingly faster and cheaper air, rail and road transport'.

Without services, globalisation would not have reached its current stage of development. Or, to put it another way, the 'globalisation' of goods cannot be conceptualised without services and vice versa; both are dependent on each other and this interdependency is at the centre of the process of globalisation. The International Monetary Fund (1997) defined globalisation as a process of 'growing mutual dependence led by a growing volume and variety of cross-border transactions of goods and services, growing international flows of capital and the speeding up of technology diffusion'.

The interrelationship between services and globalisation should not be underestimated; the development of globalisation and the expansion of services occurs at the same time, in the same places and is even of the same magnitude. Over the last few decades the globalisation of services and the process of globalisation have become increasingly important. This is supported by recent statistical surveys (United Nations, 1999; De la Dehesa, 2000). Many economies are now more open to external competition. World trade has grown 16 times since 1950 and between 1987 and 1997 gross investment stocks doubled or tripled in OECD countries, with annual growth rates reaching 6 to 7 per cent. Multinational, or even transnational, companies have become more powerful, some having turnovers in excess of the GDP of many countries. Mergers and takeovers have also increased in importance; in the 1990s the number of mergers doubled in the United States and Europe and the value of these activities rose from 2 per cent to almost 20 per cent of GDP. More and more companies operate on a worldwide scale; communication is simpler and cheaper (the cost of phones and computers represents only 6 to 7 per cent of their cost in 1960). Short-term financial flows have gained in importance compared to other periods. Between 1980 and 1996 the exchange of bonds grew by 25 per cent whilst currency exchanges and international loans grew by 24 per cent and 8 per cent respectively. Despite recent problems experienced by e-commerce companies, the term New Economy and its associated technology have become an emblematic sign of a new way of conceptualising the global economy. In conclusion, although economic globalisation as a concept has its limits[1] almost no one questions the actual significance of the global economy.

Likewise, it is difficult to deny the dominant position of services in most economies and their persistent growth trend. In 1998, in some of the most advanced economies, service employment accounted for over 70 per cent of total employment. According to the OECD (2000) tertiary activities accounted for the majority of value added in Australia (70.4 per cent), Denmark (71.3 per cent), France (70.8 per cent), the United States (72.2 per cent) and Luxemburg (76.1 per cent). By now, the service contribution to added value of countries not in this list may have also passed the 70 per cent threshold (United Kingdom (69.9 per cent), Belgium (69.8 per cent) and the Netherlands (69.3 per cent)). In terms of employment, including civilian employment, the number of countries that have more than 70 per cent of employees in services has increased: Australia, Canada, France, Luxemburg, the Netherlands, Norway, Sweden, the United Kingdom and the United States. In comparison to 1988 services value added increased by over 3 to 4 points and employment gained by between 3 to 6 points.

The growth in globalisation and the increasing rise in importance of services are undoubtedly the consequence of different processes, but these appear to be linked rather than separate processes. One of these links that must be considered is which services are growing at the fastest rates. The growth of service employment and value added has mainly been concentrated in business services (from 4 per cent of total employment in 1970 in various European countries to 9 per cent in 1994), and public services (from 14 per cent to 20 per cent). Other services experienced only limited growth (distribution from 16 per cent to 17 per cent, transport and communications from 5 per cent to 6 per cent, banking and insurance from 2 per cent to 3 per cent).[2] What is obvious is that the expansion of the service economy affects all distribution activities and that some industries are influenced by or play an important role in instigating or fomenting globalisation, for example advanced business services in particular (Rubalcaba-Bermejo, 1999; Cuadrado-Roura and Rubalcaba-Bermejo, 2000). It is important to remember that improvements in the quality of services may be linked to globalisation (increased competition) and such improvements may be associated with price reductions (for example in transportation and communication).

Advanced business services[3] continue to take advantage of the opportunities offered by globalisation and to provide solutions to the problems raised by the challenges of globalisation. Business services are one of the best examples of the interrelationship between service activities and globalisation. Telecommunication services or the Internet greatly facilitate collaboration between people and businesses located in different places. Market research provides businesses considering undertaking foreign direct investment or trade with the necessary information to make an informed decision. They can also provide detailed information regarding the ways in which customers located in countries that are not currently supplied with the product would consume the product. Minor changes to the product or service or to the advertising might be required to ensure that the product meets the expectations of consumers. International trade exhibitions provide competitors with the opportunity to explore the products produced by other countries as well as by possible competitors. They allow companies to position their products within the existing product ranges available in any one country. Strategic consulting companies can be employed to evaluate the impact of altering a company's organisational structure or the consequences of developing new production and/or markets. Lawyers provide solution to legal problems, but more importantly can be hired to ensure that the company and its products meet requirement of country specific legislation. Computer service suppliers allow clients to maximise the benefits obtained from information and communication services. Sophisticated advertising campaigns introduce products to new markets and can be especially important in opening difficult markets. All of these examples show the many and varied ways in which advanced business services function to adapt production (manufacturing and services) to the challenges imposed by producing and selling in a rapidly developing global marketplace.

Obviously, not all services contribute, or are related in the same way, to the process of globalisation. On the one hand, cleaning or security services, for instance, are 'passive' activities that do not contribute to the process of globalisation in any meaningful way. On the other hand, services related to the Internet are at the forefront of globalisation. In this sense, it can also be noted that services – particularly advanced business services – are not only *direct instruments and agents* of globalisation but also *contribute to impel it forward* through the effects that they produce in and on client companies.

THE GLOBALISATION PROCESS: SOME SPECIFIC CHARACTERISTICS

Historically, processes that tend to favour the globalisation of economic activity have always been strongly linked to specific service activities. This was the case in antiquity and in the Middle Ages, when major trading routes were established as a consequence of developments in transportation techniques and by the opening up of new markets that resulted from the activities of explorers and missionaries. From the sixteenth century, the discovery of America encouraged the development of commercial, banking, transport and social services. Later, the Industrial Revolution obscured the role undertaken by service activities by emphasising large-scale manufacturing production.[4] This led, however, a few decades later, to what has been considered the first major phase of modern globalisation (1870–1914), characterised by industrialisation, the development of manufacturing trade and the creation and exploitation of overseas colonies. The second phase began after the two world wars and the recovery from protectionism that was introduced as one of the measure to counter the 1929 economic crisis. This phase began in the 1960s and has been characterised by two related processes: the de-industrialisation and tertiarisation of the advanced developed economies. The rise in importance of new communications and increasing market integration have become important drivers of change during the last twenty years of the last century.

The IMF (1997) pays particular attention to de-industrialisation in its analysis of factors that are producing globalisation. Lower labour costs and an available labour force in developing countries have led to the development of an international division of labour or production. In other words at the same time that the developed economies were experiencing strong tertiarisation, companies based in the developed countries began to follow a process of 'delocalisation' or the transfer of production facilities to developing countries. This trend has produced and is producing multinational and some transnational or global companies. An increasing number of businesses can alter the location of their production factors by shifting investment (factories, offices) between countries and by organising production and sales globally. Companies are increasingly *footloose* and are able to locate and relocate to places with lower production costs but still retain acceptable productivity levels. In fact, differences in productivity and production costs (land, labour, environmental regulation) combined with technological developments explain the process of de-industrialisation better than other factors. In turn, services accounted for a major share of new employment creation in developed countries or, in the case of European countries, they have been able to provide employment for those made redundant due to the decline in industrial employment.

From this short account of the historical relationship between services and globalisation a number of general statements regarding the role played by services in the globalisation process can be made:

1. *Services affect the definition of the current process of globalisation.* In practically all international reports services are considered to play an

extremely important role in economic globalisation. There are two important points to be made. First, the 1870–1914 period that involved the development of a number of proto-multinational companies was explicitly orientated around manufacturing. It should be noted that the expansion of manufacturing companies overseas in the nineteenth century went hand-in-hand with the development of banking and transportation networks. The current period of globalisation that involves the extension and intensification of capitalist economic and social relationships is largely service driven; its configuration and development is determined by the dynamics of services.

2. *Services are nowadays an essential element of economic integration.* Many service functions reduce the relative distance between places, facilitate communications, introduce production into international markets or provide advice on global strategies

3. *Services impel and diffuse the most recent technological developments.* There is no new technology that is not associated with services that adds or generates value and enhances user utility. The New Economy, for example, is based on the provision of Internet and communication services.

4. *Services encourage the growth of a global economy.* Since economic growth depends on total factor productivity, services play a decisive role in growth rates. Paradoxically even though some services are not as globalised as many manufacturing companies they have a strong influence on globalisation.

5. *Service influence and the asymmetric effects of globalisation.* Globalisation does not affect all tertiary activities in the same way; some service activities are more affected than others. The reasons for this are partly related to differences in regulation and in differential degrees of service liberalisation. Given this, service industries can facilitate or hinder access to the advantages of globalisation. This implies that the current debate on service liberalisation within the framework of the General Agreement on Trade in Services (GATS) is extremely important as it provides an opportunity for all countries to benefit from the advantages that will accrue from service liberalisation. Services can emphasise or correct the asymmetric effects of the global economy.

SERVICES AND POLICY CHALLENGES FACED BY GLOBALISATION

Our argument so far suggests that the role services are playing in the internationalisation of economic activity will largely determine or define the rate of globalisation. This argument does not just involve the tertiarisation of developed countries. There are some indications of the role service activities will play in the future development of a global economic system. Important amongst these are the contribution services make to the opening up of international markets (this influences both global economic integration and trade negotiations); the level of complementarity or substitutability in relation to manufacturing industry (strong complementarity can preserve specific industries in developed countries); the evolution of total factor productivity (the lower productivity of services reduces the economic growth rate, which can both hinder and stimulate globalisation); and, finally, their contribution to technological challenges (R&D) and social ones (culture-related services or services linked to development aid) brought about by this process.

In relative terms, services are not considered to be significant global players, even if they have had a significant influence on the process of globalisation. The growth rate experienced by services since the 1980s has been extremely high, but the performance of services in relation to some indicators (participation in trade, international investments or business mergers) does not correspond to the weight these activities have in value added or employment in the advanced market economies. In the European Union (EU-15), service industries account for about 55 per cent of FDI, 44 per cent of total mergers and takeovers, and 21 per cent of international trade (slightly more in exports, less in imports). In the US, the figures are similar: 58 per cent of FDI, 44 per cent of total mergers and takeovers and close to 20 per cent of its international trade (26 per cent of exports). Additionally, for some major countries, services account for about one-third of total employees in foreign affiliates and close to half of the total production attributed to foreign affiliates (see Chapters 2, 5 and 14).

One characteristic of services that has been well documented in the academic literature explains the relatively reduced presence of services in international trade. Trade in services is hampered by the relationship between service production and consumption; in many instances a service is produced in the same space and time in which it is consumed. Additionally, there are other important characteristics of services that affect their tradability: problems of standardisation, difficulties of storage, and personal character. All these factors are reinforced by the operation of non-tariff as well as tariff barriers. The first challenge services have to face in relation to globalisation is their own *internationalisation*. New modes of service delivery have to be developed and old ways improved. It is no coincidence that the list of companies that can be classified as transnational and even global does not contain any non-financial service companies. Similarly, service companies only account for between 20 and 25 per cent of the largest non-financial multinational firms (United Nations, 2000).

By definition and characteristics it is unlikely that services will ever be able to be provided like standardised goods. Likewise, service companies will never favour direct foreign trade against foreign direct investment. For services, internationalisation increasingly implies *in situ* provision or the localisation of provision. However, it is important to note that different types of services are provided in different ways and that technologies and methodologies of service delivery are changing. The evidence provided in Parts II and III of this collection suggests that over the next twenty years service trade (direct and FDI) will grow. This growth will be partially dependent on new technologies as well as alterations in the ways in which services are consumed as well as the continued liberalisation of markets. The opening of service markets which were formally protected from international competition, such as telecommunications, is promoting strong international trade and is increasing all types of cross-border operations (mergers, acquisitions, trade).

Services are and will continue to play an important role in the integration of the global economy through the introduction of improved and cheaper transport and communications. These technical innovations are producing new types of global organisation and or network, as well as enabling companies of all sizes to enter foreign markets. All of this involves the development of new services, new forms of services and the spread of services between countries. Globalisation is not only associated with *a mere unification of production and consumption habits* but also permits and in some cases encourages *national diversity*. The place centred or localisation characteristic of services provides opportunities for 'global services' to be localised and to develop economic, cultural and social diversity. In this way it can be argued that in a globalised world geography and especially place still matters, and specifically it is especially important for service industries. Tourism, linguistic services, fairs and exhibitions and some consulting services operate and exist through exploiting difference and diversity. The development of transport, communication and leisure services are also associated with processes of integration but this *does not imply the substantial elimination of differences*. In this sense, the development of a global service economy is the best guarantee against globalisation becoming a source of or impetus towards cultural or economic homogenisation.

According to the proposals made within the GATS framework (WTO, 2000) the liberalisation of service markets and their opening to international competition aims at 'fomenting the global economy' both in services and in goods and that this process will benefit all countries. In any case, a careful follow-up study will be required to evaluate the advantages and possible maladjustments brought about by the continuing globalisation of service functions. One problem is differences in the mobility of service labour between highly mobile highly qualified professional employees and relatively immobile unqualified workers. However, there are indications that the increasing mobility of capital is being undermined or affected by the relative immobility of all types of employees. Capital may be able to become relatively placeless, but people and personal relationships (families and friends) are rooted in particular cultures and localities.

THE STRUCTURE OF THE BOOK

In this volume, we focus on understanding the complex and evolving interrelationships between globalisation and services. The key questions are 'how do services contribute to the globalisation of economic processes?' and 'how are global trends affecting service industries'. Most of the chapters deal with these two issues. The analysis of these relationships is undertaken both conceptually and empirically. Empirically the focus is on understanding service trade, foreign direct investment and identifying indicators of globalisation. An important additional theme is the consideration of the policy implications and challenges that result from the development of 'global' services, and especially the implications of the GATS 2000 negotiations. The rationale of the book can be subdivided into three themes or groups of questions:

1. What are the relationships between services and the global economy? What is the role of service functions in economic integration? To what extent will service activities play an important role in new technological developments being inspired by the New Economy and the Internet?
2. How are services affected by the new global economy? How do services internationalise and establish global links? Are trade and FDI alternatives or complementary methods of globalisation? Do services create new patterns of trading, investing and managing? What is the role played by business and advanced professional services in the globalisation of economic activity?
3. What can be expected from GATS? How is it legitimated? What are the various positions taken by those involved in the negotiations? Does a single market for services exist in Europe? Is the EU SMP the best model for GATS?
4. To stimulate thought and debate around these three themes or, at least, to provide elements of a framework that would contribute towards addressing these issues, this book contains fourteen chapters organised into three parts with an overarching introduction. The first part presents an overview of the interrelationships between services and globalisation. It explores the role of services as drivers of economic change and as catalysts facilitating the ongoing globalisation of economic activity. The second part

identifies types and models of service globalisation, for example direct trade versus FDI. The focus is on identifying the scope and form in which the globalisation of services is occurring. Part of this debate is under-standing the ways in which tertiary activities create new patterns of trade and investment as well as spreading new or even old forms of organising and managing businesses. The final part explores the policy implications that derive from the escalation in service trade, and particularly the role of GATS as one mechanism that is being deployed to try to liberalise service trade. The objectives and scope of the GATS agreements are evaluated and the interests of the negotiating actors identified.

Part I   Globalisation and Services: Concepts and Trends

Part I begins with two economists' understanding of services and globalisa-tion, Luis Rubalcaba-Bermejo and Juan Cuadrado-Roura, who explore the interrelationships between services and globalisation from two perspectives: the ways in which services affect the process of globalisation and how the latter influences services. The aim of the chapter is to develop the overall objective of this book and to provide a comprehensive framework for concep-tualising the complex relationship between services and globalisation. Specifically, they suggest that the present rate of globalisation largely depends on the ways in which services continue to grow and become increasingly inter-woven with other sectors of the economy. Services are considered to be play-ing a fundamental role in recent economic growth as well as in the development of the New Economy.

After this overview of the interrelationships between services and globali-sation, Orio Giarini develops a theoretical prospective that critically evaluates the ways in which services are conceptualised in traditional economic theory and suggests that economic theory needs to be revised to account for the diver-sity and complexity of service functions and activities. To Giarini, service functions are present in all economic activities and specifically in most cases they are the determining element in the production system. Service functions occur before, during and after all production processes from research and development to the production of tools (this includes security, quality and logistics management), storage and distribution, utilisation costs and recycling costs. In making this argument, Giarini acknowledges that the basic charac-teristics of the economy have changed and are changing and that consequently a revision of some of the fundamental principles of economics is required, specifically the construction of a revised concept of value. Value is now more and more about the utility produced by a system and this is linked to perfor-mance and costs (utilisation costs/service costs) over an unknown period of time. The duration of a period of utilisation introduces uncertainty into the calculation of the value of a product. Furthermore, costs and benefits are related to the positive performance of the system. The notion of an equilibrium price system, therefore, is replaced by one in which the price set at the moment a transaction occurs has to implicitly include the costs and benefits that will accrue through the utilisation of the product. These costs and benefits are difficult to calculate as they are determined by factors that alter depending on the nature of utilisation. To Giarini, these uncertainties come to the fore in production systems dominated by services and ultimately risk management or methodologies to manage uncertainty become vital elements of the economy.

The final chapter in this section by Luis Rubalcaba-Bermejo and Juan Cuadrado-Roura explores differences between services and goods and specifically identifies different types of globalisation: international trade, FDI, an international division of production factors and the development of international networks and frameworks. All of these types of internationalisation are influenced by the increasing importance of brands and trademarks. Rubalcaba-Bermejo and Cuadrado-Roura identify empirical evidence that highlights the increasing importance of each of these types of processes, especially FDI and mergers and acquisitions. In making this argument an index of globalisation is calculated that reveals that financial services, together with transport and communication services, are the service sectors that are most likely to develop global operations.

Part II   Global Trade, Global Investment and Global Management

The chapters in the second part of the book draw from and illustrate many of the issues examined in Part I. Though the development of a diverse range of theoretically informed case studies the significance of different modes of service globalisation are explored. The case studies range from an overview of service trade in the European Union to a detailed account of flows of management knowledges between the US and the UK.

Part II begins with a contribution from Peter Daniels on international trade and the evolving pattern of trade in services within the EU and between the EU, the US, Japan and the rest of the world over the period 1987–96. Particularly interesting are the trends identified in the pattern, value and structure of trade in the fastest growing 'other services' group, especially miscellaneous business, professional and technical services. Measures have been introduced by the EU to stimulate cross-border service trade within and beyond the EU. Nevertheless the evidence suggests that the service share of total trade (merchandise and services) has increased at a lower rate than might be expected given the significant expansion of services that has occurred in the economies of most EU member countries. There are, however, some indications that intra-EU trade in miscellaneous business, professional and technical services is expanding in response to new opportunities created by the Single European Market.

Complementing the more general discussion of European service trade by Daniels, Pierre-Yves Leo and Jean Philippe provide a detailed account of the internationalisation of business service firms located in three French metropolitan areas (Lyon, Marseille and Toulouse). Empirical studies of service globalisation have concentrated on exploring the strategies and activities of multinational companies. It is not only large companies that have developed overseas trade or engaged in FDI, but also small and medium-sized enterprises (SMEs). A survey of 121 business service firms was undertaken that shows that a significant proportion of SMEs have developed overseas markets. Two strategies are identified that are used by these companies to trade abroad: a reactive approach that involves following existing clients that have begun to trade overseas and a proactive approach that involves companies actively seeking to develop foreign markets. Closely bound up with the ability to develop foreign markets are issues concerning the mode of service delivery, FDI or networking arrangement and the ability to control the quality of the services provided. These decisions determine the competitive advantage of the supplied services. Another important issue concerns adaptations to the service provided to foreign clients as well as the diversification of supplied services. Extending the market of an existing service or adaptations to the supplied services might undermine the French company's competitive advantage.

The empirical content chosen by Peter Sjøholt to analyse service globalisation comes from a study of the Norwegian wholesale and retail trades. His chapter explores existing conceptualisations of service trade by exploring three related questions: why do firms develop international markets?, how do firms develop international markets? and where do they internationalise? The theoretical focus concentrates on the eclectic paradigm and the OLI framework (Ownership, Locational Advantages, Internalisation Advantages) and explores the peculiar behaviour of service firms and markets. Companies decide to enter foreign markets by either push or pull factors that are similar to Leo and Philippe's reactive and proactive strategies. However, where Sjøholt differs from Leo and Philippe is the emphasis that he places on cultural factors. Companies developing foreign markets need to be aware of the cultural, institutional and political factors that will affect their operations. The ability to modify behaviour and adapt services and management structures to these factors is considered to be an essential element of success.

Finally, John Bryson demonstrates how trade does not just involve the provision of services or of goods, but also involves the transfer of information and, more importantly, knowledge. In this context the development of an international or even global economy is associated with the transfer of management knowledges both as a direct result of companies engaged in FDI or via the activities of business service professionals and more specifically management consultants. In his contribution two management ideas – Taylorism and Total Quality Management (TQM) – are explored to show not only the long-term impact these theories had on the organisation of production but also the variable interpretations of these theories that were constructed by managers. Only some management ideas become popular. Popularity comes from the adopation of the idea by business magazines, the general business press, MBA courses and by consultants. The success of Taylor's ideas was less to do with the concepts he developed, and more to do with Taylor's reputation as an engineer. The tradability of a management idea is, at least in part, a function of how these ideas are conveyed to those who might be persuaded to use them by the business press, competitors or consultants.

Part III   The Liberalisation of Service Trade: the GATS

Part III of the book considers the important issue of the liberalisation of service trade and the ongoing international negotiations. Most of the contributions explore the GATS (General Agreement on Trade in Services) and the possibilities that this agreement offers for escalating service trade. The Uruguay round of negotiations was the first to explore the problems of service trade, and it was this round that produced the GATS agreement that was signed in January 1995. This agreement aimed to increase the volume of international trade with one projected consequence being increased economic growth and social welfare. This relationship between trade, growth and welfare occurred after the GATT agreement of 1947.

The GATS are a complex series of negotiations that would be impossible to explore in a single volume. The objectives of this book were chosen to highlight some of the most important aspects of service trade and liberalisation and more specifically to supplement rather than replicate the collection of essays edited by Sauvé and Stern (2000). These essays provide an in-depth analysis of negotiating strategies, agreement principles and the problems that result from conflicting national trade regulations.

This part of the book is structured around two themes: first, the problems of legitimacy and, second, the misunderstandings that result from the interpretations of the agreement held by the three most important actors in the negotiations: the European Union, the United States and developing countries. The first theme is explored by the contributors through identifying the opportunities and limitations of the GATS negotiations and trying to identify the agreement's scope and the various positions taken by the major actors in the process. Taken as a whole these chapters provide an indication of the potential that the GATS have to encourage an increase in the globalisation of service activities. The second theme involves representatives from some of the major organisations and countries involved in the negotiations discussing and justifying their positions in the trade rounds.

David Hartridge, Director of the World Trade Organisation's Service Division, begins this section with an analysis of the scope of GATS and the misunderstandings that result from conflicting interpretations of the aims and objectives of the negotiations. He begins by recognising the value of a debate that has until January 2000 being solely the preserve of specialists. Since January 2000 and the Seattle negotiations many misunderstandings of the GATS have developed in both the popular and policy press. Many of the arguments made against continued GATS negotiations, according to Hartridge, are founded upon an unfounded perceived threat to national sovereignty and democracy. The agreement excludes, for instance, services supplied by or for governments. Such services will continue to be regulated nationally even when they are provided by monopolies or are public services that are also provided by private firms. Similar confusion occurs over the rights to regulation retained by the member states of the World Trade Organisation (WTO). The WTO does not set standards and the regulations that guarantee service quality are determined and policed nationally. A good example is accountancy where the agreement has little to say about qualification or standards, but rather concentrates on transparency, access to information and equality in the treatment of foreign applicants. Additionally, the flexibility of the system is guaranteed by the right each country has to choose those sectors that will be included in the negotiations and by the principle of progressive liberalisation.

Julian Arkell's contribution develops a similar argument by exploring the legitimacy of the GATS. The GATS legitimacy is not very different from that of the organisation on which it is based, the WTO. In both cases, the issues surrounding legitimacy are similar, for instance, the representativeness of the member states during negotiations, the ethical or moral referents and the necessary balances between suppliers and customers or between winners and losers. The GATS principles can be applied flexibly and, as with the principle of progressive liberalisation, they offer one mechanism for legitimising countries that sign up to the agreements. One of the interesting aspects of this chapter is the brief summary of service sectors affected by the agreements. Each sector is affected in different ways from those that are nearly completely included in the agreement (financial services) to others which have yet to be significantly incorporated into the negotiations (tourism). It is important to note from this analysis that these sectors operate under different national regulatory structures and in some cases the national regulations were developed many years ago as is the case for professional services.

The European Union is one of the most significant actors in the service negotiations. Sergio Balibrea, of the European Commission, provides an analysis of the GATS from the perspective of the European Union. Service trade is a very important component of the European economy. The development of a single intra-European market for services and the relatively liberal position taken by the Commission for some services (financial and telecommunications) has resulted in the European Commission playing an active role in the negotiations. The Commission has both encouraged service liberalisation as well as being involved in the introduction of exceptions to the agreements, for example public services. Accordingly, Balibrea's contribution explores the definition of the GATS as well as its structure and the type of agreements. This chapter provides a useful overview of the agreement that would be especially helpful for anyone unfamiliar with the negotiations. During the course of the chapter the current state of the negotiations in each of the main sectors is identified and an analysis presented that highlights the importance of each sector and the European's Union's position. An interesting aspect of this chapter is the emphasis placed on the GATS as an agreement of potential rather than actuality. By this it is meant that the impacts of the agreement will take many years to be realised and that different countries and sectors will experience different levels of trade liberalisation. It is also worth noting that the GATS must also be understood in relation to other discussions that may extend the impact of the negotiations: MFN exemptions review; the e-commerce work programme; the air transport review and the review of accounting rates in telecommunication services.

The European perspective is countered by a brief but incisive contribution made by Robert Vastine, President of the CSI, who describes the United States' position in relation to the GATS. For the US the GATS are an extremely important instrument for furthering the development of trade and FDI of North American services. The GATS will encourage the growth of multinational service firms, compensate for the trade deficit in goods and increase economic growth. Vastine cites Hufbauer and Warrens (1999) estimate that suggests that comprehensive liberalisation of services could raise global GDP by 4–6 per cent and increase the long-term global growth rate from 3.2 per cent to 5 per cent. The US takes a highly liberal position within the GATS framework and this replicates its stance taken in the agreements on financial services and telecommunications. In particular, Vastine emphasises the requirement for the liberalisation of the delivery of services via the transfer of people. This type of service delivery has been largely neglected in the current negotiations. He also stresses the requirement for encouraging pro-competitive regulatory reforms and guaranteeing full competition in sectors such as electronic commerce.

A third position on GATS, explored by Pierre Sauvé from the OECD, is that of developing countries. There are a variety of economic and political reasons that initially prevent poorer countries from entering the GATS, for instance the perception that the GATS weakens national sovereignty or that developing countries do not have much to gain in negotiations involving service sectors in which they do not possess competitive advantages. Nevertheless, there are signs that this attitude is changing. Some developing countries are now playing an active role in the agreements that have already been negotiated on in the work being undertaken by current negotiating groups – the convenience of adopting agreements that promote pro-competitive regulations is beginning to be recognised. The mere existence of the GATS and the references to the transparency of international standards or the future liberalisation of the movement of service suppliers are beginning to be considered as opportunities. Some developing countries are introducing the necessary national reforms and are considering trying to reduce the problems of asymmetric information that prejudices reforms. These developments are one incentive to attract the human capital that these economies urgently require. Development in e-commerce and the liberalisation of this sector may provide developing countries with comparative advantage and the opportunity of developing new export markets.

The book concludes with a chapter by Jean-Yves Muylle, of the European Commission, on the Single Service Market in Europe who explores the inter-relationships between the processes of international service liberalisation and national or regional policies (European Union, NAFTA, Mercosur). The chapter begins with a description of indicators of service internationalisation and integration in Europe (this complements the discussion in Chapter 2) and follows this by highlighting the importance and growth of service trade, in general, and intra-European ones in particular. The focus of the analyses is the limited impact that the Single Market Programme has had on services. Positive effects have only been identified by 35 per cent of service firms as against 45 per cent of manufacturing companies. Muylle also suggests that the European Union needs to try to enhance attempts to increase the integration of service markets throughout Europe. The obvious problem is that services are notoriously localised and not very sensitive to liberalising measures. The principle of mutual recognition that inspired the creation of the Single Services Market in the 1990s, requires a fresh impetus. What is required is stronger coordination with other policies and a closer follow-up of the proportionality between the cases in which this principle is not accepted and the objectives of general interest on which the restriction is based. The plan of the Commission to create a single market, both effective and for the benefit of all, highlights services as the sector that requires a stronger effort to eliminate trade barriers and impede the creation of new ones. The European Council held in Lisbon followed the same line by including services within the framework of structural reforms necessary to improve economic growth.

SOME FINAL REMARKS

It is always difficult and even problematic to reduce to simple conclusions a collection of chapters that are so rich in ideas and suggestions. In fact, it does not seem appropriate to try to establish an overall conclusion. Nevertheless, this does not mean that it is impossible to select points which, in our opinion, should be emphasised, for example:

1. The globalisation of services is the result of a complex process, influenced by both historical, economic and cultural factors. The ongoing trend towards the globalisation of service functions produces mutual benefits for other parts of the production process. The development of the New Economy is closely associated with the globalisation of advanced producer services. Globalisation is predominantly the result of the quality and lower costs of many services which, over time, have gained in technological intensity, in real productivity and in their capacity to generate added value both directly and indirectly.

2. The globalisation of service functions is playing an important role in stimulating the globalisation of other activities. Service functions contribute to the overall efficiency of the economic system by stimulating creativity that is a necessary requirement for successful global trade. Service-inspired creativity reduces the uncertainty associated with globalisation by, for example, drawing upon the expertise, experiences and knowledges of management consultants, theorists and authors. Management consultancy and business management theories have trained and are training companies to compete and to develop strategies to maintain competitiveness in an increasingly global market place.

3. The globalisation of services has developed and is developing in multiple but complementary ways. The different types of international trade constitute the most visible sign of the strategies deployed by service companies as they become more global – for example networking, foreign affiliates and franchises; the latter being led by the role of trademarks, distinctive elements of the way service markets respond to asymmetric information through the use of reputational or symbolic signs. The complementarity of forms can also be observed between international trade and direct foreign investment (once considered as alternative forms) and between direct greenfield investment and mergers and takeovers.

4. Indicators of international transactions reveal the extent of the globalisation of services. The share of international service trade is still (relatively) modest, but it is increasing at a faster rate than goods. Nevertheless, the European service statistics reveal that service trade is lower than can be expected and is lower than the position of services in the US. However,

over the last few years direct investment, mergers and takeovers of service activities have experienced higher growth rates than goods. Some service industries are more open to internationalisation, according to their own characteristics and internal dynamism (financial services and telecommunications).

5. Along with traditional macroeconomic factors, internal factors increasingly determine the competitive advantages of firms. Although international expansion is often a reactive process the evidence presented in this book suggests that it is also a pro-active strategy. Each type of service tends to favour a particular method of international expansion. Networking and the quality control procedures are important factors that are a feature of most strategies. Cultural proximity and the capacity to adapt to local socioeconomic contexts constitute one of the most important factors in the international expansion of standardised services.

The chapters on the GATS and some of the chapters on globalisation provide some interesting elements that must be considered by individuals and organisations engaged in developing policy in this area. Some of the most interesting issues identified are:

1. The increasing importance of service industries and their internationalisation and the development of service markets through national and international liberalisation and deregulation can improve both economic growth and social welfare. Empirical evidence highlights the advantages of services trade liberalisation in all its aspects and forms, and for all countries. Service liberalisation, however, needs to be defined especially in relation to which sectors can be liberalised and to what extent, and which countries will benefit. Multilateral agreements on services trade are still very new (almost 50 years younger than negotiations that involve goods!) and it can be expected that they will develop over the next couple of years.

2. The GATS is not a simple transfer of the GATT to services. A new way of understanding and developing services globalisation is being formulated. It does not refer so much to removing barriers, tariffs or other cross-border obstacles but rather to creating conditions and encouraging adequate pro-competitive reforms to guarantee access-free competitive markets or contestable markets (Fernández-Martos, 2000). This difference is explained by the qualitative differences between goods and services; the internationalisation of goods can be encouraged via quantitative-based policies to encourage and regulate trade. Due to the special characteristics of services the GATS include aspects related to national regulations affecting services trade. Once the negotiations are finalised the success of

GATS will depend on the progress made by countries in the regulation of their internal markets, competition policy and information transparency.

3. The GATS have been heavily criticised, but the chapters in this book suggest that many of these criticisms are unfounded. National sovereignty and, hence, the GATS legitimacy, should not be questioned. For example, the provision of public services is still a monopoly or quasi-monopoly in many countries and is still under the GATS regulated and controlled by nation states. The national right to regulate services is recognised by the agreements and nation states are free to adhere to services they consider should be most liberalised and, last and not least, that the principle of progressive liberalisation guarantees a flexible approach to the adoption and implementation of the agreements. Developing countries have more to gain than lose from GATS, since it can facilitate their access to the competitive advantages they now lack and be an opportunity to improve national pro-competitive reforms. The positive economic effects and service liberalisation are considered to be much more important than the negative and adjustment-related costs (WTO, 1997). The GATS legitimacy depends on a wide range of aspects but, ultimately, it is the reality of globalisation that defines the need for the GATS and the GATS provides one mechanism to enable the ongoing development of service globalisation.

4. The GATS agreements should not be conceptualised as a process that is external to the rest of the economy. There are other liberalising processes that interact with the GATS and which mutually benefit from it. The experience of GATT has helped to create and develop the GATS. The GATS have benefited from the knowledges acquired during the GATT and the GATS approach to qualitative aspects of trade are also informing ongoing negotiations over the trade of goods. The blurring of the distinction between goods and services implies that a global approach to service and goods trade is increasingly essential. It also follows that all liberalising processes must advance in the same direction. It would be contradictory to increase service liberalisation whilst some agricultural or manufacturing sectors remain largely protected. This implies that some countries with higher exports of specific products could benefit more from service liberalisation that others. However, even in the highly improbable case that GATS is the only agreement to develop over the next few years, then its benefits would still be experienced in most places and countries.

The experience of Europe emphasises the benefits of service liberalisation. This does not mean a mere liberalisation or reduction of barriers according to the parameters of policies based on traditional instruments derived from policies developed for the trade of goods. Rather it means that three elements need to be incorporated into service liberalisation policies: (1) a global perspective on the services economy and its markets; (2) to understand that the only companies that can compete in foreign markets are those that compete in their own economies; and (3) to complement and search for efficiency gains through combining different policies (macroeconomic, commercial, competition promotion, transport and communications, R&D and innovation, labour markets, and so on). Services will carry on being, in any case, the protagonists of the current phase of globalisation. A good service industry policy can greatly help to increase the positive consequences of liberalisation and reduce the negative and asymmetric aspects that occur at local or regional levels.

These comments and final remarks should not be considered to be the final conclusions of this book. They only constitute some reflections extracted from our readings of the chapters.

NOTES

1. It should be noted that the most recent international trade and investment of some countries in relation to GDP are comparable to those of a century ago – at least in relative terms – and that at that historical time and during the following years strong migratory movements took place, which were more important than the current ones in relative terms.
2. Decreasing contribution of public services to services value added have also helped the gains observed in other service industries.
3. The OECD (1999) selected some strategic services which it considers essential to business competitiveness and which, in addition, have spectacularly grown over the last years. They are: services in computer software and information processing, R&D and technical testing, marketing, business organisation (management consultancy and labour recruitment) and human resource development. This set of services has been growing by about 10 per cent per year. Obviously, other services – also qualified as advanced but not integrated as such in the business service group – could be added to this list.
4. Service activities were clearly ignored by many classical economists from Adam Smith onwards, as it is well known. This was not contradictory to the fact that trade was the driving force of productive specialisation between countries or regions (Smith, Ricardo, Mill and others).

REFERENCES

Amin, A. (1997), 'Placing globalisation', *Theory, Culture and Society*, **14** (2), 123–37.
Amin, A. (1999), 'Placing globalisation', in J.R. Bryson, N. Henry, D. Keeble and R. Martin (eds), *The Economic Geography Reader*, Chichester: John Wiley, pp. 40–45.
Axford, B. (2000), 'Globalisation', in G. Browning, A. Halcli and F. Webster (eds), *Understanding Contemporary Society: Theories of the Present*, London: Sage, pp. 238–51.
Bryson, J.R. and Henry, N. (2001), 'The Global Production System: from Fordism to Post-Fordism', in P. Daniels, M. Bradshaw, D. Shaw and J. Sidaway (eds), *Human Geography: Issues for the 21st Century*, London: Prentice Hall, pp. 342–73.
Bryson, J.R., Henry, N., Keeble, D. and Martin, R. (eds) (1999), *The Economic*

Geography Reader: Producing and Consuming Global Capitalism, John Wiley, Chichester.

Cuadrado-Roura, J.R. and Rubalcaba-Bermejo, L (2000), *Los Servicios a Empresas en la Industria Española*, Madrid: Instituto de E. Económicos.

De la Dehesa, G (2000), *Comprender la Globalización*, Madrid: Alianza Editorial.

Fernández-Martos, A. (2000), 'Comercio de servicios: un complejo proceso de liberalizacin', *Información Comercial Española,* 785, May–June, 13–25.

Harvey, D. (1989), *The Condition of Postmodernity*, Oxford: Blackwell.

Held, D. (1995), *Democracy and the Global Order*, Cambridge: Polity.

Hirst, P. and Thompson, G. (1992), 'The problem of globalization: international economic relations, national economic management, and the formation of trading blocs', *Economy and Society,* **21** (4), 357–96.

Hirst, P. and Thompson, G. (1996a), 'Globalisation: ten frequently asked questions and some surprising answers', *Soundings,* **4**, Autumn, 47–66.

Hirst, P. and Thompson, G. (1996b), *Globalization in Question,* Cambridge: Polity.

Hufbauer, G.C. and Warren, T. (1999), 'The Globalization of Services, What Has Happened?', Institute for International Economics.

International Monetary Fund (IMF) (1997), *World Economy Forecasts*, May 1997, Washington: IMF.

Lash, S. and Urry, J. (1994), *Economies of Signs and Space*, London: Sage.

O'Brien, R. (1992), *Global Financial Integration: the End of Geography*, London: Pinter.

OECD (1999), *Strategic Business Services*, Paris: OECD.

OECD (2000), *OECD in Figures. Statistics on Member Countries*, 2000 Edition, June, Paris; OECD.

Rubalcaba-Bermejo, L. (1999), *Business Services in the European Industry: growth, employment and competitiveness*, Brussels: European Commission.

Sauvé, P. and Stern, R. (eds) (2000), GATS 2000: New Directions in Service Trade Liberalisation. Centre for Business and Government & Brookings Institution Press, Harvard University & Washington, D.C.

Swyngedouw, E. (1997), 'Neither Global nor Local: "Glocalization" and the Politics of Scale' in Cox, K.R. (ed.), *Spaces of Globalization: reasserting the power of the local*, The Guildford Press: New York: 137–66.

United Nations Development Program (1999), *Human Development Report*, New York: UNDP.

United Nations (UNCTAD) (2000), *World Investment Report 2000*, New York and Geneva: United Nations.

Worlds Trade Organisation (1997), *Economic Effects of Service Liberalisation*, Council for Trade in Services, 7 October 1997, WTO.

World Trade Organisation (2000), *Services Rules for Growth and Investments. Trading into the future: the introduction to the WTO*, WTO, www@wto.og.

PART I

Globalisation and Services: Concepts and Trends

2. Services in the age of globalisation: explanatory interrelations and dimensions

Luis Rubalcaba-Bermejo and Juan R. Cuadrado-Roura

INTRODUCTION

The previous chapter has shown that the service economy is increasingly affecting many economic aspects of globalisation and that it is more and more difficult to understand one without the other. It underlined the ways in which the growth of services and the continued development of globalisation are intertwined. This chapter explores key theories, examples and evidence regarding the relationships between services and globalisation and develops the overall objective of the book by providing a comprehensive framework for analysis.

This chapter will, first, explore some of the main interrelations between services and globalisation. The key interaction mechanisms will be identified and examples provided. The double relationship or dialectic will be identified – how services promote globalisation and how services are affected by globalisation. The specificity and limitations of service globalisation are also identified. Secondly, the chapter considers the main forms of service globalisation and differences between that of goods. The purpose is to identify distinctive aspects of service globalisation within the framework of the global economy. Four dimensions are identified and briefly discussed. These focus on selected variables that explain the relationship between services and globalisation.

Globalisation is a difficult concept and like most concepts in the social sciences the definition is extremely important. For the purposes of this chapter a particular definition of the vaporous concept of globalisation is deployed. Given the widely recognised ambiguity of the concept this chapter is restricted to an analysis of the economic dimension and it largely ignores the cultural, political and social aspects of globalisation. Globalisation is therefore conceptualised for the purposes of this chapter as a dynamic process in which the markets for goods, factors of production and capital are increasingly integrated.

This is not to negate the importance of cultural, political and social aspects of globalisation, but rather our restricted definition is used to explore the economic dimension of what is a complex and multidimensional process.

THE INTERACTION BETWEEN SERVICES AND GLOBALISATION

In order to understand the interrelationships between globalisation and services, it is necessary to explore both dimensions of this issue: 'how do services promote globalisation?' and 'how does globalisation affect services?'.

How do Services Promote Globalisation?

The first dimension of the relationship, *how services promote globalisation*, can be explored from a number of different positions. Seven ways in which services affect globalisation are synthesised below, and one of them, the relationship with the New Economy, is developed further. Some of these points have already been made in the previous chapter , but they are developed in this analysis.

1. *Overcoming distances*   The first way in which services contribute to globalisation is through the reduction of distance. The so called 'death of distance' would not have occurred without the development of transport or communication services that has also led to an impressive decrease in transportation costs over the last few decades (see examples in IMF, 1997 and UNDP, 1999). The reduction in relative geographic distance caused by technological developments has been a fundamental factor driving globalisation. However, other types of distance have also being reduced as a consequence of what are almost exclusively service factors, for example social, cultural or linguistic distances. Thus, many advanced services (for example, management consultancy) and operative ones (for example, linguistic) contribute to the adaptation of international initiatives and firms to local environment. Face-to-face relationships that are a fundamental part of many service transactions are also encouraging a reduction in cultural and linguistic distances. It should be noted, however, that this type of impact is sector-specific and also limited to particular service occupations. Most services are still produced and consumed locally.
2. *Promoting transnational companies*   An increasing number of firms are internationalising as a consequence of the activities of service companies. Management services may be involved in the restructuring of a client company that ultimately encourages a search for new markets. Legal and

economic services are involved in mergers or takeovers. For example the top ten mergers and acquisitions advisors undertook 1275 deals valued at $4492 billion. Many of these advisers are American companies and Goldman Sachs holds the first position in this sector. Trade fairs and market research companies operate to design and promote products. They also can encourage companies to develop internationally by providing clients with knowledge of foreign markets and of competing products and services. Advertising and marketing are involved in the differentiation of products. Computer services increasingly function to link supply chains together as well as encouraging the development of global knowledge networks. In addition, service functions are extremely important once the problem of production localisation is solved. Sales, logistics, financing, marketing, personnel are all activities which are beginning to network together and one consequence is that transnational companies (TNCs) are increasingly truly international. As a result, there is growing intra-firm service trade in all sectors. Even in a very manufacturing export-oriented economy like Germany, it has been recognised that services boost manufacturing trade and that the weakness of services may be affecting certain industries (Bullinger, 1998).

3. *Reinforcing specialisation processes*   In the first phase of globalisation de-industrialisation was identified as one of the main causes of tertiary specialisation in the advanced countries. Tertiarisation was the result of the relocation of manufacturing production to low cost high productivity areas. Currently, services are increasingly being integrated with manufacturing production and this integration is producing new specialisation processes both in manufacturing and services (Cuadrado-Roura and Rubalcaba-Bermejo, 2000). Manufacturing industries that make effective use of service functions are able to gain comparative advantages. The implication is that regions with well-developed service economies may be more competitive that those with undeveloped or under-developed service infrastructure (see Leo and Philippe (1999) for an example of how dynamic manufacturing companies use services linked to the export of goods). Likewise, the expansion of services that are produced using 'industrial' systems are generating specialisation in traditional (tourism) or in modern sectors (advanced services). As a consequence, service activities may provide significant comparative advantage for many countries. One implication is that current trade balance deficits may be compensated and service trade may increase the standard level of life.

4. *Explaining the productivity and growth paradox*   The productivity paradox according to which recent periods of strong technological progress coincide with periods of lower productivity and growth rates is very much associated with services. Services are the most important activities in total

productivity (Bernard and Jones, 1996) and consequently service productivity affects structural change and growth (Cuadrado-Roura and Del Río,
1993), the role of manufacturing industries (Petit, 1986) as well as global
life standards due to the negative effects on real wages (Krugman, 1996).
The relatively low level of service productivity has been explored ever
since it was identified in the seminal work of Fourastié (1952). It is
explained by the nature of service activities and the difficulties of substi-
tuting labour for capital (for example, Baumol, 1967, 1985; Baumol et al.
1989; De Bandt, 1991) or in segmenting service markets (Roach, 1991).
The de-industrialisation/tertiarisation process is also explained by differences in productivity between both sectors and factor mobility (IMF,
1997). However, according to the application of neoclassical growth
models (Solow, Hecksher–Ohlin–Samuelson) this would lead to convergence processes which, in general terms, are not observed.

Services reinforce new theories of endogenous growth that explain
divergence in different endowments of human capital or infrastructures.
Some services can be conceptualised as contributing to infrastructure and
some to human capital. Both types are heavily concentrated in developed
countries and regions. On the other hand, services are generating the highest possible employment in the global economy, while some contribute
positively to productivity and economic growth, although others have
apparent low productivity. The uneven role of business services must be
noted given relatively high apparent productivity levels and moderate or
declining apparent growth rates (Rubalcaba-Bermejo, 2000). The role of
outsourcing must also be considered as this links the productivity of both
the services and manufacturing sectors (Ten-Raa and Wolff, 1996). There
are major difficulties associated with the measurement of service productivity (Gadrey, 1996) and the increasing need for measures to take into
consideration qualitative aspects of services (Riddle, 1986, De Bandt,
1995) as well as indirect measures (Wolff, 1999). When these measurement problems are taken into account it could be the case that the least
productive sectors are in fact those which contribute the most to economic
growth and globalisation. This may be another service paradox.

5. *Enlarging or reducing market asymmetries*   Traditional services are less
    geographically concentrated than manufacturing; services are able to
    counterbalance industrial asymmetries. However, in the same way that
    manufacturing has generated asymmetries by delocalising parts of the
    production (the spatial division of labour) process, so too do services
    contribute to uneven development as the most advanced services tend to
    be regionally concentrated and, particularly, tend to be clustered in major
    metropolitan areas. The strong concentration of advanced services (and
    some traditional and public administration services) is a factor that

contributes to divergence. Some traditional services and, to a much lesser extent, the de-localisation of some technologically advanced services can reduce some of these differences. The uneven geography but important role of services in the changing economic geography has been widely analysed (for example, Daniels and Moulaert, 1991; Daniels, 1993; Daniels et al., 1993; Bonamy and May, 1994; Marshall and Wood, 1995; Illeris, 1996). In addition, the existence of barriers in service markets also generates additional asymmetries. Protectionism can undermine the positive advantages that result from service trade. Finally, other asymmetries can be generated in competitiveness and in the balance of payments, since it is clear that some regions and countries produce service-related competitive advantages that can even reduce commercial deficits.

6. *Promoting new global economic dynamism*   Economic dynamism is very often prompted by Schumpeterian impulses that are very strongly linked to innovation depending, in turn, on a wide range of elements. However, amongst the latter, services are once again important actors. A recent OECD (1999) report on the future of the global economy placed services in ICT and as functions that contribute to structural adjustment. Of course, not all services are innovative and in the same way not all management consultancy is innovative (some types are routine and some enhances competitiveness). R&D activities are technically the most important innovating service sector. In Baumol's words (2000: 2) 'R&D has become the current king of the services and perhaps even of the economy as a whole, at least in industrial countries'. Services are increasingly implicated in R&D expenditure, especially in financial, telecommunications and some knowledge-intensive business services. It is sectors like these that are more likely to innovate than many manufacturing companies (OECD, 2000b, 2000c). Many of these innovations are related to current technological changes and the development of a New Economy.

Services in the New Economy

The processes of technological change are so strong that the attention of observers and the public at large is no longer just focussed on services in general but on what is now called the 'new economy', or what used to be termed the 'information and communication society' or, simply, 'Internet'.[1] The changes occurring in the world of Internet and electronic business and commerce are undoubtedly some of the most characteristic aspects of current global transformations. These alterations are so important that experts and businessmen suggest that the 1990s period of expansion experienced by the North American economy is due to *increases in productivity* and lower unitary labour costs that can largely be explained by the technological revolution. They have also suggested that the 1990s growth differential between Europe and the United States can also be explained in this way. It should also be noted that such differentials enable the possible transfer of this type of American revolution to Europe. Taking into account these expectations, it is no coincidence that Internet firms experienced dramatic escalations in the value of their stock. Many of these companies were operating at a loss and by all account an excessive capitalisation. The *strong correction of the New Economy* with such shares occurred in the second half of 2000 but this period was also one in which the North American economy experienced a significant decline in its performance. The problems affecting many Internet firms have led to questions concerning the overestimation of the financial profits that can be made from such enterprises rather than the development of a more general critique of new technological developments. Value is now increasingly linked to a new or revised notion of value constructed around the concept of service value.[2]

In the context of the 'new technological revolution', there are some services that have been and are fundamental to these processes of change. Telecommunication companies, computer firms and leisure industries are leading technological markets in stock exchanges and are the promoters and protagonists of the development of the new economy. All of these are service firms that have directly played an important role in the globalisation process. However, there are other more discrete services that are ignored by the media but which, at the same time, are behind these changes. Some business services, for example, indirectly affect and support the process of globalisation. For example the advanced services related to *engineering, computers and electronic businesses* are the three business service activities most strongly associated with the 'technological revolution'. These have facilitated the production, expansion and application of new technologies, which have been behind the infrastructure that have made the technologies of the new economy possible. Computer services have been and are the major precursors of new businesses related to the Internet and its possibilities. Without the development of computer technology (hardware as well as software) many of the changes that are now occurring would have been impossible. Computer services enable and facilitate the possibilities offered by electronic commerce. Businesses that were established as small companies to exchange databases, provide on-line consultancy, or advertising pages have rapidly become the colossi of the New Economy. Large companies all over the planet are investing thousands of millions of dollars trying to identify niches in a market that is still rather more of a virtuality than a reality.

Some of these new businesses are based around telecommunication and banking firms or the media, but many operate or would like to operate as authentic business service providers that operate by integrating other types of services. In any case it is obvious that an *'e-business, business-to-business'* firm, for instance, has more to do with advanced business services than with traditional firms dedicated to telephony, transport or even commercial distribution. In a way, many Internet businesses could be considered as new business services related to new forms of commercial distribution as for instance '*e-commerce, B-to-C*', telecommunications or electronic communication.

In any case, it is obvious that this new technological revolution has required and will continue to require services to implement these changes, make them comprehensible to firms and extract the highest yields. Among business services, it would not be surprising if those particularly linked to this technology – computer, communication, engineering and design services – experienced the highest growth rates over the next few years. However, other services will also be affected. Some may be affected negatively: some intermediate providers of real estate, labour recruitment, or trade fairs could possibly suffer from alternatives that are being offered by Internet providers. Internet technology and its associated services will probably not eliminate business services but, on the contrary, will encourage the development of new or revised services. Trade fairs are a good example. All the technological developments have not eliminated the necessity for personal meeting and physical contact. On the contrary, they have increased the possibilities of such meetings and have attracted more and better customers. It will be interesting to see how longstanding service providers react to these new challenges.

It may not be a coincidence that the United States is leading the New Economy. The US has an industrial technology complex (Silicon Valley) constructed around the development of technologies that are related to the Internet and it has also encouraged the development of cultural and socioeconomic behaviour that is favourable to the world of the Internet. The US is also one of the most advanced service economies. All of these elements may ensure that the US has competitive advantage in Internet technology – developed technology, favourable culture and social behaviour, strong supporting services. Some of these elements will have to be either transferred or developed in Europe. The merger of aspects of the new and old economy will produce new ways of work and organisation and new solutions where no country either wins everything or loses everything.

How Services are Affected by Globalisation

Let us now consider the second dimension of the problem: *how are services affected by globalisation?* Once again the analysis would require an investigation that took into consideration different points of view. It is sufficient at this stage to state that globalisation requires the internationalisation of services and that services adapt themselves to new competitive environments as well as being capable of offering better and cheaper services and meeting the increasingly international needs of their clients – both firms and consumers.

Services also need to identify and construct comparative advantages and localise themselves in places where they can have better access to information, human resources and the most important clients. As a result of these challenges, services are increasing their international trade, foreign investment, agreements, alliances, mergers and collaboration networks.

It is quite obvious that services are affected by globalisation; but raising the question 'by how much?' leads us to the paradox of service globalisation. Services represent 70 per cent of the most advanced economies but only account for less than 25 per cent of international trade and almost half of direct investment, mergers and takeovers. These figures create a paradox that can be explained by two reasons. First, the *natural (the service relationship) and artificial difficulties (barriers to trade)* faced by the service sector that inhibits internationalisation. Second, the *non-inclusion in official statistics* of the share of internationalised goods that are due to services, for example intra-firm trade or the service value incorporated into exported goods. If these were taken into account the service trade figures would be extremely different. The first explanation can be subdivided into a number of elements. The OECD (2000a) identifies six reasons: services cannot be stored; client–supplier interaction requires local presence; most service firms are SMEs; products are highly differentiated; cultural differences are especially important in this field; and, finally, trade barriers and restrictions on local operations exist. However, despite all of this, globalisation produces clear advantages to suppliers.

Advantages and reasons for service globalisation

In principle, globalisation can be considered as positive for services since it provides them with new business opportunities – especially important where markets are already saturated – and forces them to be more competitive and, therefore, more productive. For most companies, its effects will *clearly be positive.* Management consultancy services will advise client firms on how to take advantage of new possibilities and the strategic behaviour they must adopt in order to remain competitive. Legal, accounting and auditing services will have to face new challenges brought by large-scale internationalisation that results from different national regulations, insecurities due to network contracting, registering and different tax systems. Quality control will have to be transferred to networked businesses because the absence of 'physical' (face-to-face) relationships increases the need for all types of guarantees. Advertising has found a new channel for its expression and service. Personnel and training services will have to be orientated towards new employment requirements. It is clear that the participation of all these services in the new processes of change will help reinforce the interactive integration of services into the developing global economy.

The advantages offered to services by globalisation can be explored by dividing them into those that are demand related and those that are supply related.[3] From the demand side, consumers and service clients will have a wider choice. This will improve the efficiency and productivity of internationalised services. From the supply side the advantages are, first, similar to those identified in theories of trade and comparative advantage. Second, Dunning's eclectic paradigm (Dunning, 1993a) identifies three approaches: trade, organisation and location theories (OLI model) and underlines the advantages of property, cost internationalisation and adequate localisation (see Chapter 7 by Peter Shojolt in this volume). This paradigm is a useful framework for investigating service TNCs (Enderwick, 1989) and is reinforced in the case of services by the increasing tradability of services and the role of goods in globalisation. This is a major cause of globalisation as suppliers follow clients into foreign marketplaces.

This is not the place to review these theories but it can be emphasised that remarkable efforts have recently been made to distinguish the importance of external country resources from that of internal firm strategy and characteristics. Roberts (1998) underlines the relevance of theories of *comparative advantage* to service trade between developed and developing countries. Factors that are important are the relative abundance or scarcity of skilled labour. *Absolute advantage* theories (or comparative ones including intangible resources) apply to trading between countries with similar factor endowments. Most service trade is produced between developed nations and product differentiation is the key factor (through knowledge, managerial skills, technology applications, reputation, and so on). Nusbaumer (1987) explores the usefulness of both approaches according to *service differentiation* (absolute advantage) or *standardisation* (comparative advantages). Rubalcaba-Bermejo and Gago (2001) show how service trade and market shares (competitiveness) can be determined by *non-macroeconomic variables* and that these enable additional room for explanations of Kaldor's paradox. In any case, the advantages and function of service trade is recognised to the extent that *people holding very diverse views commonly support the liberalisation of service trade*.[4] This is even the case for developing economies that support the linkage of goods and service trade negotiations (see Bhagwati, 1987 or Sauvé, Chapter 13 in this volume).

Specificity of service globalisation
The identification of the processes and pressures driving service trade raises the important issue of the differences between service trade when compared with that of manufactured goods. In fact, the internationalisation of services has its own characteristics that differentiates it from that of goods. In services, cross-border trade is unusual; rather trade consists of contacts between people and companies located in different countries. Service internationalisation does

not centre around the sale of the same product in various places but rather it consists of the provision of different (local) services via forms of production and global organisation. In services, what is internationalised is not so much the chain of production and distribution but rather human resources, techniques, intangibles and the property of firms. *Service endowments are certainly different from good endowments*; Daniels (1993) suggests, for instance, that services depend on human capital and political and cultural factors rather than on a strategic location based on raw materials and the relative abundance of factors of production. Therefore, for service trade the H–O–S model is of limited value (Petit, 1986) and cultural advantages need to be considered together with economic ones (Riddle, 1986). Of course, certain services stand out as exhibiting greater differences to goods. And sometimes such differences are not very evident. For example, the generation of knowledge by all parts of a professional multinational service firm is partly based on the service way of producing and maintaining competitiveness in national contexts. Such a production system undermines the narrow links that exist between headquarters, determinants of direct investment and locational home advantages (Nachum, 2000). This method of organising professional service firms may be similar to other manufacturing ones rather than to other multinational service firms. The importance of strategic managerial differences between manufacturing and services is not shared by all authors (Aharoni, 2000a).

In services, *expectations, reputation and prestige* play a decisive role (Aharoni, 2000b), particularly in business services where clients find it extremely hard to assess quality and competence reliability. Switching costs can be high and the choice of a poor supplier can produce devastating consequences. For these reasons, one of the most important signs of service internationalisation is the development of international brands which sell an image that is an assurance of a standardised quality service that is guaranteed all over the world. In this sense, service internationalisation follows the same course as the internationalisation of goods as it is founded on standardised products with identifiable branding. However, service brands play a somewhat different role as they are not associated with physical products that are easily comparable. Therefore, trust must be developed by the client and this often necessitates physical proximity and, especially in advanced services, the ability to manage a flow of external information and knowledge by the client organisation. For services, the creation, accumulation, transfer and protection of knowledge is extremely important (Grosse, 2000). Finally, the internationalisation of services requires that the limitations of service standardisation are overcome as well as the difficulty or even impossibility of storage and transport. For these reasons, the ways in which services are internationalised will be different from those of goods. Service trade is normally based on a *stage approach* similar to the one proposed by Roberts (1999): first, no exports; second, domestically located exports; third, embodied service exports; fourth, presence based on intra-firm exports and fifth, establishment of a service production facility overseas.

Limitations of service globalisation

Service globalisation has clearly identifiable limitations. For instance, there are very few truly global manufacturing let alone service firms. There are very few service companies like Nestlé, Royal Dutch-Shell, Exxon-Mobil, Unilever, Electrolux, ABB, IBM or Procter and Gamble that are major transnational manufacturing organisations (some with more than half their production outside the country of origin). The Canadian Seagram Company (beverages/media) and the Thomson Corporation (media/publishing) are representative of the major service TNCs measured in foreign assets as shown by the United Nations World Investment Report (WIR) (2000: 79). However, the majority of TNCs, whether they are global or have significant transnational capital, are based on a standardised product, for example oil companies. Such companies have simple international organisational structures and they can benefit from economies of scale by creating a truly global structure. The characteristics of the service relationship make such a structure difficult to develop. Manufacturing industries can relocate parts of their production processes. Service companies find this spatial division of labour difficult as their products are not easily divisible and require co-production with client companies. A spatial division of service co-production would require clients and suppliers to develop similar global networks and this type of network would be practically impossible to develop for interactive services. In this sense, it can be said that services globalisation is not inevitable (Daniels, 1993) since the limits to global service enterprises act together to restrict the development of truly global service companies. Related to this is the fact that domestic markets remain the core market for the majority of service TNCs.[5]

Given these problems it is hardly surprising that even amongst TNCs only some service sectors manage to develop major global service companies; the best examples are found in *banking, trading, insurance and communications*. There are some outstanding examples of TNCs that are dedicated to the provision of non-financial services: New Corporation (Australia, media/publishing), Cable and Wireless Plc (UK, telecommunications), Mitsui & Co. (Japan, diversified), Itochu (Japan, trading), Sumimoto (Japan, trading/machinery), Nortel Networks (Canada, telecommunications), Nissho Iwai (Japan, trading) and Telefónica S.A. (Spain, telecommunications). Each of these has more than 13 billion dollars in assets and all of them are integrated into the 52 largest companies in the world (WIR, 2000). In 1998, out of the 100 largest companies only 15 per cent were service providers. Certainly, Dunning (1993b) was correct when he suggested that services are less truly international that manufacturing companies, and that the advantages of being a TNC are likely to be less important than that for good producers.[6] Even reactive behaviour is very dominant in service companies. The *oligopoly reaction* of service TNCs that follow their competitors is the most important determinant of foreign investment according to Li and Guisinger (1993). They identify this type of reactive strategy in services as being very important during the 1970s and 1980s. It is also correct to argue that some service companies during the 1990s have been *more proactive and less reactive* in their behaviour with respect to developing international markets (see Chapter 6 by Leo and Philippe and Chapter 7 by Shojolt in this volume).

Another limitation of globalisation is that at the moment trade and investment is more important at a regional and national level than at an international one. The reduction in transport costs and the liberalisation of markets do not yet seem to be sufficient to encourage the expansion of international service trade so that it surpasses regional trade growth. However, this argument is valid if investment is considered rather than trade. For example, in the EU, both for goods and services, intra-EU trade has grown in a similar way to extra-EU trade. Although for some computer and business services intra-EU trade has been more important (see Daniels, Chapter 5 this volume). But intra-EU trade in services is particularly low and stable (15 per cent GDP; 20 per cent of total intra-EU trade; see Muylle Chapter 14 in this volume). The intra-EU integration of services is more associated with FDI than with trade: service flows are 70 per cent of total intra-EU investment while services only amount for 40–50 per cent with respect to extra-EU investment (WIR, 2000).

In addition, the limits on the integration of service markets can be seen in many other ways. For example, it is unusual for global service companies to develop management policies that result in the integration of employees at an intra-country level. The international transfer of service workers is still unusual as TNCs prefer to maintain local managers who inspire trust in clients and know the local social and cultural environment. Despite the recent wave of mergers and takeovers, large service firms remain largely national, except for a small number of cases.

Another factor that also greatly contributes to the factors that limit service globalisation are restrictions placed on international trade. Such restrictions can take the form of tariff barriers but they also include the disadvantageous conditions under which foreign suppliers have to operate in foreign countries, for example language, cultural and religious constraints. Most of the limitations identified so far are related to the natural characteristics of service production and consumption – or in other words the service relationship, but tariff restrictions must be considered as artificial restrictions of service trade and it is these that are explored in the third part of this book.

GLOBALISATION AND SERVICES: SOME EXAMPLES

Examples of the relationships between globalisation and services are shown in Table 2.1. Both columns of the table deal with both aspects of the relationship: the way in which each service is internationalised (how globalisation affects services) and the way in which each service contributes to the internationalisation of other sectors (how services affect globalisation).

The first part considers the most important and traditional service industries, all of which have been subjected to the logic of globalisation. First, wholesale and retail distributive trades, an industry that is changing rapidly with the introduction of large stores and hypermarket chains, and country-specific debates on licenses, permissions and opening hours. All of these are indicative of strong competition and the internationalisation of products and working methods. Hotels, restaurants and tourist activities are clearly international since they exploit geography, climate and history as well as cultural and economic differences. Transport is also affected by globalisation. Decision making is increasingly at an international level and takes into consideration the advantages of better connections and infrastructure. Many medium-sized or large firms are affected by growing competition in road transport, while air transport is undergoing a process of concentration and the formation of alliances. The banking and insurance sector is confronted with a similar situation, with an increasing number of mergers, takeovers and transnational operations. Finally, telecommunications is also experiencing strong globalisation as it incorporates the latest technology.

Compared to these large service sectors, business services are also influenced by globalisation, although in a less visible way. Consultancy, auditing, market research or advertising multinationals are increasingly offering international services to international clients and gaining increasingly greater market share. The expansion of business abroad is also a new characteristic of some activities, such as trade fairs and exhibitions, which have recently started to be organised across national borders. Networking and collaborative agreements tend to be increasingly common amongst engineering consultancy, legal services and market research firms and are one way in which SMEs can service foreign clients.

Traditional services offer many examples on the way in which services contribute to globalisation. For example, the food industry, or at least part of it, takes advantage of the sales potential of large distribution chains. Managers of industrial firms travel and use the hotel and tourist infrastructures of cities. A good transport and telecommunication network is indispensable for operation at a global level. Financial services also facilitate transnational operations.

Business services once again make a less visible contribution to the process of globalisation, but they have a much greater potential than many other

Table 2.1   Relationships between services and globalisation: some examples

Sectors	Ways in which services internationalise	Ways in which services contribute to internationalisation
Wholesale and retail distributive trades	Arrival of large stores International products Increasing competition	Use of sales potential offered by big stores Need for a comparable size to negotiate at the same level (basically food industry)
Hotels/restaurants and tourism	Foreign customers International chains of hotels Tourist concentration in international tour operators	The improvement of professional or business tourism contributes to facilitate globalisation Attraction of international businesses
Transport	Improvement of international connections Alliances and concentration in airline and road transport companies Increasing comparisons in services	High quality and cheap transport networks are key factors for goods and service globalisation
Banking and insurance	Mergers. Foreign investment Accounts and operations in foreign currencies	Facilitators of transnational operations
Telecommunications	Fast incorporation of the latest technology. Participation of foreign capital in phone companies Agreements between operators from different countries	Enables fast and fluid communications between agents. Death of distance
Business services: (some examples)		
– Management consultancy	Influence of the large multinational consultancy firms	Adoption of internationally proven organisational systems Counselling in international strategy
– Legal services	Collaboration agreements between lawyer firms.	Advice on national legal system

Sectors	Ways in which services internationalise	Ways in which services contribute to internationalisation
– Computer services	Agreements with multinational firms Use of standard software International suppliers	Counselling international support Preparation of firms for global connections and adequate use of information
– Trade fair services	Organisation of trade fairs abroad	Observation of what is produced in other countries (feel global markets)
– Market research	Networking. Multinationals. Procedure standardisation	Test on foreign markets Information improvement
– Advertising	Repetition of the same ads in different countries. Concentration. Multinationals	Entry into foreign markets Creation of the same or similar tastes. Improvement of entry potentials

sectors. Business services advise clients on the process of international expansion (consultancy, trade fairs, market research, legal services, advertising) and provide them with the necessary information required to take decisions. To this effect, services are not playing a purely instrumental role in globalisation but in fact are playing an active role as 'educators or teachers'. Client companies may benefit to a greater or lesser degree depending on whether they take advantage of this knowledge.

It is therefore clear that globalisation affects all service industries but not in the same way. On the one hand, the special characteristics of services markets will determine the nature and extent of globalisation. On the other hand, services globalisation can have similarities with that of goods. The next section explores these differences by exploring different forms of service globalisation.

How do Services become Global? Approaching the Key Dimensions

Service globalisation takes many forms; some forms are similar to those observed in manufacturing, whilst others are specific to services. What globalisation implies, in any case, is the ability to offer a similar product in any part of the world; a global conception of the market that involves the internationalisation of productive inputs and exports and the activities of multinational firms.

This chapter has stressed the special characteristics of services. Specifically attention has been drawn to the importance of *product differentiation* (which is never identical in all places) and *service customisation* (due to the interactive nature of services). Both these aspects imply that a service will have to be altered to fit the requirements of a foreign market. This means that *service internationalisation* implies *'nationalisation'*, that is to say, the adaptation to normative, economic, cultural and social parameters of foreign countries or markets. The interaction between consumers and products is at the heart of the peculiar tradability of services; it is both an advantage and a disadvantage. There are many multinational companies in which subsidiaries retain a degree of independence as well as having multilevel management structures that attempt to replicate services. The difference from manufacturing is that there is no vertical division of production in service industries and low cost or low technology parts of the production process cannot usually be relocated to developing countries. This difference means that global movements of services are not so much associated with cross-border movements but rather with the transmission of processes, knowledge and techniques or with the exchange of residents and non-residents and the transfer of workers, managers and technology. The flows are not of products but of people and of ideas.

Modes of service internationalisation have been analysed from different service-oriented perspectives. Vandermerwe and Chadwick (1989), for example, present a classification system for service firm internationalisation that contains two dimensions: the relative involvement of goods in services and the degree of consumer–producer interaction. 'Exportable' services are those embodied in goods and which have low interaction. Investment-oriented services are those that require high interaction. Nicolaidis (1993) proposed a taxonomy of modes of service globalisation according to the share of local added value and the degree of ownership and control of local units. FDI requires high levels in both dimensions. Roberts (1998) proposes a threefold classification of international services: non-traded services, traded services and factor movement related to international service transactions (including foreign investment and networking). Leo and Phillipe explore in this volume the different delivery modes of French service firms taking into consideration the types of network and the quality control procedures that are developed to ensure the quality of an exported service is maintained. Quality control is especially important given the importance of service brands and the relationship between the brand and client trust.

In our opinion, four dimensions of service globalisation can be identified. The first dimension (A) concerns international flows that involve specific transactions. This refers to *international trade* as it is traditionally defined together with the international movement of factors of production. The second dimension (B) is related to the role played by *brands*. These are decisive in the uncertain context of service markets where reputation is so important and

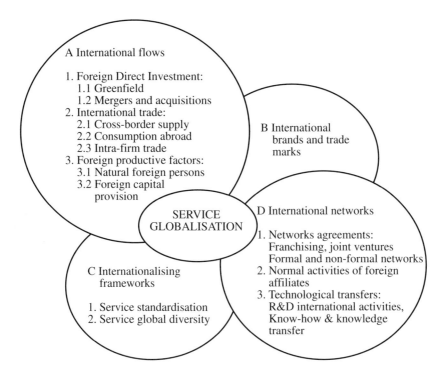

Figure 2.1 The four dimensions of service globalisation

where quality is implicitly associated to the brand. The third dimension (C) refers to the *production* and the nature of each service. Services that are or can be standardised are more likely to be internationalised. Or special services can capitalise or their distinctiveness to develop foreign clients. Finally, the fourth dimension (D) deals with the organisation of *international networks*. There are many ways of organising formal or non-formal network organisations – foreign affiliates (their mere presence is a form of globalisation through a network structure), franchise arrangements and joint ventures or international R&D teams that can be involved in technological and knowledge transfer.

Figure 2.1 explores these four dimensions of service globalisation. Although each of these dimensions may be developed on its own, service globalisation requires all four dimensions to be developed as well as explored. A consultant who travels from one country to another to share knowledge contributes to service globalisation through client transactions and the diffusion of a brand and a reputation associated with a firm. During this type of service trade networking and knowledge transfer will occur and the co-production of an international service will result in adaptation to local conditions. This process of adaptation will lead to further opportunities to develop service trade as the acquired experience may result in the provision of services to other foreign companies. A foreign firm dedicated to telecommunications will have to invest capital (investment flow, dimension A), sell and develop a brand (dimension B), present a network adapted to local conditions and at the same time transmit international knowledge (dimension D) and try to partially replicate services that can increasingly be sold globally (dimension C).

Dimension A: International Transactions

The first dimension refers to flows derived from international service transactions of both products and productive factors. As indicated, it includes the following types related to the four modes of international trade defined by the GATS and WTO:

1. International trade (IT)
    1.1 *Cross-border supply* (mode 1)
    1.2 *Consumption abroad* (mode 2)
    1.3 *Intra-firm trade*
2. Foreign Direct Investment (FDI) (mode 3)
    2.1 *Greenfield FDI*
    2.2 *Mergers and acquisitions (M&A)*
3. International flows of productive factors (IPF)
    3.1 *Presence of natural foreign persons* (mode 4)
    3.2 *Capital provision flows*

International trade is the traditional way of conceiving internationalisation. Three categories can be identified: traditional cross-border trade that is similar to that of goods; trade which implies the movement of customers (as in the case of tourism) and intra-firm trade that is increasingly more important today (both in manufacturing and service firms). FDI is the commonest form of service internationalisation and includes both greenfield direct investment (inward and outward flows) and cross-border mergers and acquisitions. Thirdly, IPF is related to the movement of labour and capital inputs. The most important, however, is the movement of people that implies the transfer of suppliers to other countries. These three broad types of service internationalisation include the four modes through which the WTO and GATS define international trade: mode 1, cross-border supply (no movement; international trade similar to goods); mode 2, consumption abroad (client's movement); mode 3, commercial presence through direct investment; mode 4, presence of natural persons (provider's movement, for example, consultancy or construction projects).

Foreign investment tends to be the favoured mode for entry into international markets. Such an investment process given the difficulties of developing a reputation in a new market usually favours the acquisition of an existing company or some form of merger or even network relationship. In contrast to manufacturing, service globalisation via trade is only one of form of globalisation organisational strategy. The most important strategies involve the movement of financial capital, technical expertise and people or embodied expertise.

It should be noted that, in some cases, these forms are neither completely *alternatives* nor *complementary options*. There are some services where investment is clearly preferred to trade (communications systems), others are a form of trade (tourism) whilst others apply the formula of the temporary transfer of professional staff (forms of consultancy). However, most sectors use the various modes of internationalisation in a complementary manner. The decision to invest, for instance, affects other strategies, but the same is not true, for example, of the trade option. Service trade can grow without affecting investment. Thus, the strength of service internationalisation is founded on the strong orientation that exists towards investment coupled with strong brands.

Service trade also encourages the development of other forms of international trade. Such trade often leads to the movement of suppliers (consultancy) and/or clients (tourism) as well as fomenting investment flows reducing transfer costs and at the same time improves the international strategies of firms. A typical example is the investment decision that may follow trade generated by a client's international strategy. A client travels to another country with the consequence that service firms may begin to develop certain types of trade. Developing new relationships in this country will finally lead to an investment (greenfield or through a merger or acquisition) or the search for a local partner to establish a collaborative agreement. For services traditional trade is often the second-best strategy and it is frequently followed by investment. It should be noted, however, that all forms of internationalisation strategy are increasingly complementing each other.

The service literature has repeatedly analysed the relationship between service trade and service investments. For instance, Noyelle and Dutka (1988) identified the international trade of business services as being both complementary and substitutive modes of expansion. Hirsch (1993) states that the choice between trade or investment depends on the type of service: specialised services with high user interaction favour FDI whilst universalised services tend to be standardised and favour the trade option. Trade and investment are complementary modes. Fontagné (1999) stresses this by exploring the relationship between these variables. During the 1980s trade led to FDI but in the 1990s this relationship switched so that FDI led to trade. One dollar of outward FDI can generate two dollars of additional exports in investing countries and short-term imports increase in host countries (although results greatly depend on the country). In the long term, effects can also be positive on host country exports through technological transfers, job creation or local subcontracting.

The strong link between international trade and FDI is also found in intra-firm trade that can be considered as trade that is linked to FDI. Coffey and Polèse (1987) and Bailly et al. (1992) analysed the key role of intra-firm trade in the context of interregional trade in producer services. One of their findings is that the nature of intra-firm flows is different to inter-firm flows: the former is largely information-intensive with a high human capital input whilst the latter tend to be office-based. Fernández (2000) explores spillovers that result from foreign affiliate trade in relation to business services. The complementarity of international trade and FDI affects trade balances in a positive or negative way through links between headquarters and affiliates. Most studies, however, suggest that foreign affiliates will favour the import of services rather than the recruitment of local service suppliers.

It is important to note that the various forms of internationalisation are not mutually exclusive; this makes it difficult to distinguish the affects of each form from one another. In fact, in some cases the forms are difficult to separate both theoretically and statistically. For instance, mergers and acquisitions are part of FDI, and although mergers are different from forms of FDI they can involve capital investment that may not be reflected in statistics of direct investment. Not every merger and acquisition can be classified as FDI, but between 75 per cent and 85 per cent of registered FDI is accounted for by mergers and acquisitions. On the other hand, greenfield FDI represents a new investment, whilst mergers and acquisitions do not necessarily add anything to the productive capacity of the country in which the acquired company is located. The existence of these types of differences between FDI and mergers and acquisitions justifies their consideration as separate indicators (for further examples of this problems see WIR, 2000).

The differences between greenfield FDI and mergers and acquisitions have been explored. One of the key factors explaining these different strategies is related to the maturity of a country's markets. The condition of a market or its state of maturity may imply that there is only one really efficient way to enter the market place. Where markets are poorly developed greenfield FDI is usually the chosen option. If the market is mature mergers and acquisitions may be selected as a means to benefit from face-to-face proximity, to overcome barriers to entry, and of acquiring intangible assets (technology, human resources, brands) (Kang and Johanson, 2000). Greenfield FDI is quite important in developed-non-developed trading but mergers and acquisitions are important between developed countries. Of course, other facts do influence the choice of strategy. *European Economy* (2000) concludes that mergers and acquisition activity between Member States correlates closely with the stock market capitalisation of domestic firms. Financial markets are thus very important facilitators in the mergers and acquisitions process. Muylle (Chapter 14 in this volume) explores the relationship between mergers and acquisitions, market structure and EU policy.

In conclusion, it must be noted that all modes of service internationalisation are clearly interconnected and complementary (coexisting in some cases with substitution processes). Although recent trends shows a shift from trade to investment and intra-firm trade, and from greenfield FDI to mergers and acquisitions, especially in developed countries. In Chapter 4 we will try to verify this hypothesis.

Dimension B: The Role of Brands and Trademarks

The relationship between globalisation and the growing importance of brands is very clear in many manufactured products, but brands are also playing a significant role in the process of service globalisation. Indeed, the presence and role of branding is increasing in all types of services: producer services (for example finance, business services), distributive services (for example trade, transport, communications) or personal services (for example hotels and catering, entertainment).

Global brand as a strategic tool and as a necessity

There are a number of reasons why brands and trademarks have become increasingly important internationally. Some authors, for instance, have emphasised the strategic significance of brand decisions in the conquest and consolidation of new markets (Aaker, 1991, 1995; Kapferer, 1992). However, other factors are equally important: the conviction of the market value of international brands (Ourusoff, 1992); the globalisation of markets and communications (Levitt, 1987; Grönroos, 2000); or the identification of branding as a factor providing firms with competitive advantages at an international scale (Hunt and Morgan, 1995). Indeed, brands not only are a means of communication between a firm and its market (investors, suppliers, consumers or users) but they constitute a well-known commercial *international language*. It is in brands that the competitive advantages of an organisation are synthesised (Cerviño, 1996) and form a key element of marketing strategies (Murphy, 1987). The function of branding is well known in the case of goods and for a limited number of services but branding is now acquiring increasing importance for many services.

Most definitions of a 'brand' usually identify it with any sign or means (a name, term, signal, symbol or a combination of them)[7] 'which distinguishes or helps to distinguish on the market the products or services of a specific producer from similar or identical ones from other producers or sellers'. Thus, branding first appears as an instrument of *identification*[8] but this is not its only function. For names, symbols and logos to act as a brand they must *add specific significance and personality to the product or service*, that is to say, something that contributes to differentiating the product or service provided by a specific organisation. A mere name (of a firm or its products) is not a brand. A name is a sign of identification to which branding contributes *a singular identity* that is transmitted to and perceived by current and potential consumers.

In the context of the current process of internationalisation or globalisation the brand of a firm or organisation is not only an *intangible asset* but is also a *strategic asset* for firms and organisations wanting to internationalise. This explains why international branding policy and strategy have become *a key issue* for both multinationals and firms wanting to develop an internationalisation strategy. Moreover, increased competitive pressures, together with enhanced globalisation are fomenting the development of *global brands* in relation to local ones. Global brands already exist but are now becoming an instrument for the expansion of service firms and organisations. Branding is important for companies engaged in direct investment or takeovers or in the transfer of *know-how*. Branding is important for organisations supplying specific services (hotels and restaurants, consultancy and other business services, finance, transport, communications, leisure industries, and so on) especially where branding plays a decisive role in the *identification* of a specific quality, *mode of provision, international respectability* or, simply, as a factor instilling trust.

The changes that have taken place in the international economic environment (opening of markets, concentration of firms, increase in international travels, global communications), together with the complexity of the 'environment' in which industrial firms evolve[9] and the increased homogenisation of consumers' tastes (both in goods and in some specific services) give *service brands* a strategic character that operates internationally. Manufacturing industries have to use services in the countries to which they export or in which they want to establish their brands. Prior knowledge of specific service firms (consultancy, finance and transport) usually encourages client companies to employ these firms in the new country. Those who travel – whether for leisure or business – frequently choose a known brand of hotel, travel agency, car rental or restaurant.[10] Branding as an instrument to identify quality becomes an instrument through which a wide variety of service firms can have access to foreign markets.

Types of brands and global brands

Service branding can be divided into four main groups (Casares and Aranda, 2000): denomination of origin; producer's brands; distributor's brands; and establishment's brands. Producer's brands can appear in tertiary activities when a firm producing a specific service is able to incorporate a distinctive sign to differentiate its service from those already existing on the market. The analysis of distributors' brands (so common in goods) is, on the contrary, less clear-cut. In principle, distributors' brands are only applicable to commercial services whose provision underlines a tangible product as is the case for commercial services and, to a lesser extent, hotel and restaurant services. Establishment brands seem to be the category best adapted to tertiary characteristics, since they can be used both for production and consumer services. This is where franchises can be most easily developed.

The theory of resources and capacities has identified brands as a source of competitive advantage and as one of the key elements in strategic decisions (Hitt et al., 1997) which support – in current circumstances – the concept of *global brands* in relation to *local brands*.[11] From this perspective, internationalisation is equivalent to the process of transferring local resources, capacities and competitive advantages to other markets in the search for additional profitability. Thus, it seems obvious that internationalising service firms will transfer the resources and capacities supporting their competitive advantage. By transferring a brand the company will be able to draw upon the advantages of a '*standard*' and *form* of service provision that has a recognised capacity to provide customers with proven knowledge and internal efficiency as well as the advantages of quality control.

Branding offers important advantages to firms and organisations intending to respond to the internationalisation challenge. First, it provides the firm with financial value (potential price of the firm, profitability in the market, higher financing ratio and capability) and increases its market power (development of client loyalty, leadership, negotiating power). In addition, branding also generates other benefits by reducing the cost of sales and acquisition transactions, both for the titular firm or those allowed to use the brand as well as for consumers and users. Likewise, it can potentially open access to a wide variety of markets and offer the user the possibility of being dealt with in a similar way in distant parts of the world. This is increasingly important as a growing proportion of clients are multinational customers.

However, the thesis developed at the beginning of this chapter can also be applied to brands. That is to say, brands are simultaneously a tool for service globalisation and, at the same time, globalisation is impelling the development of brands. The creation of *global service brands* can be observed either through *geographic expansion*, *brand acquisition* or *alliance between brands*.

The strategy of geographic extension can be undertaken through the direct exportation of products (services) and firm brands to new markets or through the establishment of representatives, foreign agents, commercial *joint ventures* or direct investment. This type of strategy, quite common in services, maintains relatively strong control over the brand. The investment made by the parent company does not have to be high and it can expand through trade (or through representatives, agreements and firms founded with national partners, and so on). Maybe the weakness is that market penetration generally takes a long time since the creation of a brand at an international level is a slow process. The process can be shortened if the financial resources are available to permit the rapid development of a brand.[12] The acquisition of existing brands, a process that is common amongst products, allows a firm to rapidly acquire a position in the market (the speed of market penetration is higher). In the case of brand acquisition consumer identification is not as focussed on the company as frequently the company will maintain many brands, but in some cases the brands may eventually be merged. Finally, there are very few examples of brand alliances in the service world compared with that of products, but this does not impede the existence of collaboration agreements or the integration of various services within a group. There are examples of groups integrating financial, advertising, insurance, consultancy, or communication services but usually each activity retains its original differentiating brand.

Dimension C: Internationalising Frameworks

There are other processes unrelated to the previous dimensions that are contributing to service globalisation. There are frameworks that companies can adhere to which can encourage the internationalisation of service functions. A good example of this process is the impact of quality standards such as ISO9000 that forces companies signing up to the scheme to maintain standards. Services require a certain degree of standardisation to be internationalised. This can come from many different sources: technological integration to make them transportable and replicable, network organisation, the presence of multinationals or international quality standards and accreditation. All of these are part of what is known as the 'industrialisation' of tertiary activities and they constitute an important factor in globalisation.

However, growing service standardisation does not necessarily imply that they will become uniform. In fact, many services (tourism, trade fairs, translation, consultancy) originate from economic, social and cultural diversity and benefit from such diversity. In addition, the diffusion of specific diversity and the reduction of transport costs are responsible for an important part of service globalisation (tourism being the clearest example). On the other hand, new technologies and global environment foment the creation of competitive advantages based on service diversity (a consultancy firm which offers a clearly differentiated service, a trade fair which distinguishes itself from others by providing diversity of exhibitors).

Dimension D: International Networks

Apart from specific transactions (IT, FDI, IPF) service firms can contribute to the process of globalisation through their everyday activities. Formal or non-formal collaboration networks, technology transfer (from R&D activities to the mere exchange of know-how and expertise) or the very activity of foreign affiliates (their functioning and growth are a key form of globalisation) represent some examples of this process. The important role of service networks has been widely recognised (for example, Daniels et al., 1989; Nicolaidis, 1993; Aharoni, 1993; Bonamy and May, 1994; RESER, 1995 or Leo and Phillipe in this volume) and will not be further explored here. However, from all the various types of organisational relationship that could be explored in this section one stands out as requiring further attention – franchise networks, as these provide a link between branding and networks that have been largely neglected by service researchers.

Franchises: visible expression of globalisation
Franchises are maybe the most visible type of international service network. Clearly associated with brands, franchises represent the most complete expression of globally standardised services with the participation of a national investor. Usually, a franchise is defined as a form of business collaboration through which the franchiser allows those who franchise to reproduce the operating systems of an established business and offers – in exchange for the corresponding economic retribution – a 'brand', know-how as well as business and commercial methods. Fladmoe-Lindquist (2000) highlights franchising as an efficient method for international business expansion through four key common elements: shared identity, collective learning, connections to local partners and network culture.

Service franchises have grown strongly in European countries, especially in France and Germany. The development trajectory they have followed over the last few years places hotel and restaurant services in a prominent position (between 25 and 35 per cent of total franchises) together with personal equipment (20–30 per cent), specialised trade (5–8 per cent) and personal services (4–7 per cent). Although the more recent growth of specialised services, both personal and firm-related, should also be noted.

A point to be emphasised is that franchising is having significant effects on service production and supply, as well as on consumers' adaptation to these changes (Casares and Aranda, 2000). These effects which will possibly increase in the future can be identified as follows:

(i)   Franchises contribute to *service standardisation*. In principle, the possibilities of service standardisation are limited. However, one of the cornerstones of a franchise is that the franchiser transfers knowledge of a business to the person or enterprise who operates the franchise. This knowledge transfer includes the characteristics of the provided services, their physical image and the type of decoration as well as staffing issues (uniform, and so on). All these features result in the standardisation of provided services.[13]

(ii)   They enable services to *industrialise* by incorporating productive processes similar to those found in the industrial sector. Service franchises results in the expansion of the firms providing these services. This takes into consideration elements such as scale economies (in supply and advertising for instance) and purchasing power which contribute to competitiveness and profitability.

(iii)   They contribute to *service internationalisation.* Among the main service features the following stand out: the personal character and the impossibility of storing and transporting services. However, franchises partly breaks down these limitations. On the one hand, by incorporating a brand in service provision personal character is (partly) included. On the other hand the franchisee (supplier) provides a service locally and this removes the need for transportation and storage.

(iv)   Finally, service franchises foment the *standardisation of some consumption and behaviour patterns.* The provision of homogeneous services, under a recognised brand and a uniform quality, often leads to an extension and widening of clients' consumption and behaviour patterns. The commercial sector is maybe the best example. Most consumers are aware that in any city they will be able to find the same products in similar 'branded' establishments.

Establishment brands in services have similar characteristics to producer brands, but they adjust themselves to the development of some tertiary activities through franchise agreements. Franchises expand markets without the requirement of enormous direct investment on behalf of the owner of the brand, and they also ensure that the quality of the service or product is maintained.

CONCLUSION

Services and the growth of globalisation are strongly interrelated through a wide range of elements acting in both possible directions. Services have been active protagonists of globalisation by reducing distance, stimulating multinational companies, reinforcing specialisation, impacting on productivity, introducing new dynamism into economies and increasing or reducing specific asymmetries. The relationship between services, especially advanced services, and the new economy illustrates this. At the same time, services are going through a globalisation process but they have reached a level of internationalisation that is less than could be expected given the size of the service sector in developed market economies. Despite the recognised advantages held by multinational firms in the service sector evidently either service specificity or natural and artificial barriers are making it difficult for services to enter the global market place.

The globalisation of services can be analysed through four main dimensions: flows of international transactions, the role played by service brands, international frameworks and networks. These dimensions affect services and their production factors as well as the range of intangibles that are incorporated into services. All service international transactions can be classified and explored using these four dimensions although each case will be different. Some services will have developed a share of the global market by developing one of the dimensions of globalisation maybe at the expense of leaving the other three dimensions in an underdeveloped state. Obviously, each dimension provides interrelated forms and modes of globalisation. Most explanatory factors within these dimensions complement one another so that they are, in fact, different sides of the same process. However, in certain cases, substitution processes take place, for example between international trade and foreign investment or between greenfield direct investment and mergers and acquisitions. In these instances, both complementary and substitution processes coexist. A common element in all dimensions and modes is the increasing role of intangibles, information and reputation required by services as they enter the global market place. Further research and more attention should be devoted to exploring the role of these factors in the relationship between services and globalisation.

At a policy level, the impact of liberalisation and market integration will not be the same for services as that experienced by goods. There will be important differences even if there is an increasing integration between trade in services and goods. The specificity of services still needs to be further investigated and understood in order to better justify, organise and implement service policies, including GATS negotiations on service trade.

NOTES

1. Nevertheless, some differences can be established between the exact meaning of these concepts.
2. See the next chapter, by O. Giarini.
3. Another way of approaching internationalisation advantages is analysing separately macroeconomic and microeconomic effects, as it is done in Rubalcaba-Barmejo (1999).
4. Producer services represent a good example through different models: from the H–O–S model reinterpreting the comparative advantage when producer services can boost both goods imports and service exports (Melvin, 1989), the monopolistic competition producer service model where free trade is efficient under certain conditions (Markusen, 1989), to the linkages between trade, specialisation and comparative advantages (François, 1993), which suggests that supporting free trade in services is highly convenient.

5. Another factor explaining the conversion of TNCs into global firms is the combination of size and economic level given in the country of origin. Small countries like Switzerland or some Scandinavian countries have provided large service TNCs (in engineering, cleaning and security services, for instance) that could become global companies in the future.
6. He also stated that TNCs service activities precede those of goods and only certain producer and business services will lead to international investment in goods
7. They are defined in similar terms by the World Organisation of Intellectual Property, the North American Marketing Association and in many legal articles and analyses related to international marketing.
8. Both attributes were already conferred to brands centuries ago, even when Guilds used them as a *guarantee* enabling the buyer to identify the producer when the product was faulty or the producer to control the commercialisation of products.
9. Requiring business services to counsel on markets, financing, technology, and so on (Rubalcaba-Bermejo, 1999).
10. Many hotel chains base most of their success on offering and guaranteeing a specific service quality or even the internal layout and decoration of their hotels so that they look familiar to clients (such as Sheraton, Hyatt, Sol-Melia, Ciga, and so on). Something similar occurs in very internationalised travel agency chains, consultancies (Andersen, PriceWaterhouse & Coopers, Little, and so on), financial advisers (Morgan, Lehman) or car rental firms (Hertz, Avis, Dollar, and so on).
11. Obviously, in the case of services, the characteristics of some of them (very personalised, based on trust and 'personal' knowledge, and so on) enable local brands to function in a specific market area. For that reason in some merger situations local brands are maintained.
12. The decision to obtain a central locations in major cities; advertising campaigns or the extension of activities beyond those specific to the firm (for example to dedicate resources to sports, cultural or social events or various charitable donations).
13. The franchiser counts on a prestigious brand which guarantees the customer the uniformity of the service they require and the supplier the existence of a specific market share.

REFERENCES

Aaker, D. (1991), *Managing Brand Equity. Capitalizing on the Value of the Brand Name*, New York: The Free Press.

Aaker, D. (1995), *Building Strong Brands*, New York: The Free Press.

Aharoni, Y. (1993), 'Ownerships, Networks and Coalitions', in Y. Aharoni. (ed.), *Coalitions and Competition: the Globalization of Professional Business Services*, London and New York: Routledge.

Aharoni, Y. (2000a), 'Introduction: Setting the Scene', in Y. Aharoni and L. Nachum (eds), *Globalisation of Services: Some Implications for Theory and Practice*, London and New York: Routledge.

Aharoni, Y. (2000b), 'The Role of Reputation in Global Professional Business Services', in Y. Aharoni and L. Nachum (eds), *Globalisation of Services: Some Implications for Theory and Practice*, London and New York: Routledge.

Bailly, A., Coffey, W., Paelinck, J.H.P. and Polèse, M. (1992), *Spatial Econometrics of Services*, Aldershot: Avebury.

Baumol, W. (1967), 'Macroeconomics of unbalanced growth: The anatomy of urban crisis', *American Economic Review*, June, 57.

Baumol, W. (1985), 'Productivity Policy in the Service Sector', in R. Inmann (eds), *Managing the Service Economy*, Cambridge: Cambridge University Press.

Baumol, W. (2000), 'Services as leaders and the leader of the services', Inaugural lecture, International Conference on the Economics and Socio-Economics of Services, Lille, France, June 22 and 23, 2000.

Baumol, W.J., Blackman, S.A.B. and Wolff, E.N. (1989), *Productivity and American Leadership: the Long View*, Cambridge, MA: MIT Press.

Bernard, A. and Jones, C. (1996), 'Productivity across industries and countries: time series theories and evidence', *The Review of Economics and Statistics*, **78**, 135–46.

Bhagwati, J. (1987), 'International Trade in Services and its Relevance for Economic Development', in O. Giarini (ed.), *The Emerging Service Economy*, Oxford: Pergamon Press.

Bonamy, J. and May, N. (1994), *Services et Mutations Urbaines: questionnements et perspectives*, Paris: Anthopos, Economica.

Bullinger, H.-J. (1998), *Service 2000plus. A Future Report on Services in Germany*, Stuttgart: Fraunhofer IRB Verlag.

Casares, J. and Aranda, E. (2000), 'Las marcas en la configuración del sector servicios: una visión en escorzo', *Inform. Comercial Española,* 787, Sept.–October, 83–94.

Cerviño, J. (1996), 'La marca en la estrategia internacional de la empresa española', *Economía Industrial,* 307, 75–90.

Coffey, W.J. and Polése, M. (1987), 'Intrafirm trade in Business Services: implications for the location of office-based activities', *Papers of Regional Science Association,* **62**, 71–80.

Cuadrado-Roura, J.R. and Rubalcaba-Bermejo, L. (2000), *Los Servicios a Empresas en la Industria Española*, Madrid: Instituto de Estudios Economicos.

Cuadrado-Roura, J.R., Del Río-Gómez, C. (1993), *Los servicios en España*. Pirámide, Madrid.

Daniels, P.W. (1993), *Service Industries in the World Economy*, Oxford: Blackwell.

Daniels, P.W. and Moulaert, F. (eds) (1991), *The Changing Geography of Advanced Producer Services,* London: Belhaven Press.

Daniels, P., Thrift, N.J. and Leyson, A. (1989), 'Internationalisation of Professional Producer Services: accountancy conglomerates', in P. Enderwick (ed.), *Multinational Service Firms*, London: Routledge.

Daniels, P., Illeris, S., Bonamy, J. and Philippe, J. (1993), *The Geography of Services*, London: Frank Cass.

De Bandt, J. (1991), *Les Services: Productivité et Prix*, Paris: Economica.

De Bandt, J. (1995), *Services aux Entreprises*, Paris: Economica.

Dunning, J.H. (1993a), *Multinational Enterprises and the Global Economy*, Harrow: Addison-Wesley.

Dunning, J.H. (1993b), 'The Internationalisation of the Production of Services: some general and specific explanations', in Y. Aharoni. (ed.), *Coalitions and Competition: the Globalization of Professional Business Services*, London and New York: Routledge.

Enderwick, P. (1989), *Multinational Service Firms*, London and New York: Routledge.

European Economy, (2000), 'Mergers and acquisitions', *European Economy, Supplement A. Economic Trends*, 5/6.

Fernández, T. (2000), 'International Trade Activities of Business Service Foreign Affiliates Firms in Spain', International Conference on the Economics and Socio-Economics of Services. Lille, France, June 22 and 23, 2000.

Fladmoe-Lindquist, K. (2000), 'International franchising: a network approach to

FDI', in Y. and Aharoni L. Nachum (eds), *Globalisation of Services: Some Implications for Theory and Practice*, London and New York: Routledge.

Fontagné, L. (1999), 'Foreign Direct Investment and International Trade: Complements or Substitutes?', STI Working Papers 1999/3, Paris: OECD.

Fourastié, J. (1952), *Le Grand Espoir du XX siècle*, Paris: PUF.

François, J.F. (1993), 'Explaining the pattern of trade in producer services', *International Economic Journal*, **7** (3), 23–31.

Gadrey, J. (1996), *Services: la Productivité en Question*, Paris: Desclée de Brower.

Grönroos, C. (2000), *Service Management and Marketing. A Customer Relationship Management Approach*, 2nd edn, Chichester: Wiley.

Grosse, R. (2000), 'Knowledge Creation and Transfer in Global Service Firms', in Y. Aharoni and L. Nachum (eds), *Globalisation of Services: Some implications for theory and practice*, London and New York: Routledge.

Hirsch, S. (1993), 'The globalization of services and service-intense goods industries', in Y. Aharoni (ed.), *Coalitions and Competition: the Globalization of Professional Business Services*, London and New York: Routledge.

Hitt, M., Ireland, R.D. and Hoskisson, R.E. (1997), *Strategic Management. Competitiveness and Globalization*, 2nd edn, MN: West Publishing Co. St. Paul.

Hunt, S.D. and Morgan, R.M. (1995), 'The comparative advantage theory of competition', *Journal of Marketing*, **59**, April, 1–15.

Illeris, S. (1996), *The Service Economy: a geographical approach*, Chichester: John Wiley & Sons.

IMF (1997), *World Economic Outlook, May 1997*, Washington, DC: IMF.

Kang, N.-H. and Johanson, S. (2000), *Cross-border Mergers and Acquisitions: Their Role in Industrial Globalisation*, DSTI DOC (2000)1, Paris: OECD.

Kapferer, J.N. (1992), *Strategic Brand Management. New Approaches to Creating and Evaluating Brand Equity*, New York: The Free Press.

Krugman, P. (1996), *Pop Internationalism*, Cambridge, MA: The FreePress.

Leo, P.-Y. and Philippe, J. (1999), 'Stratégies tertiaires des exportateurs industriels', Économies et sociétés, **XXXIII** (5), May, 17–43.

Levitt, T. (1982), 'The globalization of markets', *Harvard Business Review*, May/June, 92–102.

Li, J. and Guisinger, S. (1993), 'Patterns of International Competition in Service Industries: global oligopolistic reaction and national competitive advantages', in Y. Aharoni (ed.), *Coalitions and Competition: the Globalization of Professional Business Services*, London and New York: Routledge.

Markusen, J.R. (1989), 'Trade in producer services and in other specialized intermediate inputs', *American Economic Review*, **79**, 85–95.

Marshall, N. and Wood, P. (1995), *Services and Space. Key aspects of Urban and Regional Development*, Singapore: Longman Singapore Publishers.

Melvin, J.R. (1989), 'Trade in Producer Services: a Hecksher–Ohlin Approach', *Journal of Political Economy*, **97**, 1180–96.

Murphy, J. (1987), *Branding, A Key Marketing Tool*, London: Macmillan Ltd.

Nachum, L. (2000), 'FDI, the Location Advantages of Countries and the Competitiveness of TNCs: US FDI in professional service industries', in Y. Aharoni and L. Nachum (eds), *Globalisation of Services: Some Implications for Theory and Practice*, London and New York: Routledge.

Nicolaidis, K. (1993), 'Mutual Recognition, Regulatory Competition and the Globalization of Professional Services', in Y. Aharoni (ed.), *Coalitions and Competition:*

the Globalization of Professional Business Services, London and New York: Routledge.

Noyelle, T.J. and Dutka, A. (1988), *International Trade in Business Services*, American Enterprise Institute, Washington DC: Ballinger Publications.

Nusbaumer, J. (1987), *Services in the Global Market*, Boston: Kluwer.

OECD (1999), *The Future of Global Economy. Towards a Long Boom?* Paris: OECD.

OECD (2000a), 'The service economy', *Business and Industry Policy Forum Series*, STI, Paris: OECD.

OECD (2000b), *A New Economy? The Changing Role of Innovation and Information Technology Growth*, Information Society, Paris: OECD.

OECD (2000c), 'Promoting Innovation and Growth in Services', *Science, Technology and Industry Outlook 2000*, Paris: OECD, forthcoming.

Ourusoff, A. (1992), 'Brands – What's Hot'; *Financial World*, August, **2**, 40–50.

Petit, P. (1986), *Slow Growth and the Service Economy*, London: Francis Pinter.

RESER (1995), *Consultancy Services Networks in Europe*, Aix-en-Provence: Serdeco Editions.

Riddle, D.I. (1986), *Service-led Growth, the Role of the Service Sector in World Development*, Praeger, New York.

Roach, S.S. (1991), 'Services under siege – the restructuring imperative', *Harvard Business Review*, **69**, September–October.

Roberts, J. (1998), *Multinational Business Service Firms*, Aldershot: Ashgate.

Roberts, J. (1999), 'The internationalisation of business service firms: a stages approach', *The Service Industries Journal*, October, **19** (4), 68–88.

Rubalcaba-Bermejo, L. (1999), *Business Services in European Industry: Growth, Employment and competitiveness*, Luxembourg: European Commission.

Rubalcaba-Bermejo, L. (2000), 'Productivity in European business services: some statistical measures', International Conference on the Economics and Socio-Economics of Services, Lille, France, June 22 and 23, 2000.

Rubalcaba-Bermejo, L. and Gago, D. (2001), 'Relationships between services and competitiveness: the case of Spanish trade', *The Service Industries Journal*, **21** (1), January, forthcoming.

Ten-Raa, T. and Wolff, E.N. (1996), 'Outsourcing of Services and the Productivity Recovery in US manufacturing in the 1980s', Tilburg Centre for Economic Research, Discussion Paper No. 9689.

UNDP (1999), *Human Development Report*, United Nations.

Vandermerwe, S. and Chadwick, M. (1989), 'The Internalisation of Services', *The Service Industries Journal*, **9** (1), January, 79–93.

WIR United Nations (2000), *World Investment Report, Cross-border Mergers and Acquisitions and Development*, United Nations.

Wolff, E.N. (1999), 'The productivity paradox: evidence from indirect indicators of service sector productivity growth', *Canadian Journal of Economics*, **32** (2), 281–308.

3. The globalisation of services in economic theory and economic practice: some conceptual issues

Orio Giarini

'CATCHING UP WITH THE ECONOMY'

In New York, in January 1999, Professor Robert W. Fogel delivered the presidential address to the American Economic Association. The title of his address was 'Catching up with the Economy' and in this he had the courage to state that 'the profession is lagging behind the economy more than it has to' (Fogel, 1999). There are some basic controversial issues that follow from this statement concerning the role of services in economics and in the economy:

- Fogel highlights 'the difficulty in measuring output in the service sector'. In the present situation services are no longer a sector but a function dominating, in terms of resource utilisation, all productive activities in the economy and in particular the so-called manufacturing sector. The fact that everybody admits that services represent two-thirds of the economy, is not the determining issue: it is rather to understand that the production of value is essentially everywhere based on services.
- This implies a revision of the notion of value. Understanding will be impossible if we still insist on measuring services and their positive economic results in terms of a scheme of thinking built essentially on the predominance of the industrial revolution.
- This is related to Fogel's thesis that 'the economic profession is lagging behind the economy more than it has to'. In fact, I came to the conclusion that economic theory, as it has been developed since Adam Smith, is not a theory of the economy *per se* but a theory founded on the experience of the industrial revolution. This was more than adequate during the time when the logic of industrial production was dominant. This is no longer the case: the utility of any productive economic system must be measured in terms of performance over a future period of time.
- The notion of performance in time opens the door for a fundamental,

58

positive re-thinking of the notion of risk on the one hand, and on the possibility and necessity of integrating the complementarity of non-monetized and non-monetarized productive activities in economic analysis. The two latter activities are increasingly complementary to any production system and they are in practice also considered as alternatives to situations in which monetarized solutions become inefficient. Therefore, there is an absolute need to broaden the boundaries of economics to integrate a significant part of non-monetarized and non-monetized activities. This goes beyond the idea of Samuelson who once stated that economics also includes non-monetized (but not non-monetarized) activities.

– I strongly disagree with the ideas that there are 'commodities that lack material form' (Fogel, 1999). There is no material product, which does not need a service for its utilisation, and there is no utilisation in whatever service function that does not use a material base. The difference between traditional industrial economics and service economics is that, in the first case, the material base is dominant, whereas in the second, the priority and the dominant base in terms of economic resources are represented by service functions. The attempt that has occurred over the last 20 years to define services in terms of immaterial commodities is the last conceivable effort to integrate service functions within a frame of reference based around traditional manufacturing – industrial-based economic thinking. Today, real activities in all so-called manufacturing industries are well beyond this point.

These points will be considered in detail in the following chapters. It is perhaps useful to start from the very beginning by exploring the boundaries that are set by mainstream economics on the economy and the requirement to push them beyond their present limits.

On the Question of Limits and Boundaries

I cannot resist the pleasure of citing a text, about 2000 years old, by Lucretius, from his *De Rerum Natura:*

> . . . *homo mortalis tollere contra est oculus ausus.*
> *quem neque fama deum nec fulmina nec minitanti*
> *murmure compressit caelum, sed eo magis acrem*
> *inritat animi virtutem, effringerre ut arta*
> *naturae primus portarum claustra cupiret.*
> *Ergo vivida vis animi pervicit, et extra*
> *processit longe flammantia moenia mundi*
> *atque omne immensum peragravit mente animoque:*

unde refert nobis victo quid possit oriri
quid nequate, finita potestas denique cuique
quanam sit ratione atque alte terminus baerens.

This text expresses the idea that human beings are daring creatures that, even if the skies appear scaring and intimidating, cannot resist going to verify nature's limits. The poem ends by saying that the human being in fact succeeds in reaching the very last limits of the universe and that from there he comes back as a winner, having achieved ultimate knowledge. I very much like this inspiring poem in which we can recognise the spirit of human endeavour, the willingness to conquer knowledge and, of course, the dramas which have paved such ambition. But, 2000 years after Lucretius, I would suggest that there is no question of human beings having reached any definitive limit: conquering or understanding a limit is simply the starting point for a further leap towards the unknown in the search for new knowledge. In fact, if we could ever imagine the end of limits, of boundaries or of constraints, it could simply mean that either the human being has become God, or that we have totally disappeared. The human condition, as we live it, is therefore institutionally bound up with the discovery, understanding and overcoming of limits in a dynamic process where, today, nobody would dare to set an end.

Identifying limits especially when they are considered as boundary conditions, is a normal scientific method but it can also become a trap. Another poet from our century, Pete Hein from Denmark, has written:

... our simple problems often grew
to mysteries we fumbled over
because of lines we nimbly drew
and later neatly stumbled over.

This poem is a perfect introduction to a fundamental thought of Alfred Marshall in his *Principles of Economics* (1909): . . . 'if the subject matter of a science passes through different stages of development, the laws which apply to one stage will seldom apply without modifications to others'. These poems and quotations remind us that in ancient times as well as in modern times, in physics as well as in economics, a fundamental question concerns limits and boundaries. There are moments in history when limits and boundaries appear relatively well defined and far off. There are other periods in history where limits and boundaries have been approached and, in a sense, conquered to such a point that in fact what we need is a new vision to fix new boundaries or, as some philosopher put it, propose and discover new paradigms.

It is my contention that today we are living through a period in which a fundamental change is taking place which started about two centuries ago and which is today definitely spreading around the world: this change is the

Industrial Revolution. This phenomenon has probably been the most important social event of modern times. It has integrated scientific advances with technological improvements and has spread democratic systems of governments around the planet. All this involves a process of growing complexity and interdependency of all human beings that live on spaceship earth. When it started, the industrial revolution began a major attack against a fundamental aspect of limits on earth: the problem of poverty. The ambition of the industrial revolution has been to promote the wealth of nations. Although this process is far from being completed, it has profoundly modified all human societies.

Today, the new paradigm in economics appears to be the following: under which new conditions can the wealth of nations be developed. The approach adopted by economics to solving this problem needs deep rethinking or modification. The fact is that we no more and nowhere live essentially in an economic system dominated by manufacturing. The latter is, of course, still important, but has become secondary to many service activities and functions. The notion of value in classical and neoclassical economic theory is one of those lines or targets which has been drawn and on which we are now in Pete Hain's words neatly stumbling over. In the next sections the key elements are formulated that should allow us to redefine the future boundaries of economic and social development.

KEY ELEMENTS IN THE NEW SEARCH FOR WEALTH IN THE SERVICE ECONOMY

In the industrial revolution all efforts have been concentrated on the production of goods in order to fight against poverty and to increase wealth. More shelters, more food and more energy were essential (and still are in many parts of the world) to allow people to live better quality lives. It should not be forgotten that the founder of economics, Adam Smith, promoted the discipline of Economics as a *moral* necessity. About 20 to 30 years ago the basic assumption of the industrial revolution began to alter considerably: the revolution took place in the manufacturing sector itself. During this period service functions became more important than traditional manufacturing activities.

From the Industrial Revolution to the Service Economy

In fact, if we consider all sectors of contemporary economic activity it can be shown that services of any sort comprise the essential part of the production and utilisation systems of both goods and services. A first fundamental fact to be taken into consideration is that for each product purchased, be it an automobile or a carpet, the pure cost of production or of manufacturing is very seldom higher than 20 per cent of the final price. More than 70 to 80 per cent is accounted for by the cost of making the complex service and delivery system function. This implies that service functions now account for the greatest part of investment even within the most traditional industrial companies. It must therefore be clear that the service economy does not exist in opposition to the industrial economy, but represents a more advanced stage of development in economic history.

In the same way, from the beginning of the industrial revolution, agricultural production was not eliminated and, on the contrary, remained a fundamental economic activity. But it is through industrialisation, directly or indirectly, that agriculture has become increasingly efficient. Now both agricultural and manufacturing industries increasingly rely on the development of services in order to ameliorate their economic performance in production, distribution and utilisation.

A recent survey (published by *Business Week*) into the economic consequences of new technologies calculated that the total cost of a computer used

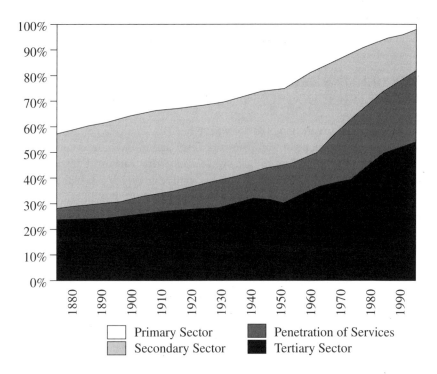

Figure 3.1 The changing structure of the German economy, 1880–1990

for a period of five years in American industry was made up of 10 per cent for the initial cost of the computer and 90 per cent for supporting services. Schindler, a leading world manufacturer of elevators, has forecast, on the basis of their 'industrial' experience, that within ten years employment in manufacturing jobs would be reduced to 8 per cent. The remaining 92 per cent of employees will be involved in the provision of services.

To illustrate this Figure 3.1 shows that since 1880 the German economy has altered so that the so-called tertiary sector *per se* has grown, but also that service functions have become dominant within the secondary sector itself. It should also be noted that a consistent part of the primary sector's output is linked to service functions. On the other hand, parts of the tertiary sector have also adopted procedures and processes that could be defined as 'manufacturing-like'. The key issues that need to be considered are:

1. To accept the idea that services are found in all sectors and, therefore, that traditional economic theory is somewhat obsolete.
2. It is advanced manufacturing industries that have developed the most and best performing services. Therefore, the old idea that services are a kind of secondary or even backward part of the economy needs to be dismissed.
3. We should not confuse pre-industrial services with services that are derived from a mature industrial society that have benefited from newer and more efficient technologies.
4. Service functions normally account for between 70 per cent and 80 per cent of 'production' costs in most 'manufacturing' companies. These functions belong to five categories (see Figure 3.2):
    ⇨ *Before manufacturing* (research, financing).
    ⇨ *During manufacturing* (financing, quality control, safety, and so on).
    ⇨ *Selling* (logistics, distribution networks, and so on).
    ⇨ *During product and system utilisation* (maintenance, leasing, and so on).
    ⇨ *After product and system utilisation* (waste management, recycling and so on).

Traditionally, costs were assigned to the 'production' phase. However, costs related to the other four phases (in both directions – pre- and postproduction) have constantly increased proportionally up to the point in which they have become dominant. The consumer, instead of being totally separate from the production process, is involved in this global production system, particularly at the level of distribution and above all utilisation and finally recycling. Alvin Toffler has described this phenomenon as the 'prosumer'.

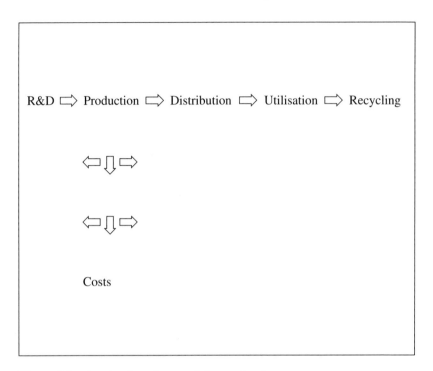

Figure 3.2   Service functions and the production system

Economic value is not only related to the existence of a material product (traditionally limited to the phase of material production), but is extended over the *performance* of the production system, whereas utility depends on the utilisation of the product or system. The notion of utilisation requires a time reference (duration), which in itself can only be defined as a probability. Costs and benefits, therefore, cannot be analysed adequately using a static system of reference, 'The General Equilibrium Theory', but have to refer to an economic system which has to optimise different levels of uncertainty.

Lessons from Insurance Pricing for Understanding the New Service Economy

The sale of a personal computer implies that 90 per cent of the actual cost of the machine (purchase price + running costs + services) must be based on an estimate of cost and prices that have to do with a period of utilisation related to a future period of time. The classical economic equilibrium between supply and demand has become a kind of uncertain system in which probabilities of future costs destroy the utopia of certainty of perfect price. Uncertainty is the name of the game in the service economy. In classical industrial economics prices are normally fixed by reference to production costs. In contrast, however, the insurance experience has always been that of a 'reversed cycle' in which a price has to be fixed on the basis of an uncertain event happening in the future.

Today, increasingly pricing systems in all economic sectors have begun to resemble insurance policies and are moving away from the traditional simplified 'industrial', equilibrium-based, price setting model. Indeed, some of the costs occasioned by product or system utilisation (including waste disposal) require judgements at the moment of sale which comes closer to the way an insurance underwriter thinks and acts: future events will affect the cost of any economic performance. This is particularly obvious in the case of leasing. Expansion of liability costs for products and services has become, for instance, a way of incorporating the future 'quality' performance of products and systems as a factor in the calculation of the 'costs of production' (*Financial Times*, 1999: 2).

With adequate information classical industrial economics could aim at 'perfect price equilibrium'. In the service economy the notion of uncertainty is an integral part of both practice and theory. Prices increasingly reflect a probabilistic judgement concerning future utilisation costs. In such circumstances, no 'scientific' information could ever generate what is thought as 'perfect' information. Economics needs to look closely at the way in which insurance price systems work.

RISK MANAGEMENT VULNERABILITY AND INSURABILITY

The notion of systems becomes essential in the service economy. When systems function properly they produce positive results or economic value. The notion of systems operation (or functioning) requires the consideration of real time and the dynamics of real life. Whenever real time is taken into consideration the degree of uncertainty and of probability that conditions any human action becomes a central issue.

The economics of the industrial revolution could, in contrast, rely on the fiction of perfect equilibrium theory (outside real time and duration), based on the assumption of certainty. During most of the economic history of the industrial revolution, risk and uncertainty has been a subject only for historians and sociologists and not for economists. The first systematic attempt to take risk and uncertainty into consideration was made with great timidity by Frank Knight during the 1920s (Knights, 1933).

Any system working to obtain some future result is by definition in a situation of uncertainty, even if different situations are characterised by different degrees of risk, uncertainty or even indetermination. But risk and uncertainty are not a matter of choice: they are simply part of the human condition. Rationality is, therefore, not so much a problem of avoiding risks and eliminating uncertainty, but of controlling risks and of reducing uncertainty and indetermination to acceptable levels in given situations. Furthermore, the systemic nature of modern economic systems and the increasing degree of complexity of technological developments require a deeper and deeper economic understanding and control of the increasing vulnerability and complexity of these systems.

Unfortunately, the notion of vulnerability is generally misunderstood. To say that vulnerability increases through increases in the quality and performance of modern technology might seem paradoxical. In fact, the higher level of performance of most technological advances relies upon a reduction of the margins of error that a system can tolerate without breakdown. Accidents and management mistakes still happen even if less frequently, but there effects have costly systemic consequences. Opening the door of a car in motion does not necessarily lead to a catastrophe. In the case of a modern aeroplane, it will. This shows that the notions of system functioning and of vulnerability control become a key economic function where the contributions of people like economists and engineers must be integrated. In a similar way, problems of social security and savings for the individual have to take into account vulnerability management. Thus, the notion of risk and the management of vulnerability and uncertainty become a key connotation of the service economy.

Let us now consider the notion of insurability (manageability of risks and uncertainties), which although unknown in most courses on economics, is a fundamental concept for the interpretation and management of the key economic problems of our time. Although pure risks (depending on the implicit vulnerability of any system) and entrepreneurial risks (depending on taking or not taking a specific action) are in many cases interrelated and interdependent, it is important to make a clear distinction as to their different nature. Here, too, we have to remark that only entrepreneurial risks as such have been considered, although belatedly, by economic theory and analysis.

In fact, entrepreneurial risk itself is increasingly conditioned, in all sectors, by an adequate understanding and control of pure risk, from the management of financial risk through the question of systemic risk. Everything seems to be pointing to one key issue: the identification of the level or the threshhold of insurability, within which the private system can operate. Beyond that level of insurability, whatever the political ideology of a government, the public authorities or society at large have to step in. But as attempts are made to minimise the vulnerability (financial, economic and social) of governments and society, it is clear that the *notion of insurability is moving, little by little, centre-stage of future economic policy making.* Governments are increasingly recognising that they have a vested interest in stimulating an efficient private insurance system in order to develop an adequate economic policy. In fact, most governments in today's world are forced into privatising many activities in order to make them more efficient, but also to reduce their deficits. Once again this process concerns key policies like social security, the effects of natural catastrophes, industrial and environmental risks (with all the consequences for liability that they involve), health insurance, crime and terrorism prevention (including fraud and moral hazard related issues). To the extent that they fall within the limits of insurability, all these activities can be transferred to private institutions.

There are of course essentially two levels of insurability:

- An upper level at which in theory all risks can be insured, provided they are sufficiently defined as a class and adequately quantified as far as their frequency and gravity are concerned; and
- A second level of insurability is determined by the capacity of the insurance industry, or of any risk management institution, to cover risks properly. The word capacity embraces both financial and management potential.

Of course, any analysis of insurability involves specific issues like: the market and regulatory conditions for adequate capacity-building; the development of professionalism in risk selection (the improvement of rating management); regulations on solvency and fiscal conditions; the control of liabilities contracted in the past and their effect on the future solvency of insurance companies and institutions; reserve constitution in cases of extreme uncertainty. But such analysis also involves, as a matter of general economic policy, the setting up of economic incentives that facilitate economic development through the control of vulnerabilities. In economic terms, this means that any optimisation process has to consider, on the one hand, the cost of services from research to waste management, and on the other, the risk management procedures relating to all possible hazards. Insurability is, finally, also the line along which a new division of labour is being developed between private insurance and private industry in general on the one hand, and the public sector on the other.

GLOBALISATION AND DELOCALISATION IN THE WORLD SERVICE ECONOMY

If more and more business (turnover or sales and utilisation) is done not where the manufacturing process takes place, but where products and systems are utilised and then finally disposed of, it is clear that a greater part of the 'production system' is displaced to where the clients are located. What was always largely true for insurance (where one knows that you cannot cover a fire in Sicily using the same criteria one would use in Holland or in Asia) is now truer for all economic activities. The sale of hardware and even automobiles produces costs where products, systems and services are distributed, used and then disposed of. Of course, the international exchange of products still exists, and is important, but it is bypassed increasingly by the fact that investments are needed in foreign countries to create distribution and utilisation infrastructures. It is quite obvious when following this logic that the internationalisation of many economic sectors leads to acquisitions and investments that strengthen the distribution capabilities of companies. The transnational sale of products directly from a foreign base, although important and favoured by the development of powerful communication technology, is increasingly only a second level priority in this context.

Therefore, because of the logic of the service economy a global business strategy tends to *combine* investment with trade (through acquisitions or other methods) to develop *local* human capital and resources. This is fundamental for understanding internationalisation and directly concerns global economic policies. The world becomes without frontiers, but it is a situation that goes much deeper than a simple increase in international trade. The reason for this is that investment in foreign countries creates a much more rigid situation. It also stimulates autonomy.

From the standpoint of the world economy the crucial difference between the classical Industrial Revolution and the present service economy is that, with the former, investment in a foreign country was an alternative to exports, whereas with the service economy exports are closely related to investment. The reason for this is that investment is linked to utilisation and, in turn, utilisation is linked to consumer presence and active participation. There is a great message of hope in this situation that far outweighs the theory of comparative advantage (sometimes effective in a classical industrial economy). There now exists a vested interest for all world producers to establish efficient local utilisation systems. Thus, we rediscover, in an economic sense, a great general interest that all can share, in that the poorer becomes richer because they are the terrain in which new markets can be developed on the basis of their ability to use as prosumers.

This situation will probably soon have a profound impact on the activities of international institutions such as the World Trade Organisation (WTO). The WTO's predecessor, GATT, had in fact already commenced its involvement in services at the time of the Tokyo Round via the discussion on non-tariff barriers to trade. All such barriers were in reality system conditions for product utilisation. On the occasion of the Uruguay Round, the initial ideas were that if services could be defined as simply another type of good then the fostering of international trade would produce no major problems. In the event, things turned out differently and the Uruguay Round negotiators, stimulated by economic reality, were finally able to establish such principles as the right of establishment and national treatment. These are, in fact, the foundation stones of any investment policy worthy of the name for the service economy.

The way will be open for more optimistic, productive and fair strategies for developing the world economy once economists and economic leaders become conscious of the realities and potentials of the service economy. In this process, the WTO could prove a prime mover in relaunching the wealth of nations worldwide. The key to the global economy is to have the right vision of the service economy.

PRODUCTIVITY, QUALITY AND PERFORMANCE

If we accept that economic value in a service economy is determined by the performance of a system, we can propose that the notion of quality be fully integrated with the notion of performance. Higher quality performances have better value than lower quality performances. The two notions of quality and performance are in fact identical. What we are lacking is a system of measurement of economic value that can actually and effectively quantify variations in wealth production generated by all types of economic system.

In practice, a bad quality performance has a lower economic value and a performance which is very bad can even produce negative or destructive results which can be termed 'deducted values' (Giarini and Loubergé, 1978). We can also observe that more modern economies become high-technology service economies; the dichotomy between quantity and quality tends to become increasingly interdependent. Even high technological mass production must increasingly incorporate qualitative aspects to function economically. For the more advanced systems and technologies, the notion of gaining in quantity at the expense of quality (performance) makes less and less sense. It must be stated that quality must be understood in relation to the performance of a system in relation to stated objectives.

In some cases, there is the requirement of having the right type of quality and performance. For instance in the case of products that must be destroyed after use the cost of destruction must not increase disproportionately. The reason for this is that the quality of the product during use has been reinforced to the extent of becoming a *negative* quality when the product passes from the phase of utilisation to that of destruction, recycling or reconditioning. This is a problem that involves optimising the duration or the life cycle of products (Börlin and Stahel, 1987).

The problem of measuring the productivity of services highlights the fact that an economy that is essentially based on service functions cannot rely on traditional productivity measures developed for the industrial economy. Many scholars have tried to exploit traditional ways of measuring services output, but only modest results have been achieved (Ascher and Whichard, 1987; Trogan, 1988). The key issue is the possibility of defining what is the product and what is the output of a service activity as compared to an industrial activity. In both cases, it is comparatively simple to quantify the cost of production factors and inputs. In the case of the industrial economy the product is identified by a material object sold on the market. Normally, productivity means the capacity of production factors to produce in a given period of time more and more units of material products. In the case of services, we have to deal with a performance and, therefore, the traditional measurement of productivity leads in most cases to erroneous conclusions.

The methodological difficulty is that traditionally economic theory is based on the assumption of price equilibrium between supply and demand. Therefore, the cost of production is easily equated with the value of demand. The result is that, in case of services, the measurement of their value and productivity is often based on the value of production factors. In this way, a public administration that doubles its employees or doubles the salaries of its employees with no additional performance whatsoever would be considered as having doubled its value in terms of gross national product. In the same way, an inefficient administration, badly paid, as is the case for one country in the European Community, has been considered as having above average productivity because its relative costs to other public national administrations is lower, and they are all supposed to fulfil the same basic functions. Once again, no measurement of the *real performance or quality* of the services produced is taken into consideration and integrated into the traditional economic evaluation.

The extension of service functions in modern economies will increasingly oblige economists and all those involved with economic issues to decide:

- either to maintain their evaluation using traditional accounting methods of value added as proposed by classical and neoclassical industrial economics; this will results in a constant diminishing in the relevance and significance of such measurements;
- or find practical, as well as theoretical ways, to integrate measurements of service performance, or (which is the same thing) measurement of the *quality* of outputs, and in particular of results, in order to re-

establish a significant and useful possibility of measuring the real wealth produced by the economic system.

This implies for instance that the measurement of the costs and productivity of health-related activity is not done in terms of the value added produced, but in terms of the level of health achieved for a given population and/or for a given individual. Once more, these quality indicators have to be integrated into a system of evaluation including, of course, the traditional measurement of the value added. Whatever the objections as to the difficulty of this task and to the problems of integrating monetarized and non-monetarized indicators, these objections cannot change the nature of the problem. It is up to modern economic thinking to face this challenge.

At a time when 70 per cent of the working population in the advanced economies (and more than 50 per cent in the rest of the world) perform service functions, it is high time to redefine the type of wealth produced in real terms, and how these activities can be realistically quantified. In other words, how can the quality of the performance be measured in economic terms in such a way that we can find an answer to the old question of identifying and quantifying 'the wealth of nations'.

WORK, EMPLOYMENT AND PRODUCTIVE ACTIVITIES

In the course of the industrial revolution employment or remunerated work became the absolute and essential priority for economic development (monetarised activities). Before the industrial revolution, self-production and self-consumption were the dominant mode through which humanity generated economic wealth or at least secured economic survival (non-monetarised activities).

Since ancient times, of course, little by little, specialisation and productive activities came into existence and as a consequence developed the basis for the growth of trade and exchange. At first, trade and exchange were based on barter or similar techniques where a unit of account or reference was either linked to a specific product or was implicit (what we call monetarised, but non-monetised activity). The growth of such social and economic relations prepared the ground for the beginning of the industrial revolution. During the transition from the industrial revolution to the current service economy the cost of production in manufacturing and services was increasingly transferred to the consumer through the latter's participation in making products and services usable. Self-service is spreading in all sectors and information technology is lending fresh impulse to this trend. It is primarily through this transfer that in all sectors of the economy those responsible for cost control have been increasingly able to reduce production costs. Self-production activities (non-monetarised ones) are clearly making a comeback.

In addition, non-market activities or unpaid work done without payment (but still related to an exchange although non-monetised) are increasing. A recent television broadcast in France on benevolent activities has estimated that 8 million people undertake at least 4 to 5 hours of voluntary work per week, frequently in addition to or even to complement monetised activity.

At the time of the industrial revolution employment (monetarised, paid work) was the key and practically sole mechanism for economic development. However, in the service economy the interdependency of all three forms of productive activity needs to be taken into consideration. Social and economic efficiency depend increasingly on how these three forms (monetarized (monetized or non-monetized) and non-monetarized) combine, integrate or, as economists are fond of saying, enable a system to be better optimised. The combining of the three forms of productive activity is not based on any declaration of good will, but on an understanding of how a service economy really works today.

It is also important to remember that the issue of employment requires an economic approach that brings supply back into the centre-stage: work, indeed any productive activity, is the most obvious and fundamental expression of our personality and of our freedom. We are, first and foremost, what we do. It is imperative, therefore, that social policy considers people as human beings deserving of opportunities to 'produce themselves'. This is not to say that demand systems need not be considered. But such systems must be understood as selection mechanisms for choosing and using what the supply system has to offer. Supply, even in economic systems, is *always in excess*, and demand selects what is offered. Inventiveness, initiative and the entrepreneur are to be found on the side of supply, including the 'prosumer'. Without demand though, supply might grow like a cancer in the wrong direction.

A key issue is the redefinition of the role of private and public initiatives and activities. Throughout the industrial revolution, one role of economic theory was to define what were deemed to be public utilities for which the government was solely responsible. According to the culture and political regime of each country, there was, therefore, a vertical allocation of productive activities, sector by sector, between the State and private institutions. In the service economy, this vertical, sector-by-sector, distribution might be replaced by a horizontal one:

1. The State, internationally, nationally and locally, could intervene at different levels and in various ways so as to provide the equivalent of basic employment for all (around 20 hours per week organised in various ways and for various periods of time). This should not be considered merely as part-time employment but the basic unit of guaranteed formal work.

2. This basic level of work should be remunerated at a minimum level. Beyond this first level of paid employment, all government or State intervention should be limited, so that in practice the guaranteed first level would, on the one hand, provide a minimum to act as a social net and, on the other, guarantee the maximum development of private initiative. The first level would correspond, more or less, to what is considered part-time work but the notion of part-time should be abandoned and considered as a first or basic unit of work. This level of employment would only occupy a small part of the time available in everyday life and would allow for a more flexible definition of individual personality reflecting the *full range* of an individual's productive activities. An individual's professional and personal identity would not necessarily be based on first-level work, but rather on second-level free entrepreneurial activities.

The following points would need to be considered. First, the basic unit of work, equivalent to a part-time job remunerated at a minimum level, would concern people between the ages of 18 and 75 years. The three major population groups (young, old and women) that belong to categories of people excluded from the industrial revolution could, through this project, achieve social re-inclusion in a productive way. The young would have more opportunities for combining practical job experience with education and, at the same time, be able to learn how to self-support themselves. This would also help to create a demand for higher education institutions (like universities) to be better integrated in society through personal and practical links between theory and practice. Women with young children and men in similar situations would benefit from greater flexibility in the organisation of their lives.

Older people at around the age of 60 would start a period of gradual retirement. They could also continue to feel useful in society and above all remain ready to use previous experience and a lifelong education to prepare themselves for new productive activities, both in the monetarised and non-monetarised systems. This would help to provide security and increase the social integration of older people who at 60 still have a life expectancy of 20 years. In such circumstances, the possibility and even the guarantee of a part-time job (remunerated or partly remunerated, or supported in a non-remunerated activity) would constitute an essential complement to the three pillars of the social security system (government pensions, occupational pensions and private savings). It would also reduce the burden upon younger generations of supporting a growing older population and thereby place young and old alike, in a better economic and cultural position.

THE PROBLEM OF DETERMINING VALUE

The changes in the economic system since the beginning of the seventies have not simply been indicative of the beginnings of a new long-term cycle of the industrial revolution. It is rather that the economy has changed from an essentially manufacturing system to an essentially service-oriented one. During the same period economic theory, particularly at the macroeconomic level, has suffered from serious shortcomings. These shortcomings are mainly due to the fact that economic theory was formalised in response to the development of the first Industrial Revolution (Adam Smith's book *The Wealth of Nations* was published in 1776). Two centuries of successful industrial revolutions have confirmed and stimulated economic theories of various types, but all are deeply rooted in the belief that the *manufacturing* system as an entity has absolute priority. Understanding the new service economy will probably require a re-consideration of the basic assumptions and paradigms of economic theory. This will inevitably stimulate a new debate on what is the focus of economic theory: the notion of value.[1]

One of the key issues in the research for a new value paradigm for the service economy derives from the obvious inadequacies of productivity measurement for service functions. The notion of value added in the industrial revolution is a tool to measure a flow (the flow of production). Production factor inputs are relatively easily measured against specific types of flows represented by manufactured products. But when we consider the performance of services, we cannot measure them in terms of flows, but rather in terms of the results of a system's functioning. The issue is really to go back to more fundamental questions: has economic wealth really increased? And how efficiently have resources been employed?

These questions always implicitly refer to wealth as a stock and not as a flow. The industrial mode of production has made it possible to accept the assumption that all value added, as a measurement of a flow, could be considered as an addition to wealth (to a stock). This assumption is no more valid when we are in a service economy. Therefore, a new notion of value is needed to define and to measure real advances in increasing the wealth of nations in the present new economic situation. This not only for general economic purposes, but also for solving the very specific problem of productivity measurements.

Many other basic issues in economic theory should be reconsidered in terms of the new service economy. This concerns, for instance, economies of scale, where the optimisation of a system is clearly not simply the addition of the optimisation of the scale of each *component* of the same system. The economy of scale of a manufacturing activity cannot be considered independently from the scale constraints and costs of all surrounding service functions (distribution, storage, maintenance, waste management, pollution costs, and so on).

A clear bias of current economic theory that favours an economic situation centred on pure manufacturing activities is Engel's law. According to this law, consumers only demand more service activities when basic needs are satisfied. These basic needs are, of course, represented by food, shelter and health, but it is clear that no one of these basic needs can be satisfied unless the products in question (food, houses, and so on) are made available. *Services are an essential condition of the utilisation value of these products.* Engel's law is nothing but a variant of the traditional three-sector theory and it reproduces a tradition clearly stated by Adam Smith – that services make no essential contribution to economic development. This was right and proper during his time, but it is an assumption that needs radical reconsideration (see Giarini and Liedtke, 1998).

SOME HINTS AT THE PHILOSOPHY AND CULTURAL BASIS THAT CONCERN THE FUNDAMENTALS OF THE VIEWS ON EQUILIBRIUM VS. UNCERTAINTY IN ECONOMICS

Probably *the* most relevant feature of changes in the socioeconomic environment towards a service economy is their relation *to the advance of scientific thinking* and of discoveries in the last century. More generally, this has to do with the relationship between social and natural (soft and hard) sciences that embody the cultural background of our knowledge, views, attitudes and behaviour with regard to our individual and community life.

There can no longer be any 'scientific' justification for considering a state of equilibrium in economics (as referred to the Newtonian model) as the premise of economic analysis. In some cases, equilibrium might be desirable, but economic progress could well depend much more on specific and *desirable states of non-equilibrium* in cases where the isolated industrial system opens up to a multiplicity of new functions and interactions typical of the service economy. The key economic question of the future might well become not 'how shall we achieve a perfect (certain) equilibrium?', but rather 'how shall we create or stimulate productive non-equilibrium situations?', situations which, contrary to Newtonian philosophy, have a real time dimension. However, the model still subsumed by the mainstream of current economic thinking has as its fundamental paradigm the hypothesis of perfect equilibrium and of certainty, that belong to the static Newtonian scientific model. Unfortunately, this means that the current economic model often refers to scientific premises which science itself has long ago abandoned.

Intuition suggests that the idea that modern societal and economic development depends not so much on achieving perfect, deterministic and sure objectives. Rather it depends on developing creative activities, in a world where uncertainty, probability and risk are a *given* condition, providing a circumstance of real opportunities and choice. This would not be a step backwards towards irrationality. Quite the contrary, more intelligence, more rationality and more initiative are required to cope with situations of uncertainty, which after all are the daily experience of every living being. The simplistic vision of mechanised pre-programmed robots belongs much more to a deterministic world: the attempt to achieve abstract 'certainty' and 'perfect' information can only lead to a dogmatic, pseudo-religious system on the one hand or, on the other, to the annihilation of all intelligence, to the destruction of all hope for development and creativity. The marriage of contemporary scientific thinking with social sciences, and in particular with economics, in an increasingly complex world, which is interactive even beyond the limits of planet Earth, is providing a rich source of moral and intellectual stimulus for reconstructing an Image of the Future.

Learning to face uncertainties and to manage risks under these new horizons could in turn lead to an advance in the human condition. Even in terms of equity or of social justice, the problem is not to produce or to distribute *security*, which is in any case a self-deceiving notion in political (look at the dictatorships of our century) as well as in economic terms. State or Community protection policies should avoid protecting individuals in such a way as to make them increasingly vulnerable, inefficient, and ultimately prone to greater psychological and physical insecurity. Equity has more to do with increasing the physical and cultural capacity of individuals and communities to face uncertainty. The very risks that confront all living species render them creative. *Absolute poverty* is a situation in which no risk can be faced, no choice taken. It is the opposite of progress.

Finally, *in cultural terms*, no enterprise is built by dreams alone. But equally none gets off the ground without some dreaming. Successful action is by necessity guided by practical circumstances. The goal of any action is defined, implicitly or explicitly, by the deep nature of the human species, including dreams, visions of life and culture. The dynamics of life and the challenge of risk and uncertainty, require from us a new creative effort leading to the renewal of our philosophic approaches. Today we need to reconsider the notion of progress, which the philosophies and the ideologies of certainty have shuttered so much and almost destroyed. There is no real human culture other than that to be found in the real-life process of creation. This involves producing and the continuous testing, in each of our many endeavours, of an Image of the Future that we could fashion for ourselves. It is the fundamental intellectual challenge facing a modern society. Let's face risks. Let's become conscious, Risk Managers.

NOTE

1. Proposals on this point have been made in the report to the Club of Rome 'Dialogue on Wealth and Welfare', Pergamon Press, Oxford, 1980. Research in this area is also promoted by the Product-Life Institute, Geneva. This type of debate is also inevitably linked to a series of philosophical implications (see in this sense L'Incertitude de Newton à Heisenberg, un nouveau Paradigme pour l'Economique, par Orio Giarini, Vol. 9, n° 33 of *The Geneva Papers*, October 1984). See also 'The Limits to Certainty' by Orio Giarini and Walter Stahel, Kluwer, 1993.

REFERENCES

Ascher, B. and Whichard, O. (1987), 'Improving Services Trade Data', in O. Giarini, (ed.), *The Emerging Service Economy*, Oxford: Pergamon Press, pp. 255–82.

Börlin, M. and Stahel, W. (1987), *Stratégie Économique de la Durabilité*, Zurich: Swiss Bank Corporation, Zurich.

Financial Times (1999), 'EU faces up to product liability shift', *Financial Times*, 25 August, 2.

Fogel, R.W. (1999), 'Catching up with the economy', *American Economic Review*, March, 1–22.

Giarini, O. and Loubergé, H. (1978), *The Diminishing Returns of Technology*, Oxford: Pergamon Press.

Giarini, O. and Liedtke, P. (1998), *El Dilema del Empleo*, Barcelona: Galaxia Gutenberg.

Knight, F. (1933), *Risk, Uncertainty and Profit*, London: London School of Economics and Political Science.

Marshall, A. (1909), *Elements of Economics of Industry: Being the First Volume of Elements of Economics*, London: Macmillan.

Trogan, P. (1988), 'Les Statistiques de Production sur les Services Marchands et la Mesure de la Productivité', in O. Giarini and J.R. Roulet (eds), *L'Europe Face à la Nouvelle Économie des Services*, Paris: PUF, pp. 95–112.

4. A comparative approach to the internationalisation of service industries

Luis Rubalcaba-Bermejo and Juan R. Cuadrado-Roura

INTRODUCTION

This chapter explores service internationalisation trends including levels, growth rates, leadership and the relative position of service industries. The analysis draws upon the most recent available data and a comparative approach is developed that explores differences between countries, sectors and internationalisation modes. This chapter addresses four specific questions: (1) How service-oriented are the processes of internationalisation? (2) How has service internationalisation grown?; (3) Who are the leaders in service internationalisation?; and (4) How internationalised are specific service sectors? The first two questions are partially answered by comparing goods versus service trade and their different internationalisation modes. The third question compares countries and modes while the fourth compares service sectors and modes resulting in the development of an index of internationalisation.

These four questions guide the interpretation of the empirical evidence. Several hypotheses will therefore be explored. On one hand, one can expect that economic 'servicisation'[1] is reflected in international exchanges (tertiarisation) and service trade is growing more than the trade in goods. Otherwise, limitations to service internationalisation could be more important than they are supposed to be, and goods would still *lead global processes*. On the other hand, one can expect that particular sectors and countries dominate or lead the process of service internationalisation: such sectors include transnational service companies (TNCs) (banking and telecommunication) and the parent countries of transnational service firms, especially American firms. Otherwise, *new service processes and new service trading countries would continue to emerge as active players in global service markets*. At the same time, the previously mentioned hypothesis (see Chapter 2) on the shift from pure trade to investment and new competitive investment modes (for example, mergers) will also be explored by evaluating the *complementarity* of these modes of service internationalisation.

The following sources have been used for each indicator: WTO (2000) and Eurostat (2000a, 2000b) for IT; Eurostat (1999a) for FDI; and WIR Report (2000) for M&A. Complementary sources have also been used for specific aspects not covered by these sources. Additional information on methodology and statistical aspects can be obtained from each of the above sources. The analysis is mainly based on three indicators: international trade (IT), foreign direct investment (FDI) and mergers and acquisitions (M&A) (see interrelations and complementary/substitution processes in Chapter 2). The statistics used in this analysis only provide data related to supply rather than demand. Consequently, there is limited evidence concerning the global demand for services provided within agricultural or manufacturing firms, despite the fact that these are also faced with an internationalisation process and are a very important part of growing intra-firm trade. Unfortunately, there is not enough data to include these issues. In addition, with respect to statistics, the most recent and available data have been used. However, it is well known that all these sources have important methodological limitations, as well as quantitative and qualitative deficits. The implication is that specific empirical findings need to be analysed cautiously. Nevertheless, the statistics that describe service trade trends at the global levels are sufficiently reliable.

Despite these limitations the consulted sources are the best available statistics to analyse service internationalisation and they also enable the disaggregation of trends. For each question, suitable indicators are identified and treated in the most appropriate way for analytical purposes. This is the case, for instance, for internationalisation levels in direct investment, which can be measured both through outward and inward investment flows and through the stock of assets or liabilities. The former is very volatile but permit the identification of short-term trends while the latter allow the identification of real service weight in total FDI and long-term trends. The volatility of many variables related to internationalisation necessitates the use, in some cases, of annual averages and cumulative values.

SERVICE ORIENTATION OF GLOBAL TRADING

The total volume of global trade in services (commercial services) has recently been estimated by Karsenty (2000) using the four WTO modes of international trade. Conventional modes 1 and 2 have been rising to US$1.3 trillion and modes 3 and 4 may have accounted for another US$850 billion in trade in 1997, bringing the total to about US$2.2 trillion or a figure equivalent to 7–8 per cent of world GDP. These figures make up 16 per cent of total goods and service trade, or an increase of 6 points since 1985.

Although these figures indicate the growing process of tertiarisation the rate of growth identified is too low. It is necessary to point out that these figures are rough estimates since there are many methodological limitations. The figures give an indication of the total volume of world-wide trade where traditional ways of trading represent up to 80 per cent of total service trade. It is frequently stated that most modes of international service trade are under-estimated. That is the case of cross-border IT but also of FDI (for example, non-equity arrangements and inter-sectorial FDI are excluded), so these statistics are not completely comparable. In addition, FDI has increased in importance. For example, cross-border service mergers and acquisitions represented around US$400 billion in 1999, more than twice the 1997 figure. Recent developments in other FDI has also been very strong during the last years, so the balance between trade and FDI is increasingly in equilibrium. In addition, other indicators should be taken into account to estimate the real and current importance of global service trade. For example, the important and increasing role of service foreign affiliates (see Box 4.1) is a major source of international flows, many of which are not accounted for in current statistics.[2]

BOX 4.1: THE ROLE AND WEIGHT OF FOREIGN AFFILIATES

Foreign affiliates (FA) make two contributions to the globalisation process. First, when they are established, through a green-field investment or a merger or acquisition. And afterwards, when they develop their normal business activities. The employment, sales, value added, exports, and so on, generated by foreign affiliates contribute to the globalisation of services. Recently, some studies have provided the first preliminary data (not too reliable but indicative) on the activities of service foreign affiliates. The OECD/Eurostat survey on the activities of service foreign firms (FATS) estimate global value added by these firms to be US$500 billion in 1997, or 1.9 per cent of world GDP (Karsenty, 2000). From the same survey, Knauth (2000) underlines how foreign-owned enterprises account for almost 20 per cent of the turnover generated in service markets in Denmark, Sweden, Finland and the UK, even if they only represent 1 per cent of total enterprises and employ 8 per cent of people. Foreign-owned enterprises had the greatest impact on distribution trades in terms of their presence and economic weight. In second place come real estate and business service activities. Most European people working in non-EU firms were employed by US companies.

The OECD (1999a) study on multinationals provides a preliminary analysis of foreign affiliates based on a few main countries (US, Germany, Japan and Canada). These statistics are not fully comparable; methodologies vary and not all countries include the same items (for example, US hotels and business services are not included). There is a clear under-representation of FA service firms in terms of turnover and employment compared to manufacturing FA. However, this does not hold for the number of enterprises. The number of FA service firms in these four countries represents 64 per cent of total foreign affiliates. Germany shows the highest relative service percentage, 75 per cent (47 per cent in trade, hotels and restaurants). Japan and Canada have a similar rate, 64–66 per cent, but distributed in a very different way (Japan 56 per cent in trade, hotels and restaurants, while Canada 36 per cent in finance, insurance and business services). The figures for the US are lower (57 per cent, of which 36 per cent in finance and insurance) but this is probably due to statistical problems. The high proportion of service FA does not correspond to figures related to employees or turnover. German, Japanese and US service FA firms only employ 31 per cent and produce around 46 per cent of total turnover. On the contrary, 22 per cent of manufacturing firms employ 47 per cent of employees and produce between 35 per cent of total turnover in US and 56 per cent in Canada.

This different behaviour is explained by the role of small and medium-sized enterprises (SMEs) in service firms, or even in TNCs developing services activities. The average size of manufacturing FA was 587 employees in 1996 (618 in 1992), while the average size of service FA was 273 employees (266 in 1992); 224 in trade, hotels and restaurants and 43 in finance, insurance and business services. The reduced size of business service firms is clearly reproduced internationally suggesting different way of production even amongst the largest TNCs. The average service FA firm is bigger in US (215) than in Japan (55) or Germany (41). In spite of differences in statistical methodologies and coverage (US exclusion of business services enlarges the US total size of service firms), US FA firms seem to be substantially larger than those of other countries. What should also be underlined is the fact that, in all three countries, average size is stable or decreasing between 1992 and 1996 for all categories except for manufacturing in Japan and trade, hotels and restaurants in Japan and US, where average size is growing by 3 per cent annually.

International Trade

In relative terms, international trade in commercial services accounted for 19.6 per cent of total world trade in 1999. However, this percentage greatly varies depending on the country or region. US service exports represent 27 per cent of its total trade while EU exports amount to 21 per cent and Japan only 13 per cent. Nevertheless, US service imports make up 16 per cent, EU 22 per cent and Japan an extremely high 29 per cent. That means that the relative balance of services with respect to the trade of goods is very positive for the US, relatively balanced for the EU and negative for Japan. Adding together exports and imports, the rate of service trade is extremely different from one country to another but the following groups can be identified: Austria, Egypt and Greece trade more that 30 per cent in services. Canada, Germany, Finland, Portugal, Nigeria and South East Asian countries trade between 14 and 17 per cent in services. The level of trade in manufacturing goods in some countries and tourism in others are key variables explaining these rates.

It is clear that the service share of total international trade is becoming rather stable and constant. Total world service imports and exports represented 19 per cent of total trade in 1999; this was also the 1991 percentage. European service exports and imports are around 21 per cent of total trade. In 1993, this figure increased to 22–23 per cent but this was the maximum experienced over the 1989–99 period. In the US, both imports and exports represented 20–21 per cent at the beginning of the 1990s, just slightly more than today. Japanese services account for around 21–22 per cent of the total, and this percentage was relatively constant throughout the 1990s. Most EU countries are around the European average with some (France, Portugal, Finland, Sweden, Benelux) experiencing decreasing trends during the last five years (a 3–5 per cent loss) while most retained stable shares. Only Ireland showed an increasing share of services in the 1990s: from 17.5–18.5 per cent to 20 per cent in 1998.

Within the service sector, the most relevant activities are transport (around 5 per cent of total trade in Europe and the US), travel (9.5–10 per cent in Europe, 14.2 per cent US exports and 6.6 per cent US imports) and royalties (5 per cent in Europe, less in the US). During the 1990s trade increased very strongly in other commercial services (from 37.7 per cent of total service trade in 1990 to 44.2 per cent in 1999). See further details and comments in Chapter 5 by Peter Daniels in this volume.

Foreign Direct Investment

Of all foreign direct investment, investment in services greatly varies from one country to another but in general it is above 50 per cent. Estimates of world FDI (no detailed data are available due to the lack of disaggregation in some countries) show that in 1998 services represented approximately 50 per cent of inflows and 60 per cent of outflows. In 1988 the percentages were between 42 and 45 per cent respectively. In stocks, service participation and evolution it is estimated are very similar to flows.

Table 4.1 shows the main figures for the EU and US direct investment stocks in the world in 1997.[3] EU service investments represent 51 per cent of the world total and 68 per cent of the US total. Services are also very important for EU inward FDI: 58 per cent of these come from outside the EU and 46 per cent of these come from the US. Taking into account both inward and outward FDI between the EU and the world, the highest figure is given by manufacturing and construction sectors (37.4 per cent), followed by financial services (21.6 per cent), other business services (15.5 per cent) and trade (9.9 per cent). Business services account for 16.1 per cent of all investment stock. The specific investment stocks with the US are less service-oriented: 45.5 per cent versus 54 per cent with respect to the whole world. There is a large concentration of investments in manufacturing (42 per cent). Investments in trade and financial services are less important due to the very active position

Table 4.1   Stocks of EU investments in the world and the US, 1997

To/From:	EU outward FDI		EU inward FDI		EU relative % weight (in+out)	
	World	USA	World	USA	In World	In USA
Primary and energy	97 183	22 138	85 057	42 179	7.4	11.3
Manufacturing and construction	544 610	136 303	373 033	102 314	37.4	42.0
Trade	110 326	15 208	132 647	20 777	9.9	6.3
Hotels and restaurants	16 153	3 552	12 182	2 425	1.2	1.1
Transport	12 144	1 549	8 020	966	0.8	0.4
Communications	9 251	1 077	10 073	1 924	0.8	0.5
Financial services	312 531	50 345	218 193	43 129	21.6	16.5
Real estate	28 758	8 866	26 651	3 487	2.3	2.2
Computer activities	6 055	1 636	5 397	2 163	0.5	0.7
R&D	1 324	171	1 463	1 001	0.1	0.2
Other business services	171 698	44 883	208 936	41 469	15.5	15.2
Other services	14 993	7 817	19 141	6 063	1.4	2.4
Total	1 343 949	298 135	1 112 729	270 094	100.0	100.0
Services	683 233	135 104	642 703	123 404	54.0	45.5

Source: Based on Eurostat (1999a).

of these sectors throughout the world and the difficulties of entering the US markets. However, regarding some small service sectors, capital exchange between the EU and the US is quite important in computer activities, R&D and other services.

Mergers and Acquisitions

In 1999, the world value of mergers and acquisitions amounted to US$720.109 million. Services represented around 50 per cent of the total. However, in 1987 services only accounted for 28 per cent of the total. In service sales, operations in financial services (16 per cent) and transport and communications (23 per cent) stand out. Business services and trade represent 7 per cent and 5 per cent of the total respectively, while hotels and restaurants only 1 per cent. With respect to purchases, the same figure of 720.109 has 47 per cent in services, but this time banking services are the leaders with 23 per cent, followed by transport and communication services (16 per cent) and, far behind, business services (4 per cent). The manufacturing and financial sectors are, in a way, gross purchasers of other sectors; over the whole 1987–99 period, both have represented 75 per cent of purchases (25 per cent financial services) and 61 per cent of sales (15 per cent banking and insurance). The remaining service sectors have been largely sellers rather than purchasers.

Global Assessment

Table 4.2 provides a summary (estimates) of the 'servicisation' of global processes taking into account the three indicators identified above. The service share of international trade is the lowest (around 19–20 per cent), whilst the service share of FDI is the highest (around 55–58 per cent), more similar to the weight of services in economies. Mergers and acquisitions are still non-service oriented, but the service share is close to half (around 44–50 per cent). Comparing cumulative rates with recent rates highlights the international trend towards further 'servicisation'. Mergers and acquisitions show the biggest difference between rates based on cumulative 1987–99 data (44.5 per cent) and 1999 data (50.4 per cent); these two percentages are much higher than 10 years ago. International trade rates have been similar during the whole 1989–99 period, but slightly increasing trends are identified in 1999 data (19.6 per cent). FDI shares are very similar in 1998 flows and 1997 stocks but certain rates are decreasing for 1998, particularly in the US. The 'servicisation' of FDI has, rather, been stopped in the EU; service share in FDI flows fluctuating between 50 and 65 per cent during the 1990s. Mallampally and Zimny (2000) show that the long-term reorientation of FDI

Table 4.2   Service orientation of global trading: some key indicators

	World	European Union	United States
IT (exports + imports, average 1989–99)	19.1	20.2	20.0
IT exports (average 1988–99)	19.3	20.6	25.8
IT imports (average 1988–99)	18.9	19.8	15.0
International trade (exports + imports; 1999)	19.6	21.6	20.2
FDI stocks (inward + outward; 1997)	57[(*)]	55.0	57.7
FDI stocks (outward; 1997)	59[(*)]	52.1	58.4
FDI stocks (inward; 1997)	55[(*)]	58.5	56.8
FDI flows (inflows + outflows; 1998)	55[(*)]	55.4	36.4
M&A (sales + purchases, cumulative 1987–99)	44.5	44.2	43.8
M&A (sales, cumulative 1987–99)	45.2	45.7	45.3
M&A (purchases, cumulative 1987–99)	43.7	43.1	41.6
M&A (sales + purchases, 1999)	50.4	48.2	57.0

Note: * Rough estimates due to the lack of data in many developing countries.

Source: Based on WTO (2000), Eurostat (2000a), WIR (2000) and own estimates.

towards the service sector has occurred in almost all home developed countries (in 1980, service FDI share in major developed countries was around 37 per cent).

The comparison between the EU and US gives no clear answer to the question concerning which of these economies is more service orientated. In 1999, mergers and acquisitions have been more servicised in the US than in the EU, especially sales operations (services account for 65 per cent in US total sales), but percentages are very similar in rates based on cumulative data (EU is, however, slightly more servicised). In relation to trade, the US is much more servicised in exports, but much less in imports. With respect to FDI, stocks are more servicised in the US, specially outward ones, but recent 1998 flows show more 'servicisation' in the EU (inflows in particular, but not outflows where the US is always very service-oriented). Using a long-term approach Mallampally and Zimny (2000) show the *catching up* of West Europe as large home countries and the loss of US dominance. Already in 1980, Western European firms were quite well established in important service industries such as banking, insurance, publishing, airlines and other transport services. The EU position was reinforced following the fulfilment of the Single Market program and investment in US markets.

GROWTH OF SERVICE TRADING

International Trade

Considering the global growth of service trade, Figure 4.1 shows the evolution (growth rates) of EU goods and service trade (import and exports) between 1989 and 1999. The results are clear in the sense that trends are quite similar between goods and services, but service trade is slightly more stable. There is a link between the two cycles, which could also reflect the increasing interrelationship between all economic sectors. The average of world goods and services growth rates between 1989 and 1999 are 6.4 and 7.4 respectively, reflecting the slightly superior growth of service trade (more important at the start of the 1990s than at the end, with several years in which goods trade grew at a faster rate). On average, EU growth rates have been similar to the world total (7.3 per cent) but US services grew at a faster rate (8.2 per cent). US

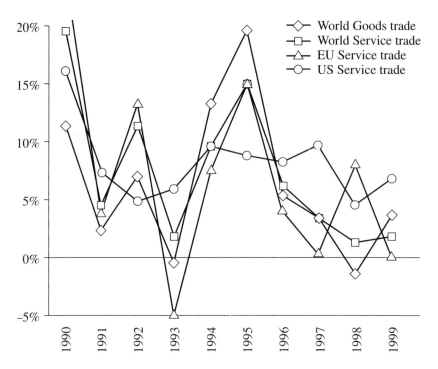

Source: Based on WTO (2000).

Figure 4.1   Trends in service international trade, 1990–99 (annual growth rates)

growth rates in service trade have been much more stable than service trade in the EU.

The EU data contains some interesting details relating to specific sectors. There are no major differences between sectors except for the very important 1992 growth rates in other business services, transport and, to a lesser extent, travel services. There was also a strong 1995 decrease in trade in financial services and the leading position in growth rates of computer and information service trade (which is the only one that retained a high figure in 1997/98, 25.9 per cent). In general, business services have been the most important service sector in international trade, as reflected in the relative growth rate figures (1989–98 average of 17 per cent annual growth), the highest of any other service activities, followed by insurance services (15.5 per cent), air transport (14.1 per cent) and communication services (12.4 per cent).

Foreign Direct Investment

Global FDI trends in European services can be seen in Figure 4.2 (no detailed data are available at a world scale). In general, FDI levels in services are quite superior to those of manufacturing industries, particularly inward FDI, which can be clearly appreciated from 1996 which were years of strong FDI expansion. However, growth rates have been superior in the FDI of manufacturing industries (1992/98 average of 33 per cent annually in outflows versus 23 per cent in services; 23 per cent versus 20 per cent in inflows), which explains the slowing-down of FDI tertiarisation.

Between 1992 and 1998 European services that have shown the strongest growth rates in outward FDI have been real estate and business services and transport and communications, while other services and hotels and restaurants have experienced lower growth rates. In inward FDI, foreign investment has been concentrated in hotels and restaurants, real estate and business services and other services. Foreign banks have not significantly increased their participation (except in 1998) whilst transport and communications have had periods of growth and decline. A clear difference throughout the whole period is that, although both European manufacturing industries and services have higher outward investment than inward, this positive balance is clearer and more stable in manufacturing industries than in services (except in 1994 and 1995). Tertiary industries have positive balances but with volatile growth rates (positive one year, negative the next).

At a world level, long-term data on FDI stocks reveals increasing servicisation of FDI and also relatively high service growth rates in FDI (Mallampally and Zimmy, 2000). Between 1985 and 1995, the nine main home countries grew in service outward investments by 38 per cent (annual growth rate) compared with 28 per cent for the whole economy. As for host

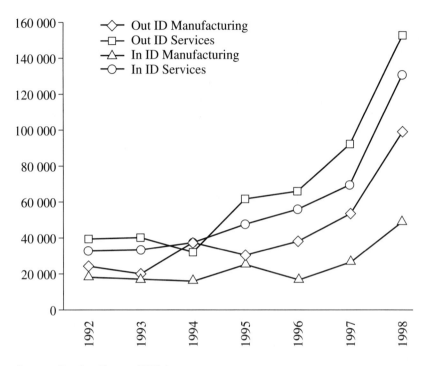

Source: Based on Eurostat (1999a).

Figure 4.2   Trends in EU foreign direct investment, 1992–98 (absolute values)

countries, service growth rates reached 31 per cent compared with 26 per cent for all goods and services. This means that during this period the main FDI countries experienced a strong growth of service FDI. However, growth over the period 1985 to 1990 was more than twice that of 1990–95. Over the 1990–95 period service FDI growth was only slightly higher than total FDI. These results, together with the analysis of the EU case, confirm a slowing-down of service FDI growth over the last decade.

Mergers and Acquisitions

Figure 4.3 shows the evolution of world purchase and sale value in service sectors. What stands out above all is the strong growth of these operations from 1995 to 1996, especially in financial and transport and communication services. The increase in service operations towards the end of the 1980s was slowed down by the 1991–94 recession. However, once economic expansion

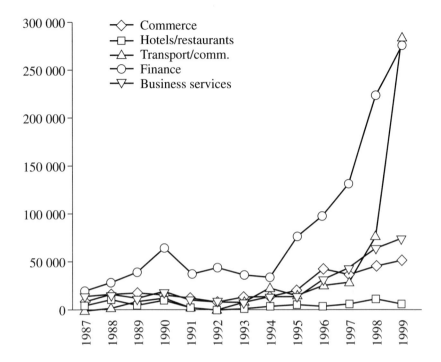

Source: Based on WIR (2000).

Figure 4.3   Trends in world mergers and acquisitions in service sectors, 1987–99 (sales and purchases absolute values)

continued growth was spectacular, particularly in transport and communication services that experienced an annual average increase reaching 101 per cent between 1989 and 1999 in sale and purchase operations. Hotels and restaurants present an annual growth of 45 per cent. Lower rates of growth were experienced by financial services (32 per cent), business services (26 per cent) and wholesale and retail trade services (25 per cent). World manufacturing mergers and acquisitions grew on average by 23 per cent annually. Services (32 per cent in total) have grown much more rapidly than manufacturing industries, especially in countries like the United States (in Europe the growth rates of the two main sectors have been similar).

Global Assessment

Trade in services has been *growing faster* than trade in goods in two of the three analysed indicators. The fastest average annual growth rates (1987–99) are in mergers and acquisitions (32 per cent); 9 points above manufacturing mergers and acquisitions (EU service mergers and acquisitions increased by 38 per cent, only 4 points above manufacturing). World trade also shows positive growth rates for trade in services; 7.4 per cent on average for 1989–99 compared with 6.4 per cent for goods. FDI (figures apply only to Europe and 1992–98) shows higher growth rates for manufacturing (around 25 per cent) than in services (22 per cent). However, other service FDI data reveals high annual growth rates for the countries that are the most important investors in services (35 per cent of both service inward and outward FDI; 7 points more than for the total FDI). Nevertheless, annual growth rates between 1990 and 1995 were 10–11 per cent for both the total figures (manufacturing and services) and for services by themselves.

All this suggests a *shift in service international growth* from international trade to FDI and from greenfield FDI to mergers and acquisitions. In the 1980s and the first half of the 1990s service trade was expected to take off and surpass 25 per cent of all trade. In fact, service trade has grown more than manufacturing due to the increasing tradability of services, outsourcing processes, manufacturing internationalisation, the growing size of service suppliers and advances in trade liberalisation. But international service trade could not really emerge as it was predicted. The prominent role of FDI in services since the mid 1980s was due to a number of reasons: the increasing integration of markets at that time and manufacturing delocalisation; the internal consolidation of the service economy; the increasing importance, dynamism and growth of TNCs; the growing competition of top firms; the initial liberalisation of some service markets, and the limits of international trade. Service trade was shifting towards FDI as a result of the processes identified above, but in some measures it still lags behind that of manufacturing. Recently, the mature condition of international service markets is forcing mergers and acquisitions between companies from developed countries as one way of facing competition and of rapidly acquiring the intangible resources and reputations that are an essential feature of all service firms.

LEADING COUNTRIES IN SERVICE INTERNATIONALISATION

US versus the EU

World service trade is highly concentrated in the EU and US. One indication of this concentration is the dominance of the US and EU in listings of major service multinational firms. The available data also confirms a strong concentration of service trade in these two regions. Together these regions account for around 60 per cent of world service trade: 61 per cent of world exports, 55 per cent of world imports, 66 per cent of world outward FDI, 59 per cent of inward FDI, and 75 per cent of world mergers and acquisitions. Of course, there are other economies that play an important role in service trade, but their market shares are rather low. For example, Asia, as a whole, accounts for 25 per cent of service imports and 20 per cent of service exports. Of this Japan accounts for 8.5 per cent and 4.5 per cent respectively. More recently, Southeast Asian Countries and China are becoming involved in service trade with these countries experiencing high growth rates in international trade during the 1990s. In FDI, developing countries only began to open their markets to service FDI in the second half of the 1980s. This explains why these countries only play a relatively important role in terms of the inward stock of FDI.[4]

EU and US service market shares of international trade exports and inward FDI are somewhat higher than those existing for the trade in goods, but goods trading concentration is higher in outward FDI and US imports. For mergers and acquisitions sales and purchases are similarly EU–US concentrated for both goods and services. This means that service trade produces a contradictory set of flows: in the developed regions service exports are concentrated more than goods and they also attract more service FDI. However, outward investment in goods is so strong that service outward investment seems relatively unimportant. These flows need further research especially the Japanese economies relatively high levels of service imports.

Of course, the EU and US experiences of service trade are different (Table 4.3). The US is a service export oriented economy since it almost accounts for 20 per cent of total world exports; 5 points higher than that for the market share of goods and services combined. The opposite is the case with respect to imports. The EU is strong in both service exports and imports and its market shares are only slightly higher than those for goods. In FDI stocks the US market share is higher than in trade – always above 20 per cent. The power of American TNCs is well represented by the 24 per cent market share of outward FDI they have in goods and services. For international trade and FDI indicators, exports and outward market shares are higher than imports and inward FDI, indicating the strong net position of these economies. However, the EU market share is more important than the US and this is explained by the catching-up process explained above. Nonetheless, in mergers and acquisitions the EU purchases take half of total purchases while the US is only slightly over 20 per cent. This difference is reduced when considering sales: the US accounts for more sales (35 per cent of the total) than can be expected from other indicators. The EU only takes 40 per cent of total sales.

Table 4.3   Service trading in the EU and the US: a comparative outlook

	Services		Goods and services	
	EU	US	EU	US
Market Shares in World (%)				
IT, 1999				
Exports	42.6	18.8	39.5	13.6
Imports	41.7	13.4	38.7	17.2
FDI, stocks 1998*				
Outward	41.7	23.9	47.2	24.1
Inward	38.4	20.9	36.1	20.2
M&A, cumulative 1989–99				
Purchases	53.2	21.9	53.9	23.0
Sales	40.5	35.2	40.1	35.2
Balance of trading (million $)				
IT, 1999	13 105	72 943	−38 675	−290 968
FDI stocks, 1997	49 562	101 328	231 220	156 061
M&A, 1989–99	138 325	−179 729	388 847	−344 103

Note: * Estimates given the difficulties in calculating total service FDI stocks.

Source: Based on WTO (2000), Eurostat (2000a), WIR (2000).

The FDI and mergers and acquisitions data confirm the importance of capital flows from the EU to the US in the 1990s. For example, for both the 1998 flows and 1997 stocks, EU services invested 12 per cent more in the US than American service companies did in the EU. This contrasts with the total balance (goods+services) which was positive for the EU in 1998 (by 10 per cent) but US stocks in the EU were still larger by 36 per cent than the EU stocks in the US. The EU positive balance is extremely high in real estate, transport, hotels and restaurants, and financial services are the strongest EU services in relation to the US (1997).[5] In terms of investment the US is much more significant than the EU in R&D, computer services, communications and distribution trades (note the impressive role of US exports in some strategic business services, 6.6 per cent billion exports – 44 per cent in computer services (OECD, 1999b)). The size of the US market, its strong growth during the 1990s, the currency position of the Euro with respect to the dollar and the reorganisation on many European TNCs partially explain this finding.

The uneven distribution of the share of the world market for services results in a current net balance for the EU and the US. In international trade and FDI the US service balances are extremely positive and the EU service balance is also positive but not to the same level as the EU. In both cases, positive international trade service balances compensates for the high or very high (US) negative balance in goods trade. However, in FDI, service balances reinforce the positive flow of goods stocks. In mergers and acquisitions there is an interesting difference between the EU and the US since the former yields more positive results (more purchases than sales) while the latter shows the opposite, both in services and in goods. In short, market shares are larger in the EU than in the US but in similar proportions with respect to market shares in goods and services (more deviation in international trade). The balance of services (import/export) is more positive for the US except in the case of mergers and acquisitions. This *asymmetry* between the high European market shares of service trading and higher net position of US service trade can be explained by the leading role of top American companies in many service sectors.[6]

The peculiar position of the EU and the US in terms of mergers and acquisitions is further explored in Table 4.4. In total, Europe surpasses the United States both in sale and purchase of service companies and in purchase growth rates. In relation to levels, the EU sells 13 per cent more than the US but the latter purchases twice as much as the former (58 per cent). With respect to growth rates, there is a 14 point difference. Differences in levels can be explained by growth rates. European services have been acquired much more frequently than North American ones, although there have also been more European sales in other sectors, except in the primary sector. However, in purchases, the strong difference is due to the manufacturing sector which accounts for more than half of European purchases; but it should be noted that financial services and transport and communication sectors have also been important. The service sector has been more active in Europe than in the United States: EU acquisitions grew by 39 per cent compared to 32 per cent in US. However, American companies were more active in business services, distributive trades and transport–communications. In service sales, American companies have been more active in all service sectors.

Details of Leadership by Country and Sector

Some additional information on international trade and FDI by service activities can be added to the evidence already presented. The second box, produced by Teresa Fernández, focuses on service countries and sectoral profiles. In addition, Chapter 5 by Peter Daniels in this volume develops some of the details in relation to international trade.

Table 4.4   M&A in Europe and the US: annual growth rates and cumulative values, 1987–99

	Sales				Purchases			
	Growth rate (%) 1987–99 (aver.)		Cumulative M&A 1987–99		Growth rate (%) 1987–99 (aver.)		Cumulative M&A 1987–99	
	US	EU	US	EU	US	EU	US	EU
Total	25	39	993 553	1 132 537	20	33	649 450	1 521 384
Primary	90	174	32 672	14 140	79	182	13 014	22 301
Manufacturing	40	46	488 400	522 748	16	38	305 788	768 091
Trade	99	66	78 532	81 227	76	30	21 473	69 852
Hotels/restaurants	41	40	19 434	20 125	45	1035	6 718	9 665
Transport/comm.	283	122	103 800	111 699	231	202	23 796	132 798
Finance	61	52	129 085	185 860	28	50	145 587	370 954
Business services	75	65	63 599	83 540	75	54	35 103	54 432
Services	50	42	394 450	482 451	32	39	232 677	637 701

Source: Based on Eurostat (1999a)

BOX 4.2: SERVICE TRADE AND INVESTMENT IN ADVANCED COUNTRIES

By Teresa Fernández Fernández, University of Alcalá

The aim of this box is to identify the position of a number of countries in trade and investment in services and to try to quantify whether there is complementarity between both forms of internationalisation. The analysis has been conducted on Western developed market economies and for the purposes of this analysis this includes all member states of the European Community as well as the US and Japan. These countries have been chosen due to the availability of disaggregated data by service activities at NACE three-digit level. The availability of this data permits a joint investment–trade study.

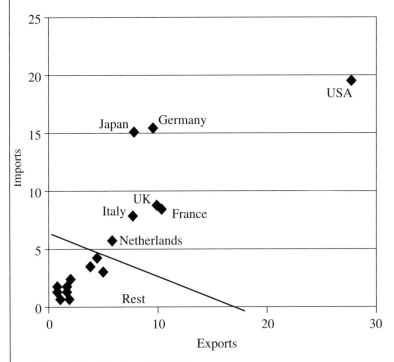

Source: Based on Eurostat (2000b).

Figure 4.4   Main traders in services in the advanced countries (% sum EU, US and Japan, 1994–98)

Main Dealers in Service Trade and Investment

Longitudinal empirical evidence for manufacturing highlights that there are countries with a significant presence in trade and investment, for example the US, Germany and Japan. Figures 4.4 and 4.5 reveals that these countries are also relatively important in terms of service internationalisation.

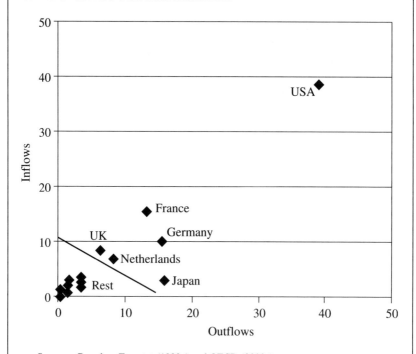

Source: Based on Eurostat (1999a) and OECD (2000c).

Figure 4.5   Main dealers in services investment in the advanced countries (% sum EU, US and Japan, 1994–98)

For the period 1994–98 the US is the most important country being responsible for about 40 per cent of investment and around 25 per cent of trade within the group of countries considered. Germany, Japan, France, and The United Kingdom, Italy and The Netherlands are all behind the US. These countries as a group account for 70 per cent of total trade and more than 80 per cent of the investment flows. The other countries in the analysis account individually for 5 per cent or less of the total flows and exchanges considered and as a group account for no more than 30 per cent of these international exchanges. The differences identified can be directly related to the relative importance of these countries in terms of GDP (for example the US, Germany, United Kingdom and France) and also to the small market size of the Netherlands that has to search for complementary demand abroad.

These countries, more or less, maintain their position in the ranking of investment and trade, but there are differences in their behaviour between their net position related to trade and investment. That is to say, there seems to be a complementarity between trade and investment but this relationship is not static and in fact seems to be affected by a reversed product cycle pattern. The product cycle theory developed by Vernon (1966), in the framework of the neo-technological theories, shows that, in relation to manufacturing, internationalisation is carried out first by trade and is followed by investment. It states that it is the normal path to internationalisation along which countries advance. Therefore, the exporting background of countries and their manufacturing tradition allows them to rapidly develop overseas investments.

Services seem to follow a reversed product cycle pattern compared to the one existing for manufacturing. That is, internationalisation in services seems to happen first through investment and later by exports. Figure 4.6 shows how more tertiarised countries like the US, France or United Kingdom, for which services have a long tradition and account more than 70 per cent of GDP and employment, are mainly exporters, while Germany and Japan, with a relatively low weight in the service sector, are mainly investors, being in the first stage.

Service characteristics, for example, the need for proximity between producers and consumers and their intangibility make them more prone to investment as a first stage. Once a branch is located in another country, the distance to near markets is reduced and the company begins to export with more intensity.

However, it can be said that since there are services more prone to trade (tourism) and more prone to investment (business services), the observed pattern for services can be affected by the relative share of different service activities in trade and investment in each country.

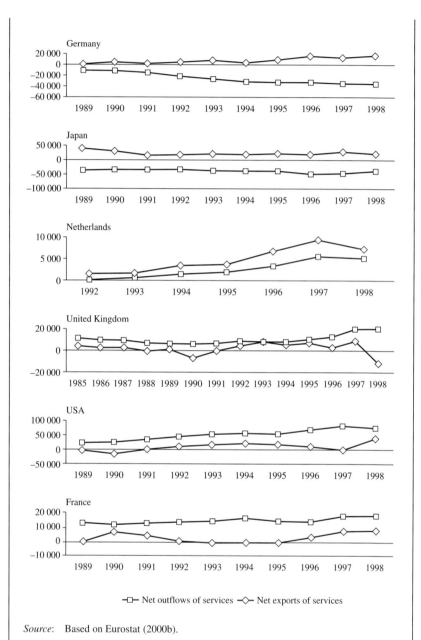

Source: Based on Eurostat (2000b).

Figure 4.6   Net exports and outflows of services in selected countries, 1985–98 (mio ECUs)

Table 4.5   Net outward investment position in services (millions of ECU in 1998)

	USA	United Kingdom	Germany	France	Netherlands
Tourism	(– 4 904)	3 207	(–37)	3 953	(–858)
Transport & Communic.	–13 648	8 713	994	(849)	(2 256)
Financial	223 525	8 084	44 330	(17 687)	28 913
Business services	(6 283)	(14 278)	–20 319	(–408)	57
Total net assets	166 667	38 636	40 158	19 742	29 263

Note: Figures between brackets mean that the trend observed in net flows during 1994–97 does not coincide with the sign observed in 1998 assets. Data on stocks for Japan are not available during the last four years.

Source: Based on OECD (2000c).

Net Positions in Service Trade and Investment

It is important to know which service activities are most important in terms of trade and investment (tables 4.5 and 4.6).

The US has quantitatively the biggest share of net assets (assets minus liabilities), followed in this order by Germany, the

Table 4.6   Net exports of services (millions of ECU in 1998)

	Germany	France	Netherlands	United Kingdom	USA	Japan
Tourism	–27 254	10 848	–3 746	–8 106	23 011	–22 360
Transport & Communications	–4 864 –6 763	610		4 992	–3 531	–8 424
Financial	644	(–456)	–609	12 966	5 228	–2 543
Business services	–4 817	4 948	2 863	16 404	15 725	–11 799
Total net exports of services	–38 442	16 837	4 675	18 114	71 897	–44 084

Note: Figures between brackets mean that the trend observed in net flows during 1994–97 does not coincide with the sign observed in 1998 assets.

Source: Based on Eurostat (2000b).

With respect to net trade (exports minus imports) it can be seen how Germany and Japan, despite their relative amount in exports shown in figures 4 and 5, are really net importers in almost all the service considered. United Kingdom despite its loosing of competitiveness in business services regarding investment, is a net exporter considering all the activities. USA keeps a good position as a net exporter and that France is very important again in tourism. In trade the trends for each service/country seem to be more stable than in investment.

United Kingdom, The Netherlands and France. Both in Germany and the US, financial services have the lion's share. The changes of trend indicate that in business activities foreign investors have been investing in the US more than the US abroad during the period 1994–98 and vice versa with tourism. The United Kingdom, despite its quantitative importance as a net investor in all the activities, seems to experiment with a change of trend in business services. France is losing importance as an investor in financial services and transport & communications and gaining in business services. The Netherlands are improving in tourism and worsening in transport & communications.

With respect to net trade (exports minus imports) it can be seen how Germany and Japan, despite their relative amount in exports shown in Tables 4.4 and 4.5, are really net importers in almost all the service considered. United Kingdom despite its loosing of competitiveness in business services regarding investment, is a net exporter considering all the activities. USA keeps a good position as a net exporter and that France is very important again in tourism. In trade the trends for each service/country seem to be more stable than in investment.

THE INTERNATIONALISATION OF SERVICE INDUSTRIES: TOWARDS AN INDEX OF INTERNATIONALISATION

This final section presents some key comparative findings for the three main indicators using available data. The objective is to verify at which point various service industries are internationalised and whether they internationalise in the same way. Using the different analyses, it is possible to identify which services are more oriented towards international trade, FDI or mergers and acquisitions. Previous studies classify service activities according to the identification of preferences towards types of service internationalisation.

Vandermerwe and Chadwick (1989) have grouped engineering and advertising with services that can be considered as FDI-oriented (low goods, high face-to-face interaction) and the maintenance of financial services (medium goods, higher interaction), and IT-oriented as requiring the least investment, control and presence. Some of these latter services could be provided via mail delivery. Sapir (1993) or OECD (2000a), amongst others, identify international trade with tourism, post, education and medical services (mode 2) and some transport, financial and professional services (mode 1). FDI (mode 3) is linked to retailing, banking, business services or telecommunications, while temporary movement of suppliers is exemplified by consultancy, construction and transport services. The FDI mode requires low mobility of both provider and clients and, normally, overcomes high reputation costs (for example in banking, telecommunications and some business services). The role of the wholesale and retailing trades is recognised in mergers and acquisitions and service foreign affiliates (Knauth, 2000). Although business services are increasing in importance and now lead the number of mergers and acquisitions operations in Europe (2800 in 1998–99, 64 per cent in computer programming services; European Economy, 2000). Telecommunications and insurance have been behind the main mega cross-border mergers and acquisitions that have occurred in services (WIR, 2000). A different taxonomy for EU service internationalisation will now be presented.

This section is based on European data, but it could be applied to other countries and time periods. Table 4.7 shows, first, the relative shares of total exchanges for each service industry and, second, annual growth rates. Percentile data are provided for the last available year and a recent series of years (1992–1998/99). Some categories contain data that has been approximated for the purposes of comparison (see footnotes in Table 4.7).

Following previous results, the first important outcome from this table is that the European internationalisation of services with respect to goods is a phenomena associated with FDI and mergers and acquisitions rather than with international trade. The opposite is the case for manufacturing where the emphasis is on international trade rather than on mergers and acquisitions. The asymmetry between manufacturing and services internationalisation would be modified if growth rates showed convergence ratios in manufacturing FDI and service trade. However, this is not the case during the last period, 1992–98.[7] For FDI and trade, 1997/98 rates are higher for manufacturing. This means that EU service internationalisation during the 1990s was still led by manufacturing processes, even if EU services had been incorporated into the global arena during the 1980s. Results were only slightly different for world trade as explained in the previous section.

Service industries are quite heterogeneous and, as expected, their internationalisation has shown different patterns. The *most global service activities* are financial one. This is due to their relatively high share of FDI (21.6 per cent) and mergers and acquisitions (20.4 per cent), even if shares on trade are rather poor (1.5). Transport and communications and real estate and business services have similar global positions, but in a different way. The first prefers mergers and acquisitions and trade to be internationalised (shares of 14.3 per cent and 5.9 per cent respectively), while FDI has little relevance (2.1 per cent). The second prefers FDI (18.8 per cent), but trade and mergers and acquisitions are also relevant (around 5 per cent of the

Table 4.7   *Summary of service internationalisation indicators: sectorial distribution and annual growth rates of EU global exchanges in the world (all figures in %)*

	FDI (Inflows + Outflows)		IT[2] (credits + debits)		M&A (sales + purchases)	
Shares of total = 100	Flows 1998	Stocks 1997[1]	1998	1992–98	1999	1992–99
Manufacturing/Goods	29.3	36.5	78.5	77.9	43.5	44.8
Services	55.4	55.0	21.5	22.1	48.2	46.3
Commerce/Merchandising	6.4	9.9	1.2	1.1	4.3	4.8
Hotels, restaurants/travel	0.1	1.2	6.5	6.7	0.4	0.9
Transport and communications	4.0	2.1	5.6	5.9	19.6	14.3
Financial services	27.3	21.6	1.2	1.5	17.5	20.4
RE & business services	15.7	18.8	5.6	5.1	5.1	5.4
Personal services	1.9	1.4	0.3	0.4	1.2	1.4
Annual growth rates[3]	Flows 1997–98	Flows 1992–98	1997–98	1992–98	1998/99	1992–99
Manufacturing/Goods	87	25	5	8	65	40
Services	76	22	5	8	90	41
Commerce/Merchandising	17	15	4	9	38	36
Hotels, restaurants/travel	290	7	7	10	–52	61
Transport and communications	38	19	13	20	629	132
Financial services	174	11	–3	28	23	37
RE & business services	34	32	36	33	50	54
Personal services	27	3	1	9	30	45

Notes:
(1)   Stocks of inward and outward direct investment.
(2)   Goods exchanges have been allocated to the manufacturing sector, travel trade to hotels and restaurants, and merchandising to wholesale and retail trade (commerce). These equivalences are only partial, but they permit an approximate comparative outlook.
(3)   Annual growth rates average of annual growth rates between 1991/1992 and last available year change. Arithmetical averages were selected instead of other possible measures to clearly include high growth rates at the end of the 1990s.

Source: Based on WTO (2000), Eurostat (2000a) and WIR (2000).

share). The least relevant global services are personal services (less than 1.4 per cent share in all indicators) and commerce (9.9 per cent in FDI and 4.8 per cent in mergers and acquisitions), which is rather poor considering the size of this sector.

In terms of growth rates, the *most dynamic service industry* in the global economy is transport and communications. This has the highest annual growth rate (an impressive 132 per cent) found for mergers and acquisitions but growth rates in FDI and trade has also been remarkable (19 per cent and 20.5 per cent respectively). The second sector is probably real estate and business services. This sector has the highest trade growth (32.7 per cent) and very high rates in FDI (32 per cent) and mergers and acquisitions (54 per cent). Financial services also yield very important rates, even if they already are the most glob-alised service activity: 28 per cent in trade, 37 per cent in mergers and acqui-sitions, 11 per cent in FDI. The least internationally dynamic service activities are commerce (distributive trades; despite the relatively high 15 per cent growth in FDI), and personal services (due to the low growth rate in trade). Anyway, it is necessary to point out that most growth rates in service activi-ties are very high and extremely significant in terms of the ways in which they are being affected by internationalisation.

Finally, an *internationalisation index* can be constructed taking into account the average size of each sector. The objective is to present a simple synthetic index which is valid for sectorial comparisons not influenced by sector size (large sectors have normally more international presence than others, so this effect should be removed in order to measure actual interna-tionalisation in each sector). Table 4.8 shows the main results. A first *size index* is built using available recent information on sectorial service contributions to value added and employment and their importance in terms of number of firms. For example, the value of 0.673 for services is the average of certain measures around the 67 per cent of service shares of total employment, value added and others. The remaining indexes are built in a similar way: average of shares divided by the size index. Finally, the internationalisation index is based on the three former ones. A value of 1 means that the sector has a rela-

Table 4.8   *Internationalisation index for services in the European Union, 1998*

	Size index	Relative FDI	Relative trade	Relative M&A	Internationalisation index
Manufacturing/Goods	0.308	1.19	2.53	1.45	1.72
Services	0.673	0.82	0.33	0.67	0.61
Commerce/Merchandising	0.190	0.52	0.11	0.25	0.29
Hotels, rest./Travel	0.060	0.19	1.11	0.14	0.48
Transport and communications	0.056	0.38	1.05	2.53	1.32
Financial services	0.081	2.67	0.19	2.52	1.79
RE & business services	0.121	1.55	0.42	0.44	0.81
Personal services	0.085	0.16	0.04	0.16	0.12

Source: Based on WTO (2000), Eurostat (2000a) and WIR (2000).

tive weight fully in coherence with its economic size. A value bigger than 1 means that internationalisation is much more important than is expected from its economic weight.

Results are fully coherent with the previous ones. Manufacturing internationalisation is always above manufacturing weight, particularly in international trade (2.53). Services are always below it as could be expected from its contribution to value added and employment, particularly in international trade (0.33). The service internationalisation index is 0.61 while the manufacturing one is 1.72. This is due to the very low rates of some activities. Personal services (0.12), commerce (0.29) and hotels and restaurants (0.48) have extremely low indexes, so they are clearly influencing the overall service sector index. However, real estate and business services have an internationalisation weight (0.81) similar to the sector's economic weight, transport and communications are clearly above (1.32) and financial services (1.79) lead the relative internationalisation processes, even more than manufacturing. The role of financial services is particularly important since they have the highest rates in FDI (2.67) and mergers and acquisitions (2.53; nearly the same as transport and communications).

In relative terms service industries prefer FDI to international trade. The exceptions are tourism (for obvious reasons) and transport and communications (probably due to the typical transport of international products and the tradability of some communication services using long-distance technology). In contrast, the relative mergers and acquisitions index stands out for transport and telecommunications and financial services. This confirms the analysis presented earlier in this chapter. In the remaining service sectors mergers and acquisitions is still lower than could be expected given their economic size. In general, these results do not contradict previous studies that explore the links between sectors and internationalisation modes.

The different international profiles of parts of the service sector can be explained by *many determinants*, but important amongst these are the nature of services, standardisation and regulatory environments. It is no coincidence that the most international sectors (transport and communications and financial services) are the ones with the greatest number of multinationals, the most standardised services as well as being in areas that are some of the most relatively liberalised service markets in Europe. Services that are associated with local environments, with more segmented markets and which are subject to narrow regulations tend to be less international than can be expected given their economic size. What it is impossible to identify in this analysis is the importance or weight of each of these factors as contributory variables that explain the ongoing internationalisation of service functions.

CONCLUSIONS

The heterogeneity of the service sector means that the internationalisation of service industries has different profiles, trends and dynamics. The heterogeneity of the sector necessitates comparative analysis by sector, country and mode of internationalisation. Thus, this chapter has explored some of the main issues related to service internationalisation based on comparisons between goods and services (and different service industries), between the US and the EU (and other EU countries) and between trade and investment (and different forms of investment). Certain hypotheses were formulated: the 'service orientation' of global processes; the American leadership of service globalisation and other relevant countries; and the uneven growth of service globalisation according to specific service sectors (not all services are internationalised to the same extent and in the same way). The chapter provides empirical evidence by comparing three main internationalisation indicators: IT, FDI (greenfield and mergers and acquisitions) and cross-border mergers and acquisisitons.

It has been shown that levels of tertiarisation are still modest in FDI, very low in international trade and high in mergers and acquisitions. Except in mergers and acquisitions, the 1990s does not suggest that services will play a more important role in global trade. The globalisation of manufacturing industry is still very significant and it is manufacturing that is at the forefront of international trade and FDI processes. Nevertheless, it is important to note that growth rates for service trade have often been higher than goods trade during the last two decades. Nevertheless, although differences in relation to goods have not being reduced significantly during the last years, service internationalisation is still growing strongly and services will continue to become more internationalised over the next few decades. Moreover, services continue to play an important role in contributing to the globalisation of goods trade.

In terms of the different modes of service internationalisation the evidence suggests a shift away from international trade to FDI and, above all, in the 1990s, from international trade and greenfield FDI to mergers and acquisitions. One of the reasons for this shift is the increasing maturing of key service markets. In mature markets it is vital for new companies to rapidly acquire the intangible assets that lie behind the competitiveness of many service functions. The acquisitions of such assets has become a priority for firms attempting to internationalise today and it has become especially for European and American companies.

The EU and US dominate the global market in service trade (around 60 per cent), despite the recently increasing importance of some Asian countries. Europe is the first region in terms of the share of the global service market followed by the US. Nevertheless in terms of import/export balances and the presence of multinationals the US is the clear leader. The exception is mergers and acquisitions in which European net investment in the US and other countries has been notorious. In Europe, only the UK possesses features similar to those of the US: active exports and investors in many services, hosting many service TNCs headquarters and at the forefront of many service globalisation processes. Most EU countries have positive trade balances in some specific services for example, German, French and Dutch investment in financial services and French and Spanish exports in tourism, and so on) and possess comparative advantages in selected markets.

Concerning the complementarity of substitution processes that exist between trade and investment in different countries further research is required. However, certain initial evidence is suggested. Some highly tertiarised economies (the US and UK) are at the forefront of service trade since they have higher levels of service trade than investment. However, less service-oriented economies like Germany or Japan tend to be greater investors than traders. International specialisation within service trade modes seems to be related to the uneven development of the service economy.

Service internationalisation is being led by financial, transport and communication industries. These sectors are internationalising at levels that are similar in relative terms to those of the manufacturing sector. Business services – especially advanced business services – are also important and play a very active and growing role in the internationalisation process (including mergers and acquisitions). The different internationalisation rates of service industries are related to a set of diverse factors: service features and required mobility, the cost of establishing a reputation, the introduction of technology, market structure and regulations. It is more than probable that further liberalisation of service markets would improve the level of service internationalisation and, as a result, increase the advantages of service trade. Furthermore, markets will continue to push for the multiplication of the manifold and fertile interactions that exists between services and globalisation. Further research and political attention is essential if academics and the policy community are to follow these coming trends and to develop appropriate national and international trading institutional frameworks.

NOTES

1. The term 'servicisation' is less common than the word 'tertiarisation', but it seems to fit better with the role of services as global activities and not only as a sector. It will be used sometimes.
2. A complete approach to service internationalisation should consider all dimensions explained in Chapter 2, or, at least, all modes representing international transactions and flows (dimension A of that model). Unfortunately, few or no statistics are available in most cases. Most of the detailed quantitative measures refers to those indicators used in this chapter: IT, FDI and M&A.

3. Flows provide results somewhat different. In the European Union, services represent 56.3 per cent of FDI in 1998, but the average between 1992 and 1998 is 60.9 per cent. In the United States, figures are similar (around 58 per cent in the last years). The highest European percentages by countries (averages superior to 70 per cent) are found in Austria, Portugal and France, while the lowest percentages (averages inferior to 60 per cent) are in Sweden, Finland, the UK and Spain. Growth or decline trends strongly vary according to the country and the sub-period. In general, the weight of European inward investment in services seems more important and increasing than outward investment.

4. Mallapally and Zimny (2000) show data for which 13 developing economies have more inward stock in services and in total FDI than 10 developed countries including the main ones. The relative share of services with respect to the total is approximately the same for the two groups, around 50 per cent. However, WIR (2000) data, quite different in value, do not concede to developing countries more than 30 per cent of total world inward FDI stocks (that share has only become larger and increasing in the recession periods of 1980–82 and 1990–94, reaching 40 per cent). Nevertheless, developing countries have a prominent position considering inward FDI standardises by market size and GDP (close to 25 per cent in 1999, reducing to less than 15 per cent in developed countries).

5. The balance between outward and inward *stocks investments* is very positive for Europe in transport services (51 per cent more outward than inward), manufacturing and construction (46 per cent), financial services (43 per cent) and computer activities (12 per cent). All these activities make EU net exports of direct investments in the world (by +21 per cent). However, in certain activities EU imports more capital: other services (outward FDI is 78 per cent of inward investment), other business services (82 per cent), trade (83 per cent), and R&D (90 per cent).

6. Dunning (1993) provides a very detailed table indicating national competitive advantages in 50 services. US firms had advantages in 39 service sectors. The UK followed with 28 service sectors and Switzerland was third with advantages in 13 sectors. Germany and Japan only held advantages in 10 and 8 sectors respectively.

7. Manufacturing and goods exchanges grew annually more than services in the two key indicators: 25 per cent in FDI (3 points more than services), and 8.2 per cent in trade (0.6 point more than services). In M&A both manufacturing and services share grew by 40 per cent annually. Growth rates for the last available year only indicate a difference with respect to M&A: service transactions grew by 91 per cent while manufacturing by 'only' 65 per cent.

REFERENCES

Dunning, J.H. (1993), 'The Internationalisation of the Production of Services: some General and Specific Explanations', in Y. Aharoni (ed.), *Coalitions and Competition: the Globalization of Professional Business Services*, London and New York: Routledge.

European Economy (2000), 'Mergers and acquisitions', *European Economy, Supplement A. Economic Trends*, No. 5/6 – 2000, European Economy.

Eurostat (1999a), *European Union Direct Investment. Data 1988–1998. Yearbook 1999. Detailed Tables*, Luxembourg: Eurostat.

Eurostat (1999b), *Services in Europe. Data 1995*, Luxembourg: Eurostat.

Eurostat (2000a), *Geographical Breakdown of the EU Current Account. Annex to the publication EU international transactions. Detailed Tables*, Luxembourg: European Commission.

Eurostat (2000b), *International Trade in Services – EU. Annex to the publication EU international transactions. Detailed Tables*, Luxembourg: European Commission.

Eurostat (2000c), *Eurostat Yearbook. A statistical eye on Europe, Data 1998–1998*, Edition 2000, Luxembourg: European Commission.

Karsenty, G. (2000), 'Assessing Trade in Services by Mode of Supply', in P. Sauvé and R. Stern (eds), *GATS 2000: New Directions in Service Trade Liberalisation*, Harvard University and Washington, DC: Centre for Business and Government and Brookings Institution Press.

Knauth, B. – Eurostat (2000), 'Foreign owned enterprises', *Statistics in Focus*, Theme 4, 5/2000, Luxembourg: European Communities.

Mallampally, P. and Zimny, Z. (2000), 'Foreign Direct Investment in Services: Trends and Patterns', in Y. Aharoni and L. Nachum (eds), *Globalisation of Services: Some implications for theory and practice*, London and New York: Routledge.

OECD (1999a), *Measuring Globalisation: the Role of Multinationals in OECD Economies*, Paris: OECD.

OECD (1999b), *Strategic Business Services*, Paris: OECD.

OECD (2000a), 'The service economy', *Business and Industry Policy Forum Series. STI*, Paris: OECD.

OECD (2000b), *OECD Economic Outlook*, No. 67, June, Paris: OECD.

OECD (2000c), *International Direct Investment Statistics Yearbook 1999*, Paris: OECD.

Sapir, A. (1993), 'The structure of services in Europe: a conceptual framework', *European Economy*, **3**, 83–98.

Vendermerwe, S. and Chadwick, M. (1989), 'The Internalisation of Services', *The Service Industries Journal*, January, **9** (1), 79–93.

Vernon, R. (1966), 'International investment and international trade in the product cycle', *Quarterly Journal of Economics*, **80**, May, 190–207.

WIR (2000), *World Investment Report, Cross-border Mergers and Acquisitions and Development*, United Nations.

World Trade Organisation (WTO) (1999), *Statistics*, Web page.

World Trade Organisation (WTO) (2000), *International Trade Statistics 2000*, Geneva: WTO.

PART II

Global Trade, Global Investment and Global Management

5. EU services trade, with particular reference to business and professional services

Peter W. Daniels[1]

INTRODUCTION

It is commonly asserted that trade in services has played a large part in the internationalisation of economies that has been one of the hallmarks of economic change during the late twentieth century (Sauvant, 1986; Bhagwati, 1987; Jones and Kierzkowski, 1990; Landesmann and Petit, 1992; Moshirian, 1993; American FSA, 1995). Innovation and efficiency in the production of services have become crucial to economic growth (Feketekuty, 1998). In common with other advanced economies, there has been a long-term shift in European GDP and employment in services. A number of EU Member States are leading participants in world commercial services trade (Table 5.1). Steadily rising disposable incomes combined with rapid advances in information and communications technology (ICT), for example, have contributed to significant job growth since the early 1980s in hotels and catering, finance and related activities, business, professional and welfare services. Even so, in Europe job creation by the service sector has been slower than in the US or Japan. In the US between 1980 and 1993 service jobs increased by 33 per cent and by 28 per cent in Japan. The equivalent increase in Europe was less than 25 per cent (European Commission, 1996, see also Petit, 1986).

The inferior performance of European services compared with the US or Japan is attributable to a number of factors. These include the distortion of the market for services in Europe by high non-wage labour costs, differential rates of output growth for services between the Member States, and differences in the level of regulation of the markets for services amongst the EU states. One of the most important effects of these variations is a degree of inflexibility in innovative capacity, adaptability and mobility of labour within the European service sector. This has possibly prevented it from fulfilling its service employment potential (see also European Commission, 1999) which is considerable given that ICT continues to evolve rapidly, is becoming relatively less

Table 5.1 Top ten exporters and importers of commercial services, 1998 (billion dollars and percentage)

Exporters	Value	Share	Annual % change	Importers	Value	Share	Annual % change
United States	240.0	18.2	2	United States	165.8	12.7	8
United Kingdom	100.5	7.6	9	Germany	125.0	9.6	3
France	84.6	6.4	5	Japan	110.7	8.5	-9
Germany	78.9	6.0	3	United Kingdom	78.8	6.0	11
Italy	66.6	5.1	0	France	62.9	4.8	7
Japan	61.8	4.7	-9	Italy	65.4	5.8	5
Netherlands	51.6	3.9	2	Netherlands	46.6	3.6	4
Spain	48.7	3.7	12	Canada	35.2	2.7	-4
Belgium-Luxembourg	35.4	2.7	4	Belgium-Luxembourg	33.9	2.6	8
Hong Kong, China	34.2	2.6	-10	Austria	30.1	2.3	6
Total of above	802.3	60.9	–	Total of above	754.4	58.6	–
World	1 320.0	100.0	0	World	1 305.0	100.0	1

Note: Compiled using IMF, Balance-of-Payments Statistics; National Statistics, and WTO Secretariat estimates.

Source: Trade in Services Section of the Statistics Division, WTO (2000).

expensive to access and use, and is a core component of knowledge-based activities that are vital to EU international competitiveness. With the manufacturing sector continuing to outsource many of its functions to services, competitive manufacturing depends on competitive services (Feketekuty and Hauser, 1986; Lanvin, 1993; European Commission, 1996; Daniels, 2000). As well as stimulating demand, ICT triggers the supply of completely new services that may not have existed before. The potential of these, as well as existing services, can increasingly be fulfilled by using ICT for long-distance, cross-border transactions, or to complement the physical transfer of labour and expertise that is essential for the supply of many services across international borders. This is certainly very important for the relatively recent growth of cross-border trade of services such as finance, communications, business and professional services that are used as intermediate inputs in the production process for traded and non-traded goods. Market structure and the impact of domestic regulatory conditions have an important effect on the distribution of service output and the principles of comparative advantage do not necessarily provide a good starting point for explaining the patterns of international trade in services (Dunning, 1977; Nachum, 1999). Perhaps more so than goods trade, services trade is a function of market structures and demand. Since these vary considerably across the EU it explains why the institution has in recent years been actively devising measures that will create a more level playing field for intra-community service transactions and the firms involved.

While it has taken some time, the EU therefore does now recognise the existing and potential value of cross-border trade in services for employment growth and sustainable economic development.[2] It has been estimated, for example, that some 50 per cent of the EU services market in terms of employment has been directly affected by the Single Market programme (European Commission, 1996). Actions such as the removal of restrictions on the cross-border provision of services, measures that make it easier for service companies based in one Member State to establish a presence in another, or relaxation of the rules governing the mobility of labour all help to create an environment that is conducive to the growth of service activity and employment.[3] From the perspective of this chapter, these initiatives have had the effect of increasing opportunities for cross-border transactions by business, professional and financial services which, until quite recently, have essentially operated within their own national markets.[4] For many of these services to be delivered effectively it is essential for them to be located near to their clients. The trend towards removal of restrictions on their ability to operate in this way should be reflected in increases in trade, both within the EU and with third party countries.[5]

More readily comparable and comprehensive data on services trade compiled by the IMF, OECD, Eurostat and the WTO are now becoming available. It remains the case, however, that the evidence they provide is still only broadly indicative rather than conclusive, since service transactions are very varied and are much more difficult to 'capture' than those for goods. This problem is getting worse as more transactions are undertaken using the Internet and e-commerce. Grubel and Walker (1989) and Sampson and Snape (1985), amongst others, have shown how service transactions may require one, or combinations of, the following: movement of providers to consumers, movement of consumers to providers, movement of both consumers and providers, or no movement by either party to the transaction. For the latter, either the service is embodied in a good that is then traded separately, or the service can be encoded and transmitted electronically. Strictly speaking, only these services are 'traded' and these are the focus of attention in this chapter. Those services that involve movement of the factors of production such as personnel are classed as investment (Nicolaides, 1989; Sauvant, 1993). An appreciation of these classifications and definitional problems remain fundamental to any meaningful analysis of trends in international trade in services, for the design and implementation of EU Services Directives, or the new round of GATS negotiations.

TRENDS IN WORLD SERVICES TRADE

It is helpful to begin with a short overview of recent trends in world services trade before turning to examine some empirical aspects of services trade

Table 5.2   Trends in exports (mill $US) of commercial services, world regions, 1980–99

Region[1]	Period (Change %)				Share (%)	
	80–85	85–90	90–95	95–99	1990	1999
North America	61.06	106.73	47.9	27.63	19.2	21.2
Latin America	3.45	65.00	49.83	20.22	3.8	4.0
Western Europe	–8.81	114.88	35.82	11.61	53.2	47.1
European Union (15)	–10.57	116.44	36.82	11.80	47.3	42.2
Africa	–11.02	64.60	35.48	12.70	2.4	2.1
Asia	21.36	116.12	99.32	1.79	16.8	19.9
World	4.63	104.60	51.79	12.82	100	100
[World: Merchandise]	[–4.13]	[76.36]	[47.60]	[10.54]		

Note: 1. No aggregate data available for economies in transition, and Middle East.

Source: Trade in Services Section of the Statistics Division, WTO (2000).

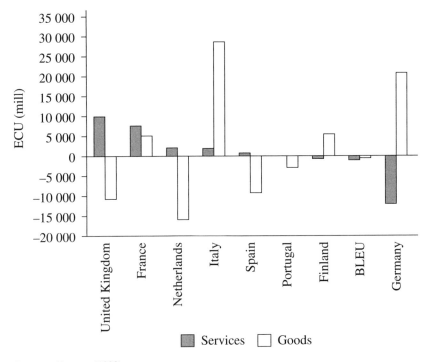

Source: Eurostat (1998).

Figure 5.1 Services and goods BOP, EU9, 1996

within the EU and between the EU and other parts of the world.[6] In relative terms, since 1980 exports of commercial services at world level have been growing faster than merchandise exports (Table 5.2). However, the value of the latter has been approximately five times larger than the former since 1985 even though the services share of all exports had increased to 23.8 per cent by 1999, compared with 18.3 per cent in 1985. The growth in the value of both merchandise and services exports slowed down between 1990–95 and 1995–99 (see Table 5.2) but the change was less marked for services exports than for merchandise exports. This must be interpreted carefully, however, because there have been substantial fluctuations during the past ten years in, for example, relative prices, currency exchange rates, and the performance of the global economy as a whole. This makes it difficult to analyse trends in service exports using absolute currency values of the kind collated by Eurostat (1998). Although its share of world commercial services exports declined between 1990 and 1999, Western Europe has consistently been the world's leading source for both merchandise and commercial services with the EU15 dominating the transactions (Table 5.2). Asia was also a significant player between 1985 and 1995 but starting from a much lower baseline than North America which is generally regarded as the dominant influence on global service exports. During the 1990s its service export growth has been higher than Western Europe and although a strong advocate for greater liberalisation of trade in services, it remains a long way behind Western Europe in terms of the value of trade in commercial services.

However, an examination of the size of service trade balances shows why the North American region is undoubtedly a major influence on the pattern of global services exports, with the US being especially important (Table 5.3). Although Western Europe is the only other major world region showing a positive balance of trade in services, the impact is dissipated because to aggregate disguises the national economies with diverse development trajectories and service trade profiles that can deviate quite significantly from the regional norm. Thus, balance of payments (BOP) data for goods and services shows that Spain, the Netherlands and the UK have a positive balance for services that compensates for a negative balance of trade in goods (Figure 5.1). On the other hand, Finland, Portugal, BLEU (Belgo-Luxembourg Economic Union) and, most notably, Germany, are net importers of services. Italy and France have surpluses in both the goods and services trade. Indeed, in 1996 France had a larger positive balance for services than for the goods trade.

The structure of trade inevitably becomes more complicated when the BOP is disaggregated using the three major service sub-categories used by Eurostat (Figure 5.2). Transportation services[7] make the major contribution to the positive balance for the Netherlands where Rotterdam, for example, is a major

Table 5.3   *Trends in balance of trade (mill $US) in commercial services, world regions, 1980–99*

| Region[1] | Services balance (exports–imports) | | | | | [Mechandise] |
	1980	1985	1990	1995	1999	[1999]
North America	6.2	2.5	25.1	60.4	64.6	−347.42
Latin America	−11.1	−4	−4.9	−9.6	−6.7	−36.5
Western Europe	23.2	28.5	24.2	35.2	31.5	−68.4
European Union (15)	20	23.3	20.3	13.6	11.8	−56.6
Africa	−14.7	−9.6	−8.2	−10.8	−9.1	−18.9
Asia	−19.8	−16.2	−47.2	−65.9	−70	−18.9
World	−31.3	−14.1	−28.3	−2.5	4.9	−265.0

Note: 1. No aggregate data available for economies in transition, and Middle East.

Source: Trade in Services Section of the Statistics Division, WTO (2000).

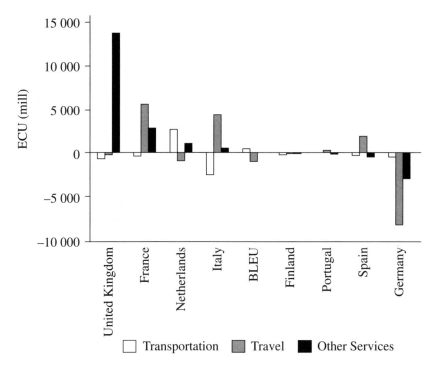

Source: Eurostat (1998).

Figure 5.2 Transportation, travel, and other services BOP, EU9, 1996

entrepôt for neighbouring countries. They are also an important source of revenue for BLEU. Spain, France and Italy and, to a smaller degree, Portugal generate significant positive balances from travel services,[8] reflecting the importance of tourism (mostly by travellers from within the EU) for all of these economies. Finally, while France, Italy and the Netherlands also have positive balances of trade in other services, these are dwarfed by the size of the UK surplus, which is equal in size to the combined deficit on trade in all three sub-categories of services in Germany. Of the nine countries shown in Figure 5.2, Germany has by far the largest deficit for trade in other services.

The BOP statistics provide a crude evidence for some national specialisation in service exports within Europe. The Netherlands is relatively specialised in transportation services; France, Italy and Spain in travel services, and the UK in other services. In the remainder of this chapter the general pattern of services trade in 1996 within the EU, between the EU and three major markets (US, Japan, the rest of the world) is examined. This is followed with more

Table 5.4 Value of exports to all markets and relationship with population and GDP per head, EU9, 1996

Country	Pop. (1998)	GDP/Head 1997[1]	Value of exports (ECU)/head, 1996				
			Services/ Head	Goods/ Head	Transportation/ Head	Travel/ Head	Other services/ Head
Germany	82 060	23 585	0.82	5.02	0.19	0.17	0.46
United Kingdom	59 084	19 234	1.09	3.46	0.24	0.27	0.58
France	58 723	20 869	1.12	3.78	0.27	0.38	0.45
Italy	57 563	17 276	0.96	3.43	0.21	0.41	0.31
Spain	39 348	11 887	0.89	2.06	0.14	0.55	0.20
Netherlands	15 650	20 392	2.50	8.85	1.02	0.33	1.15
BLEU	10 616	20 998	2.70	11.46	0.70	0.48	1.51
Portugal	9 957	8 919	0.65	2.02	0.12	0.38	0.16
Finland	5 147	20 368	1.12	6.21	0.33	0.24	0.56
r squared:							
Population (1998)			0.46	0.43	0.47	0.29	0.39
GDP/Head			0.45	0.61	0.45	0.53	0.57

Note: 1. Gross domestic product at market prices (current prices) per head of population.

Source: Data in New Cronos Database, EU, June 1998, and Eurostat (1998).

detailed scrutiny of the attributes of transactions involving other business services.[9] The chapter concludes with a brief comparative analysis of the trends in services trade for the period 1987–96 for those Member States that have been able to provide the appropriate statistics (Eurostat, 1998). Particular attention is again given to the other services category and especially miscellaneous business, professional and technical services.

SERVICE EXPORTS FROM THE EU9, 1996

Service Exports, Population and GDP

The share of total service exports for each country in the EU9 is of course in part a function of differences in the size of each national economy. In order to compare the relative significance of exports for each country it is useful to calculate the value of exports per head of population and this is undertaken for goods, services and the three major service sub-categories (Table 5.4). Service exports per head range from 2.70 ECU for BLEU to 0.65 ECU for Portugal. Countries that would be expected to perform well on this measure, such as France and the UK, are in the middle of the range with service exports valued at just over 1 ECU per head. This is matched by the much smaller economies of countries such as Finland and far exceeded by the small economies of the Netherlands and BLEU. Some of these inter-category differences are replicated for each of the three major service sub-categories, especially for exports of other services and transportation. On the other hand, Spain, Portugal, Italy and France generate higher export revenues per head from travel services than the UK, the Netherlands or Finland. Indeed exports of travel services are weakly correlated with population size (0.29) but exports per head of other services or of transportation services are more positively dependent on population size (see Table 5.4). While the correlation coefficients are not statistically significant at the 0.05 level they suggest, along with a similar distribution of coefficients for GDP/level and value of exports, that there are some underlying sources of variation in the export performance of EU9 countries. GDP/head is quite a good predictor of goods exports per head ($r = 0.61$) compared with services (0.45). This demonstrates the importance, for example, of differences in physical factor endowments for the export of travel services ($r = 0.53$) or of agglomeration or information intensity for exports of other services ($r = 0.57$).

Service Exports by EU9, by Major Sub-category, 1996

Worldwide exports of services from the nine Member States for which data are

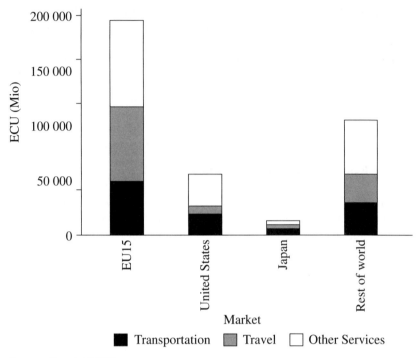

Source: Eurostat (1998).

Figure 5.3   Markets for service exports, major sub-categories, EU9, 1996

available were valued at just under 200 million ECU in 1996. Services
accounted for some 22.8 per cent of all exports. Transactions with other countries within the EU15 dominate; the US and Japan are relatively minor markets
compared with those in the rest of the world (Figure 5.3). The market for transportation, travel and other services is broadly similar with a significant emphasis on transactions within the EU15. In all four markets (EU15, US, Japan, rest
of the world) exports of other services are the largest single component (by
value) except for Japan which is, in any event, a very minor market. It is not
only the smallest market, it is also almost equally shared between each of the
three major sub-categories of services. A significant proportion of the transactions between the EU9 and the US and markets in the rest of the world involve
other services whereas exports of transportation and travel services (especially
the latter) represent more than 50 per cent of the transactions within the EU9
and between them and the EU15.

   The actual value of service export transactions for countries within the
EU15 are broadly similar although as a share of all national exports they are

less important for some countries than others. This relative uniformity within the EU15 is not matched by exports for markets outside the EU15. Here, there is a much greater variability. Thus, the value of service exports from France and the UK is more than double that for Italy or the Netherlands and almost three times larger than Spain or BLEU. Other services are the principal source of service export revenue for the UK, Germany and BLEU, whereas France, Italy and Spain rely on larger shares of their export income from travel (tourism-related) services (Figure 5.4). At the more specific level of services trade with the United States, the UK is the leading partner, closely followed by Germany, with other services comprising more than 50 per cent of the transactions by value. The value of service exports from the EU9 to Japan in 1996 was less than one-third of the total for the United States with Italy, the UK and Germany heading the list of partners. Italy's position at the top of the list is explained by the overwhelming importance of income from travel services

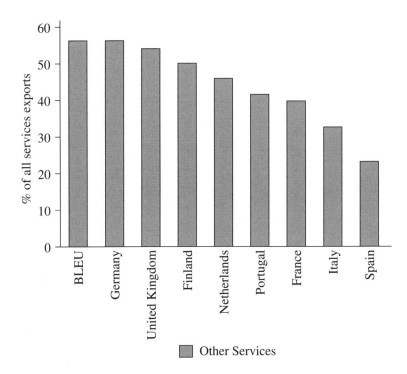

Source: Eurostat (1998).

Figure 5.4   Exports of other services (per cent of all service exports), EU9, all markets, 1996

whereas a large share of the UK–Japan transactions is linked with the provision of other services.

Miscellaneous Business, Professional and Technical Service Exports, 1996

Almost 38 per cent of the exports of other services by the EU9 in 1996 were transactions undertaken by activities classified as miscellaneous business, professional and technical services (BPTS). Along with finance and insurance, these are amongst the most tradable services that can benefit from ICT but which also often require (or prefer) a direct presence in their selected markets. Some BPTS, such as architectural, engineering or legal services, must also operate according to tightly defined roles of professional practice and these tend to vary across the Member States. As harmonisation and mutual recognition of professional qualifications is implemented there will be increasing opportunities for cross-border transactions by these services. The distribution of BPTS transactions by market broadly mirrors that for other services as a whole with 54 per cent involving countries within the EU15.

There are, however, some variations in market orientation between the different types of BPTS (Table 5.5). Although the pattern for the majority broadly mirrors that for the group as a whole, advertising, market research and polling (AMP) firms, for example, trade much more heavily than average (70 per cent) with EU15 partners. R&D associated with basic and applied research and experimental development of new products and processes (excluding market research, technological studies and consultancy)is also dominated by intra-EU15 transactions. By contrast, 40 per cent of the export transactions of architectural, engineering and other technical services (AET) firms are with clients in the rest of the world, often reflecting historical trade and administrative links between countries such as France, the Netherlands or the UK and their former colonies. The only sub-category in which the US and Japan take a larger share of EU9 exports than expected form their overall share of BPTS is services between affiliated enterprises not included elsewhere (SAE). This reflects the extensive presence of US and Japanese manufacturing and service MNEs in Europe. It covers payments by affiliates to their parent companies (for example, contributions to the parent company to cover for general management costs of the reimbursement of expenses settled directly by parent companies) and funds transferred by parent companies with headquarters in the EU9 to affiliates located outside the home country. These transactions therefore tend to be internal to the organisations involved even though they are recorded as national exports of services.

More than 60 per cent of BPTS exports by the EU9 originate from just three countries (UK, France and Germany) with the UK just heading the list (21.3

Table 5.5 Exports of miscellaneous business, professional and technical services (%), by market, EU9, 1996

Origin	Destination	LAMP[1]	AMP	R&D	AET	OMBT	SAE	Misc. BPTS	Other Services
EU9	EU15	15.6[2]	70.2	62.9	47.3	52.0	50.5	54.0	48.5
	United States	17.1	11.4	14.5	11.1	11.0	18.2	14.0	18.5
	Japan	2.2	2.0	1.3	1.6	2.6	2.8	2.2	2.6
	Rest of World	29.1	16.3	21.4	40.0	34.4	28.4	30.5	30.5
	Value (mill ECU)	6051	5185	7032	10743	16375	15834	61637	162483

Notes:
1. See footnote 6 for details of abbreviations.
2. Per cent, column sum = 100.

Source: Eurostat (1998).

per cent). This is achieved primarily as a result of its dominance (35.8 per cent) of the sub-category other miscellaneous business and technical services (OMBT) which is the largest sub-category by value of transactions. Germany has the largest of EU9 legal (27.5 per cent), advertising (19.5 per cent) and R&D (37 per cent) exports, placing it well ahead of France and the UK. France heads the list for architectural, engineering and other technical services (25.1 per cent) with Belgium (26.5 per cent) topping the list for services transactions between affiliated enterprises not included elsewhere, just ahead of the UK (22.6 per cent).

TRENDS IN SERVICES EXPORTS, EU15, 1992–96

While a five-year period is not long enough to allow very clear trends to emerge, if the Single Market initiative is having any effect a modest increase in service trade between Member States might be expected (Figure 5.5). While the aggregate annual value of service exports to markets outside the EU15 is lower their growth has actually lagged only slightly, especially towards the end of the period. But service exports to partners outside the EU15 have grown more slowly in absolute terms, their share falling steadily from just under 40

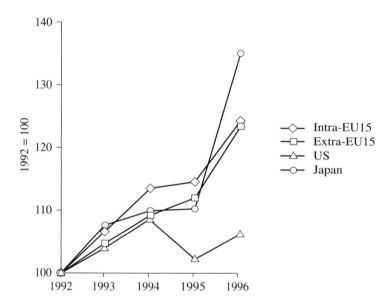

Figure 5.5   Growth of all service exports, by market, EU15, 1992–96

per cent of the total in 1992 to around 33 per cent in 1996. The marginally
slower growth in extra-EU15 trade contrasts with the rather stagnant trend in
transactions with the US and a much clearer upward trend, although admit-
tedly from a lower baseline, for exports to Japan. These figures could be interpreted as signifying the limited impact of attempts to create a more open and
integrated market for services within the EU (see below). On the other hand,
other services transactions with the US have been well established for two
decades and more so that its rather 'flat' performance should not be surprising
whereas, despite its global success in manufacturing, Japan has continued to
rely on the purchase of producer services from elsewhere (Daniels, 1998). In
all cases the value of other services transactions has consistently grown faster
than for transportation and travel services and this suggests that the main bene-
ficiary will be tradable services previously held back by differences, for example, in national standards and practice (Figure 5.6).

A closer look at the net balance of other services trade for individual EU
countries over the longer term (1987–96) does suggest that, with the exception
of the UK, the level of intra-EU transactions has not changed very much since
1987. Italy, Spain, Portugal and, most recently, Germany have all operated net
deficits. Germany had a larger surplus than the UK throughout the late 1980s
and the early part of the 1990s although its position was deteriorating steadily

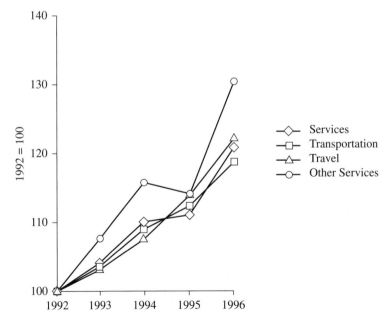

Figure 5.6   Growth of service exports, all markets, EU15, 1992–96

throughout the period. The fortunes of the UK have fluctuated but it has always shown a positive balance for other services which, by 1996, had almost returned to the level reached during the peak of the economic boom in 1986–87. The volume of exports (by value) has remained much the same throughout even though Single Market initiatives, such as the Financial Services Directives introduced in the mid-1980s have been in place for some time.

Trade in other services between the EU15 and the US is notable for substantial annual fluctuations. This is a function, no doubt, of macro-economic influences and the behaviour of multinational firms investing in the respective markets. Germany started the period with a larger surplus than the UK but by 1993 it had decreased below the level of the UK surplus and contin-ued to plunge into a net deficit for 1995. France was in surplus at the begin-ning of the period and has since experienced two periods of deficit, the most recent in 1995 and 1996. The only country to retain a positive balance throughout the decade is again the UK, which recorded a steady improvement after 1990 when its surplus had diminished to its lowest level since 1987. While most of the other countries retained a relatively consistent negative balance throughout, all fared better in their other services transactions with Japan. The absolute values are of course much smaller than for US or intra-EU trade, but only Spain has persistently operated a very small deficit with Japan. France and the UK are consistently the preferred service trade partners for Japan, although France's position deteriorated sharply in 1995 whereas the UK steadily increased its surplus so that it accounted for well over 50 per cent of the overall total in 1996.

Exports of Miscellaneous Business, Professional and Technical Services, 1992–96

Inevitably, the picture becomes more complex as the level of disaggregation is increased. There are seven countries for which comparable data for exports of BPTS between 1992 and 1996 can be extracted (Eurostat, 1998). The trends they reveal in intra-EU15 and extra-EU15 trade vary consider-ably relative to all other services, for example, or for sub-categories of BPTS relative to trends for BPTS as a whole (Table 5.6). While exports of other services to partners outside the EU increased by 32 per cent, they increased by only 19 per cent within the EU. The reverse occurred for BPTS which increased by 32 per cent within the EU between 1992 and 1996 compared with a 28 per cent increase in extra-EU transactions. There has therefore been a shift in the share of exports of BPTS towards the EU15, a trend largely confirmed with respect to the major sub-categories of this group (see Figures 5.7a and 5.7b).

Table 5.6 Trends in intra- and extra-EU exports of miscellaneous business, professional and technical services, EU7[1], 1992–96

	Year	Other Services	Misc BPTS[3]	LAMP	AMP	R&D	AET	AMO	OMBT	SAE
Intra-EU exports[2]	1992	64 033	24 688	2 074	2 310	3 606	4 243	180	4 140	8 135
	1996	76 194	32 395	3 002	3 538	4 395	4 845	231	8 249	8 138
	% change 92–96	19.0	31.2	44.7	53.2	21.9	14.2	28.3	99.3	0.0
Extra-EU exports[2]	1992	61 441	21 191	1 849	1 159	2 375	5 134	607	4 743	5 325
	1996	81 039	27 178	2 759	1 506	2 472	5 343	154	7 448	7 495
	% change 92–96	31.9	28.3	49.2	29.9	4.1	4.1	–74.6	57.0	40.8

Notes:
1. BLEU, Germany, Spain, France, Italy, Netherlands, UK.
2. Million ECU.
3. See footnotes for explanation of abbreviations.

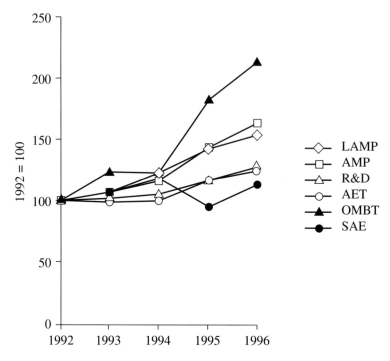

Figure 5.7a   Change in exports of MBPTS, intra-EU15, EU7, 1992–96

Apart from OMBT the growth rates for exports by advertising-related services (AMP), legal and related services (LAMP) within the EU and outside have not been very different. It may well be that OMBT, which have shown more modest expansion of exports outside the EU15, are more readily able to respond to the new opportunities created by the SEM because they are less restricted by national codes of professional practice, and/or are able to supply clients without the necessity for direct representation in the appropriate national market. For the AMP or LAMP sub-categories there is some scope for transmitting their expertise across borders, whether within or outside the EU, but they do rely much more on face-to-face contact with clients and inputs of local knowledge in order to be able to compete with domestic firms. These groups of services have therefore been actively engaged in internationalisation strategies involving foreign direct investment, as well as cross-border transactions, in their target markets. This has involved a considerable degree of merger and acquisition activity, involving UK and German legal firms for example, in order to establish European-wide or global networks of offices that can provide the highest quality

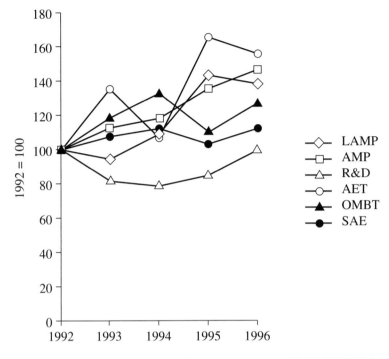

Figure 5.7b   Change in exports of MBPTS, extra-EU15, EU7, 1992–96

knowledge and expertise at local level. The deregulation of markets or the harmonisation of qualifications within the EU can be expected to encourage foreign direct investment of this kind. This underlines the necessity for using the information on trade, of the kind explored in general terms in this chapter, as only a partial indication of the true level of market integration for EU services.

Intra-EU exports of BPTS for each of the EU7 grew at a faster rate than extra-EU exports between 1992 and 1996. Starting from a small base, Spain heads the list but the 48 per cent increase for the UK and 36 per cent for BLEU provides a more significant measure of the increasing importance of the EU Member States as a market for business service transactions involving EU partners. Germany, and especially the Netherlands, contradict the overall pattern, reflecting the comparatively weak position of the former as an international source of advanced business services and the consistent weakness in the performance of the latter across the full range of sub-categories. None of the other countries in the EU7 displays the slowdown in intra-EU exports recorded for the Netherlands.

CONCLUSION

This has been a very preliminary and selective (in terms of coverage of services) attempt to summarise some broad features of recent EU international trade in services. While there continue to be many difficulties associated with the compilation of comparable data and the development of appropriate tools for measuring trade in services, the statistics now available are rather better than they have been in the past. There may therefore be some value to be derived from trying to unravel some of the key features of recent trends in services trade. There is an underlying assumption that this trade will make a growing contribution to national BOP, will stimulate growth and diversification of employment, and is one mechanism for enabling the exchange and transfer of the knowledge and skills (especially within the EU) that promotes national/regional innovation and competitiveness. Thus, the initiatives taken by the EU to remove barriers to the cross-border movement of factors of production in services, especially human resources or the recognition of professional qualifications in countries other than those where they were obtained, are a response to this changing perception of the role of services. Given the relatively recent introduction of these initiatives it is perhaps too early to assess their effects. However, they do assume that cross-border trade in services will continue to grow and that a substantial part of this activity will be increasingly focussed on intra-EU transactions.

In some respects, at first sight, the signs are not encouraging. Although by 1997 the average share of services in total employment for the EU15 was 65.3 per cent (SD8.2) merchandise exports continue to account for 70–80 per cent by value of trade. Of course, goods incorporate significant service inputs (pre-production and post-production) and many services are not tradable (many non-market services and some market services). Perhaps it should not therefore be surprising that the export of services both within the EU and between the EU and its major partners has grown only very slowly and in many cases comprises less than 20 per cent of national exports (by value). This reflects the situation for world commercial services trade more generally, as illustrated by the WTO. However, it is certain that the real scale (or share) of services trade flows is underestimated because, for example, in the statistics provided by Member States financial services transactions are recorded on a net basis. This has the important effect of underestimating the credit flows (exports). In addition, for a full analysis of international trade it is essential to examine foreign direct investment by services since this is a prerequisite for the activities of many BPTS which tend to be heavily dependent on human resources to provide the expertise and knowledge.

Although the overall growth of international trade in services may be disappointing the data summarised here does suggest that those services that are more tradable than others, such as BPTS, reveal a level of cross-border trade (within and outside the EU) that has been growing somewhat faster than most. Whether this reflects the continuation of organisational and market strategies in favour of internationalisation that were already underway in the 1980s, or is a product of the deregulation of markets by national governments and via EU Directives, is difficult to say. It is probably a combination of both but the general consequence seems to be increased national specialisation in services trade. In relation to 'other services' and to BPTS a large share of EU cross-border exports originates from the UK, France and the Netherlands. They have developed competitive advantage based on a mix of historical factors, progressive attitudes towards regulation (the UK and the Netherlands, much less so in the case of France) and a predominance of the larger BPTS firms that are more likely to be seeking to enter international markets.

NOTES

1. School of Geography and Environmental Sciences, The University of Birmingham, Edgbaston, Birmingham B15 2TT, UK (email: p.w.daniels@bham.ac.uk).
2. Includes transactions between the Member States as well as with third countries outside the EU.
3. Most recently, on 27 January 1999 the European Commission put forward proposals for two further Directives on the free movement of services in the internal market. The first covers the rights of businesses established in the EU to provide services in another Member State using non-Community staff who are lawfully established in the EU. The purpose is to make it easier for businesses to exercise their right to provide services and to clarify the situation of non-Community nationals in the framework of provision of services with the EU.
4. In some instances markets remain very fragmented at the European level. The markets for technical services (including engineers and architects) still tend to operate within national borders because of the difficulty of conforming to local rules and requirements of membership of national associations. Exports of these services to third countries (that is outside the EU) are therefore much higher than to other Member States (European Commission, 1996).
5. For a complete picture it is necessary to include foreign direct investment by services. In many respects this either complements the financial transactions examined in this chapter or is a prerequisite for supplying an international market.
6. While the data on international trade in services are becoming more comprehensive it remains important not to lose sight of the continuing difficulty, considering its intangible nature, of recording international trade in services. The task remains much more difficult than it is for merchandise trade. The Eurostat (1998) data that is used in this chapter is 'collected by means of complex systems combining enterprises' direct declarations, surveys, the census of bank transactions, and estimates' (para 1.1, 42). There are three principal problems. 1. *Conceptual*: the definition of services such as insurance or construction services is difficult to establish. 2. *The problem of mixed transactions*: the value of certain services is incorporated with the value of other transactions on the same invoice (transportation, transport insurance, financial services for example). 3. *The difficulty of identifying gross flows*: offsetting mechanisms are often used for certain transactions between related companies that is instead of paying the full debt outstanding between two branch offices (gross flows), a branch only pays the difference between what it owes and is owed to it (net flows), For a full discussion see Eurostat (1998: 42–4).
7. Transportation services cover all transportation services that are performed by residents of

one economy for those of another and that involve the carriage of passengers, the movement of goods (freight), rentals (charters) of carriers with crew, and related supporting and auxiliary services.

8. Travel services primarily cover the goods and services acquired from an economy by travellers during visits of less than one year in that economy.

9. This is the equivalent to the coverage of *Other business services* in BPM5. For the purposes of the present analysis, attention will only be given to the sub-category *Miscellaneous business, professional, and technical services*. This includes the following: legal, accounting, management consulting, and public relations services (LAMP); advertising, market research and public opinion polling (AMP); research and development services (R&D); architectural, engineering and other technical services (AET); agricultural, mining and on-site processing services (AMO); other – miscellaneous business, professional, and technical services (OMBT); services between affiliated enterprises not included elsewhere (SAE). For a more detailed description of each of these business services see Eurostat (1998), para 3.1.1.2.9, 47–8.

REFERENCES

American FSA (1995), *World Trade in Services (Highlights from a Conference at the US Department of State, Washington, DC)*, Washington: American Foreign Services Association.

Bhagwati, J.N. (1987), 'International Trade in Services and its Relevance for Economic Development', in O. Giarini (ed.), *The Emerging Service Economy*, New York: Pergamon.

Daniels, P.W. (1998), 'Producer services and the Asia-Pacific Region in a global context', *Asia Pacific Viewpoint*, **39**, 145–59.

Daniels, P.W. (2000), 'Export of services or servicing exports?', *Geografiska Annaler*, **62B**, in press.

Dunning, J.H. (1977), 'Trade, Location of Economic Activity and the MNE: a search for an eclectic approach', in B. Ohlin, H. Pere-Ove and P.M. Wijkman (eds), *The International Allocation of Economic Activity*, London: Macmillan, pp. 25–40.

European Commission (1996), *Putting Services to Work: A Communication from the Commission to the European Council*, Brussels: European Commission, November (CSE96.6).

European Commission (1999), *Sixth Periodic Report on the Social and Economic Situation of the Regions of the European Union*, Luxembourg: Office for Official Publications of the European Union.

Eurostat (1998), *International Trade in Services, EU, 1987–1996*, Luxembourg: Office de publications officielles des Communautés européennes.

Feketekuty, G. (1998), 'Principles of sound regulation in services: the key to long term economic growth in the new global economy', Paper presented at an International Symposium on Trade in Services: China and the World. Centre for American Studies, Findon University (mimeo).

Feketekuty, G. and Hauser, G. (1986), 'Information technology and trade in services', *Economic Impact*, **52**, 22–28.

Grubel, H.G. and Walker, M.A. (1989), *Service Industry Growth: causes and effects*, Vancouver, BC: Fraser Institute.

Jones, R.W. and Kierzkowski, H. (1990), 'The Role of Services in Production and International Trade: a theoretical framework', in R.W. Jones and A.O. Krueger (eds), *The Political Economy of International Trade*, Oxford: Blackwell.

Landesmann, M.A. and Petit, P. (1992), 'Trade in producer services, international specialisation and European integration', Paris: CEPREMAP (mimeo).

Lanvin, B. (1993), *Trading in a New World Order: The Impact of Telecommunications and Data Services on International Trade in Services*, Boulder CO: Westview Press.

Moshirian, F. (1993), 'Determinants of international-trade flows in travel and passenger services', *Economic Record*, **69**, 239–52.

Nachum, L. (1999), *The Origins of the International Competitiveness of Firms: The Impact of Location and Ownership in Professional Service Industries*, Cheltenham: Edward Elgar.

Nicolaides, P. (1989), *Liberalizing Service Trade*, London: Routledge.

Petit, P. (1986), *Slow Growth and the Service Economy*, London: Frances Pinter.

Sampson, G. and Snape, R. (1985), 'Identifying the issues in trade in services', *The World Economy*, **8**, 171–81.

Sauvant, K.P. (1986), *International Transactions in Services*, Boulder, CO and London: Westview Press.

Sauvant, K.P. (1993), 'The tradability of services', in K.P. Sauvant and P. Mallampally (eds), *Transnational Corporations in Services*, New York: Routledge, pp. 300–315.

Tucker, K. and Sundberg, M. (1988), *International Trade in Services*, London: Routledge.

World Trade Organisation (1999), *Report on World Trade in Services 1998*, Geneva: WTO.

World Trade Organisation (2000), *A review of statistics on Trade Flows in Services*, Geneva: WTO.

6. Transaction modes and the internationalisation of business service firms in the Haute-Garonne

Pierre-Yves Leo and Jean Philippe

The internationalisation of service activities appears to be entering a new phase. The WTO Seattle conference and the last GATS agreement clearly show that the international trade of services has become extremely important. It is now essential to explore service trade as well as to identify mechanisms deployed by service companies to develop overseas markets. Service trade liberalisation is still in the early stages of development and the GATS agreement provides a framework which still has to be implemented.

Empirical studies of service globalisation mainly rely on case studies of multinational companies: the most common case studies are American Express, McDonalds, British Airways, Federal Express, Sodexo, Accor, Cap Gemini. Direct investment abroad involves more and more companies and sectors and it is important to note that these investments also alter the status of domestic competition. Information and communication networks operate globally and are increasingly encouraging companies to trade internationally. As a result ways of management are modified and new forms of organisation or of service delivery are appearing. This implies that empirical research is required to understand the management dynamics of firms that have internationalised and entered foreign markets.

This chapter explores the findings of an exploratory study undertaken with the Toulouse Chamber of Trade and Industry to identify and explore the mechanisms of business-to-business service internationalisation of companies located in the Haute-Garonne area. The aim of this chapter is to, first, identify the strategies developed by firms and, second, to compare them to the globalisation strategies of multinational service companies. After an account of the methodology, two questions will be explored. First, how Haute-Garonne companies initiate foreign trade business and, second, the identification of strategies that have been implemented to develop cross-border trade, for example, the type of customer relationship and the service provided.

THE SURVEY

The research is based on a questionnaire survey conducted in the administrative district of Haute-Garonne. The initial aim was the production and publication of a directory of business service firms that have developed international operations. To identify such companies a preliminary postal questionnaire was sent to all 1600 service establishments located in the district. To increase the response rate it was stressed that one outcome of the research would be the publication of a professional directory. The questionnaire enabled managers to decide rapidly if they matched the characteristics of the companies included in the survey. About 300 companies were identified using this method and another 100 were identified from lists obtained from the Telexport yearly survey.

A twelve-page questionnaire was sent to 400 establishments. The questions explored the characteristics of the companies and the nature of their international operations. After follow-up telephone calls about 150 completed questionnaires were obtained. Of these 121 companies matched the sampling frame. Fifty-three per cent of responding companies are very small (less than 10 employees) and 33 per cent have between 10 and 49 employees. The rest of the respondents have between 50 and 200 employees, but two companies have 250 and 650 employees. Eighty-eight per cent of respondents are located in the Toulouse agglomeration and more than half are located in the city. Seventy-two per cent are small or medium-sized firms whilst the remaining 28 per cent are branch establishments controlled by large companies or groups of firms. The headquarters of about ten of these are located in Paris.

Company turnover ranged from 46 thousand to 64 million Euros. Just under a quarter (23 per cent) have turnovers of less than 300 thousand, 28 per cent have turnovers between 0.3 and 0.8 million Euros, another 28 per cent between 0.8 and 3 million Euros, and 21 per cent more than 3 million Euros. For the majority of companies most of their turnover comes from the provision of services; for 64 per cent of respondents the provision of services is responsible for more than 95 per cent of turnover. On the other hand, for 7 per cent of respondents service delivery contributes less than one-third of the total value of sales. This is explained by the core activity of these companies, for example, engineering services that are incorporated into goods or fittings. Seventeen per cent of respondents obtain more than half of their sales from abroad, 20 per cent export 20 to 50 per cent of their sales, 25 per cent export between 5 and 20 per cent and 13 per cent obtain less than 5 per cent of their sales from foreign markets. The remaining 25 per cent did not provide data as their international activity is provided by local subsidiaries or other partners.

Respondents were mainly concentrated in three sectors: technical engineering (47 per cent), business and management consultancy (33 per cent) and logistics (16 per cent). In each of these sectors there is a range of activities. Technical engineering includes engineering consultancy, software activities, research on materials, high-tech industrial consultancy or multimedia activities. Business consultancy consists of legal consultancy, international accountancy, market and opinion research, management and strategic consultancy, recruiting, advertising and training. Logistic activities include road and air transport as well as international parcel delivery, travel agency and transport organisation.

This overview of the characteristics of firms in the sample identifies a group of small and medium-sized enterprises (SMEs) that are involved in the provision of services internationally. It shows that internationalisation does not just involve large global firms but is also being undertaken by SMEs.

THE BEGINNING

Developing an international business or going overseas creates a number of problems for service companies including the organisation of the customer relationship as well as responding to competition from local or established international companies. This research suggests that multiple factors determine the development of international business.

Economists often privilege macroeconomic determinants of exchange and their explanations traditionally involve the comparative advantage (or disadvantage) of countries as an explanation of performance gaps between companies. The general idea underlying these works (Mucchielli, 1991) is that macroeconomic variables mainly determine the competitive advantage of companies. Comparative advantage is country-specific and incorporates a number of related factors: production traditions, consumption modes, technological abilities and the availability of factors of production. These factors produce for any one country, over a period of time, relative advantage or disadvantage in the production of goods or services.

This production-costs approach does not include other parameters of competitiveness which are associated with a company's internal characteristics. Other authors (Nyahoho, 1993), without neglecting macroeconomic factors, place more emphasis on the role played by firms that develop international business though considering logistics and the form that the internationalisation of their activities will take. These works are based upon observed behavioural differences between companies and suggest that internationalisation can be explained by considering the characteristics of countries, industrial sectors and market structures.

Competitive advantages are constructed by firms. They can support a country's comparative advantages or they can compensate for comparative disadvantages at a country level. This type of competitiveness comes from company-specific factors that provide company-specific competitive advantage. Researchers have tried to explain behavioural differences and performance gaps that exist between companies. Using statistical databases these studies bring into light the relations between strategic variables and the economic performance of companies. The underlying idea conflicts with established approaches to understanding the international economy; performance differences or gaps between countries are due to the internal characteristics of firms or activities.

The service debate on this topic is still ongoing. Lindahl and Beyers (1999) consider that applying traditional concepts derived from the study of industrial economies, for example prices, productivity or costs, to service activities is very hazardous. Many studies highlight the difficulties of identifying the comparative advantage of countries in the field of services. Research into company selection of target markets has concluded that the characteristics of the markets (size, similarity, competition, risks) influences the comparative advantage of countries (O'Farrell and Wood, 1994).

Our survey of Haute-Garonne companies develops aspects of this debate especially in the identification of how firms began operating internationally. The first finding is that the number of companies entering the international market greatly increased after 1995 (GATS agreement), much more noticeably than after 1992 (European Union market). Both of these events probably do contribute to pushing Haute-Garonne firms into considering operating overseas. Between 1996 and 1998, 35 firms from our sample entered the international market compared to 23 between 1993 and 1995 and only 21 between 1990 and 1992. Thirty-three firms began the internationalisation process during the 1970s and 1980s. These waves of internationalisation affect more or less all producer service sectors, but during the most recent period technical consultancy as well as management consultancy were particularly involved, and the companies to internationalise first are more likely to be logistic activities. In the same way the most recent companies to develop overseas markets tend to be smaller firms rather than the subsidiaries of large groups or from firms that already have multiple offices in France. For most firms internationalisation occurred after saturation of the French market place in their area of activity had occurred. This suggests that companies developing an international market appear to do so on the back of an established French national market. The process by which enterprises enter overseas markets occurs in stages.

Two Prevailing Attitudes: Reactive or Proactive

The sudden growth in international markets is often the consequence of demand arising from already internationalised French clients (52 per cent of firms), but very often service providers want to develop new markets abroad (48 per cent). Few firms explain their entry into the international market by drawing upon both these explanation; this suggests that there are two distinct attitudes to internationalisation – the 'reactive' approach is frequently specific to a particular service activity and occurs more frequently than the 'proactive' approach.

In our sample 'proactive' behaviour is undertaken by independent SMEs rather than by groups or subsidiaries whose internationalisation often follows a group strategy. The other factors mentioned derive from more passive attitudes: spontaneous demand from foreign clients (29 per cent of firms) and service activities that support international exchanges (19 per cent). These proportions remain the same when we consider only the most recent entrants into this marketplace. For half the service companies internationalisation is the result of an autonomous decision taken by the enterprise whilst for the other half the service providers follow the client overseas.

Export without Direct Investment

The methods used by manufacturing companies to develop international markets (exportation and then eventually the establishment of a branch plant) are often different from the methods used by service companies. For service companies direct investment in a foreign market is perceived as a preliminary to service delivery due to the constraint imposed by the provider–client relationship. This constraint does not appear to have prevented the majority of respondents (84 per cent) from exporting before the construction of a service delivery network; the customer or the service provider had to travel to provide the service. Since 1995, 90 per cent of companies that have entered foreign markets have used this technique. It would appear that producer services that possess knowledge and expertise of great value have less difficulty in acting in this manner. Furthermore travel costs have diminished and new types of telecommunication have been established. However, entry into overseas markets by the establishment of a branch plant/office was not completely absent from the sample (16 per cent) and maybe a more frequent occurrence amongst service firms than manufacturing companies. Most companies that are part of a group can draw upon networks established by the group all over the world. It is not as simple or as easy for independent SMEs to enter the international marketplace. One strategy being encouraged by European policy is the development of a European consortium that uses its resources to develop overseas business opportunities.

The Countries

Most of the companies in the sample (84 per cent) did not begin to trade in more than two countries simultaneously. The only companies to develop their activities in three or more countries are subsidiaries of larger groups. Most companies began exporting to other Western Europe countries: Western Europe accounted for 65 per cent of business, other developed countries (USA, Canada, Japan, Australia) 24 per cent, and developing countries only 11 per cent. The emphasis on the European market is even greater for companies establishing offices in foreign countries; 83 per cent of countries mentioned by these respondents are in Western Europe.

A limited number of criteria determine the choice of the first country for a service company to identify as suitable for market development. The most frequent factor identified was market potential (54 per cent) followed by image potential (21 per cent), proximity (21 per cent) to minimise transportation costs, membership of the European Union (19 per cent), language (16 per cent), cultural similarities (14 per cent) and technological potential (12 per cent). The choice of a country as a test-market is very rarely mentioned and only in the case of export. Companies that established branch offices did so usually only after detailed preliminary research. Geographic proximity and, in some cases, cultural similarities play an important role in the choice of country.

SERVICE STRATEGIES AND MODES OF DELIVERY

Offering services to clients located in other countries forces service providers to resolve two difficulties: how to establish and maintain client relationships and what kind of services are to be provided. The first point is a well-known characteristic of services that distinguishes them from manufactured goods: personal interaction between client and service provider is often essential to the effective delivery of a service. For a long time this characteristic restricted the development of international service trade. The emergence of distant services delivered via telecommunications and the reduction of travel costs partially undermined the importance of personal interaction. During an earlier GATS negotiation a framework was proposed (Richardson, 1987) for analysing the tradability of services:

1. Some tradable services can be produced in one country and sold in another.
2. Some tradable services have to establish a temporary or permanent commercial presence in order to facilitate their sales.
3. Other services are traded with some difficulty as they require the movement of staff for service delivery. These services are difficult to trade as they can be developed only through the creation of local establishments.

About twenty years later the analysis of this framework reveals that important transformations have occurred that have been induced by the development of information technologies: many services considered as difficult to export without an appropriate network are now exported without local support. Furthermore, the way a service is provided influences the content and nature of the service provided. Internationalisation compels companies to reconsider their services and to adapt them to local markets. Standardisation is often the preferred method used to expand the market for a service, but this depends on the sector- and company-specific factors. Consequently, the service delivery policy adopted by a company is one of the most important decisions that has to be taken. In the rest of this chapter types or modes of service delivery are identified and the ways in which companies choose a particular delivery mode are explored.

Types of Service Delivery

The most common method used by a company to develop an international market is by exporting a service. The establishment of a subsidiary or branch plant/office is undertaken by fewer companies and is more likely to be a large company strategy. Different types of service delivery were identified by respondents. The majority of companies export (81 per cent) but a significant number of companies (52 per cent) have also developed networks abroad. Consequently in many cases these different types of relationship (export/branch plant) complement each other both at an operational level and according to country.

The internationalisation of services raises a series of organisational as well as statistical problems. For companies, internationalisation involves the management of business contacts and offices located in numerous countries as well as the development of solutions to qualitative and cultural problems. Even for governments, the framework for international trade has not been completely formulated either by regional (EU market and NAFTA) or international (GATS) agreements. The continuing development of communication technologies that alter modes of service delivery also undermine aspects of these agreements.

This suggests that any discussion of international services needs to commence with the definition of service exchanges used by the main trade negotiation agencies, GATS and the World Trade Organisation. Four types of international trade have been identified and consequently four types of internationalisation can be conceptualised:

1. *Cross-border transactions* take place without the provider or customer travelling to each other. This type of service trade entails the provision of

remote services or teleservices through the medium of telecommunications. The provision of information, the analysis of databanks, software, insurance, banks (both private and corporate), computer maintenance (whether on land, sea or air) belong to this category of service trade.

2. The provision of a service internationally by the *movement of the provider* to the client's country. In this case the provider travels to the customer's country in order to deliver the service. This method of service delivery is usually undertaken by legal and engineering consultants as well as by some training providers. Transportation is also included in this category.

3. An international transaction that involves *customers* travelling to the service provider's country to obtain the service. Three services are included under this category, only one being a business-to-business service: tourism, health and training. In order to consume these services customers have to travel to the service supplier's country.

4. International delivery of a service *through foreign affiliates*. All services can be provided through foreign affiliates. Direct investment in a foreign market can become a necessity for companies that have developed significant international business. This mode of service delivery includes most consumer services (fast food restaurants, hairdressing, beauty salons), joint services (hotels, cars and equipment renters) and some business-to-business services (legal consultancy, auditing, advertising and engineering).

These four types of trade involve not only service firms but also include manufacturing companies that sell goods that are supported by services. During the course of a company's life relationships with customers can change and take different forms (marketing, market presence, service delivery).

Companies responding to the survey provided services to foreign clients in the following manner: 76 per cent move staff abroad to provide the service, 36 per cent let their foreign customers travel to obtain the service in France, 23 per cent have some local affiliates abroad that deliver the services and 16 per cent engage in cross-border exchanges (Table 6.1).

With the exception of cross-border exchange these different forms of relationship are not mutually exclusive; two delivery modes and sometimes three are used simultaneously by 43 per cent of companies. Most frequently, when only one form of relationship is used the provider travels to the foreign customer, very few firms restrict the provision of services to France forcing foreign customers to travel to France to obtain the service. Similarly, it is quite rare for a company to entirely entrust the delivery of services abroad to foreign affiliates.

In 64 per cent of cases service delivery is linked with new telecommunication technologies (Internet, EDI, data banks), but 74 per cent of companies use

Table 6.1   Types of relationship with foreign customers depending on service sector

Delivery Mode	Technical consultancy		Management consultancy		Logistics	
	No.	%*	No.	%*	No.	%*
Cross-border	6	11.1	5	12.8	6	35.3
Provider movement	42	77.8	32	82.1	9	52.9
Client movement	23	42.6	17	43.6	1	5.9
Foreign affiliates	13	24.1	8	20.5	4	23.5
Total number of firms	54	100.0	39	100.0	17	100.0

Note: * Because companies use more that one delivery mode this figure exceeds 100 per cent of the total sample.

traditional technology (telephone or fax) or postal services (62 per cent). The growing importance of new telecommunication technologies is shown by the significant proportion (56 per cent) of firms that have a website. A relatively small number of cross-border traders rely on these technologies: 72 per cent operate using new types of telecommunications, but the same percentage use more traditional technology; two-thirds rely on postal services.

At the sectoral level the type of delivery mode is similar for technical and management consultancy (Table 6.1). Client movements are more unusual for

Table 6.2   Types of network by the geographical location of the market

Type of network	Western Europe		Other developed countries		Rest of the world	
	No. of firms	%*	No. of firms	%*	No. of firms	%*
No network	47	47.5	19	42.2	23	38.3
Subsidiaries	18	18.2	9	20.0	8	13.3
Joint ventures	7	7.1	4	8.9	9	15.0
Franchises	1	1.0	0	0.0	1	1.7
Agents	4	4.0	2	4.4	6	10.0
Other partners	21	21.2	11	24.4	12	20.0
All together	99	100.0	45	100.0	60	100.0

Note: * Because companies use more than one delivery mode this figure exceeds 100 per cent.

Table 6.3 *Quality control procedures depending on network type*

Type of network	Training of local staff		Recurrent auditing		Supervising by expatriates		Partners' quality certification		Network inner rules	
	No. of firms	%*	No. of firms	%*	No. of firms	%*	No. of firms	%*	No. of firms	%*
Subsidiaries	12	54.5	11	50.0	12	54.5	6	27.0	3	13.6
Joint ventures	5	50.0	5	50.0	1	10.0	2	20.0	3	30.0
Franchises	1	50.0	0	0.0	0	0.0	0	0.0	2	100.0
Agents	5	71.4	3	42.8	4	57.1	1	14.3	1	14.3
Other partners	9	45.0	5	25.0	5	25.0	5	25.0	3	15.0
All together	23	41.0	19	33.9	14	25.0	13	24.2	7	12.5

Note: * Percentages of the total number of networked firms.

logistic companies, but cross-border delivery much more common. Respondents identified partnerships as the most common form of foreign network relationship (57 per cent) followed by the establishment of a subsidiary (46 per cent). Twenty-three per cent of networks are joint ventures, 14 per cent are established via a contract with a commercial agent and only 4 per cent are franchises. Franchise operations are difficult to establish in the field of business-to-business services.

Some interesting differences exist between countries that receive French services: services supplied to developed countries outside Europe are provided using similar methods to services provided to clients located in Western Europe (Table 6.2). Fewer companies, however, operate in these markets without developing a network. Joint Ventures or agents under contract tend to be more common in developing countries. To control standards of service quality companies establish inspection procedures that vary from one kind of network to another (Table 6.3).

In subsidiaries quality is controlled by training local staff, supervision by expatriates and by regular auditing. Joint ventures have the same quality controls, except that supervision by expatriates is rare. Franchises are controlled through their rules or charters. Agents under agreement have mostly been trained by the exporting company and in some cases are supervised by expatriates. Generally speaking, service quality appears to be less controlled in less formalised partnerships.

Does one type of relationship prove to be more efficient than another? A variance analysis identifies two significant relationships. First, a firm's total international turnover (export plus the turnover of foreign subsidiaries) is more dynamic when it has developed a controlled (supervised) network, that means a network made up of subsidiaries, joint ventures or franchises. It is less dynamic when this network only consists of commercial agents or other contracted partners ($F = 2.48$; $pr > F = 0.0892$). On average, the performance of firms without a network is somewhere between the two types of networks (controlled/uncontrolled). Seemingly it is better not to develop a network rather than to establish an uncontrolled one.

The second performance indicator associated with the mode of service delivery is the number of countries in which a firm operates. Firms operating abroad through subsidiaries, joint ventures or franchises work in the greatest number of countries (around 26 on average). The same is also true but to a lesser extent for companies that deliver services through cross border transactions (19 countries). These companies are very different from those that only provide services to foreign clients that travel to France to obtain the service (2 or 3 countries only). Service providers that move staff between countries to deliver a service operate on average in between 5 and 10 countries depending on whether this delivery mode is used alone or is associated with a local network of associates. An international network appears to be the best method to manage the delivery of a service to a number of different countries. Another efficient method is through the use of new telecommunication systems by which services can be sold in the same way as if they were physical goods.

The way in which service providers operate and the multiple networks they are using has encouraged us to consider the notion of stages in the process of the internationalisation of services activities. Often the firms operate simultaneously using several methods; they use the most convenient method and these vary from country to country or from one context to another. Actually measuring a firm's degree of internationalisation is difficult (Huault, 1998) and the criterion of the establishment of a network is not the only discriminating criterion for judging the quality of international activity.

Changing the Contents of Service Delivered Abroad

Generally speaking, an analysis of the strategies developed by companies is complicated by the heterogeneity of services activities which makes it difficult to generalise (Tannery, 1999). For international markets additional factors make it difficult to identify patterns of strategic behaviour:

1. Different service activities internationalise in different ways.
2. Countries do not possess the same opportunities.
3. A firm's competitive advantage is not automatically retained abroad because of cultural, linguistic and social differences that exist between countries.
4. Market deregulation presents new opportunities for international expansion.

Linked to these problems is a fundamental question concerning the nature of these strategies. Are international strategies developed specifically for foreign markets or are they only adaptations of home-based strategies? Many authors (Gadrey and Moulaert, 1992; Heskett, 1995) disregard the internationalisation of companies by suggesting that existing strategies are adapted. Other authors (Lovelock and Lapert, 1999; Van Dierdonck, 1998) identify some international strategies that can be considered as autonomous. In order to understand the development of service firms we need to appreciate the individual position of a firm and its relationship to wider economic structures. Our analysis tries to deal with these two issues by exploring the types of services provided by companies and their alteration to meet the demands of clients in other countries.

Specialised activities

Respondents were provided with a list of 27 activities (Table 6.4). Relatively few firms (28 per cent) provide only one service to clients located abroad,

Table 6.4 *Service activities provided abroad by delivery mode (only frequently mentioned activities are listed)*

Type of service	Firms providing the service	Delivery mode: (1) indirectly through local affiliates	(2) directly by the firm
	Number	% of number of firms	
Technical consultancy	65	18	95
Computer and data processing	38	29	97
Staff training	31	29	94
Technical assistance	24	17	100
Transportation storage	22	41	73
Management consultancy	17	47	88
Commercial intelligence	15	47	67
Brokerage	15	33	87
Installation and fitting	14	14	100
Advertising	14	14	100
Translation, interpreting	12	25	83
Telecommunications, telematics	11	36	82
Human resources consultancy	11	45	91
Intern. trade fairs, travel agencies	11	36	91
Repairing, maintenance	11	18	100

Note: The following activities have been mentioned less than ten times: after-sales service, patents and licence transfer, legal consultancy, auditing and accounting, insurance and financial services, audio-visual, motion pictures, equipment rental, temporary staff, administrative works, cleaning.

either directly or through local affiliates. Two-thirds of respondents provide less than five and one-third more than four kind of services (four firms: up to 10 or 13 types of services). No firm provided security or catering services.

Table 6.4 shows the importance of consultancy (particularly technical consultancy), software services, transportation and training activities. This is not surprising as it is a well known specialisation of the Toulouse district. The recourse to local affiliates for service delivery is particularly common for management consultancy, commercial intelligence, human resources consultancy and transportation. In general, secondary services (non-core services), maybe those for which competitive advantage is less visible, are often entrusted to local providers.

Adaptations or diversification can be necessary

Companies developing an international market have to decide on the services they want to provide abroad. Two types of behaviour can be identified: some

Firms adapting more or less the service
(in percentage of firms providing the service)

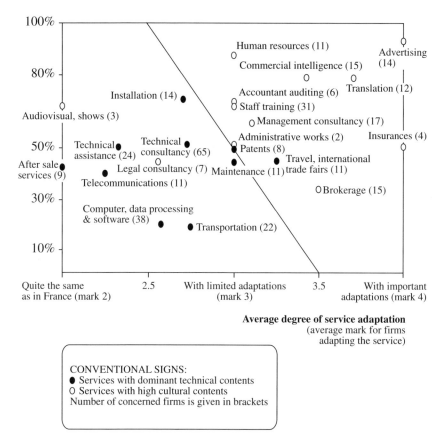

Figure 6.1   Adaptations of services to foreign markets according to the service provided

sell services abroad that are identical to those provided in France whilst others adapt services to a greater or lesser degree (Figure 6.1). The first option is usually taken by services that have a high technical content: transportation is provided in this way by 81 per cent of the firms in the sample, followed by software (80 per cent) and telecommunications (60 per cent). The second option affects services that incorporate cultural content: advertising is adapted in 92 per cent of cases, human resources (87 per cent), translations-interpreting (78 per cent), commercial information (78 per cent) and training (68 per cent). Consequently, the cultural content of a service exerts a considerable influence on its tradability.

Essential adaptations to services provided abroad include altering the delivery mode (34 per cent), pricing practices (34 per cent), conditions of payment (28 per cent), target customers (23 per cent) and advertising and marketing (21 per cent). Major alterations to the service concept are rarely made. Such a strategy would increase risk and could undermine the competitiveness of the services. Firms were asked to classify these adaptations by their level of importance. Quality and control of distant delivery is the most important factor (an average of 3.8 on a scale ranging from one to five), followed by care taken to alter the service so that it conforms to local customs and habits (3.7), conforming to local rules and regulations (3.6) and with other environmental conditions (3.6). Competing against local companies was identified as the least important factor (3.2).

Theories developed from studies of service multinationals underline the importance of service standardisation and the formalisation of procedures. Another question concerns the range of services that can be provided to a foreign market: is it acceptable to concentrate on the delivery of a core basic service or should the basic service be accompanied by secondary services to make it more attractive to client companies? For SMEs it is difficult to develop truly global services, but service adaptations may make the development of global services possible in the future

The majority of firms altered services provided to overseas clients. This involves the diversification of services provided overseas: 57 per cent have diversified their provision of both basic and secondary (complementary) services. Another 21 per cent limit their diversification to basic services. On the other hand, 10 per cent reduced the range of their basic and complementary services provided to overseas firms. These evolutions often match changes been made in the provision of service to the national market. However 26 per cent of respondents increased the diversification of their services abroad rather than in France, whilst 16 per cent implemented the opposite strategy.

Back office procedures evolved towards more codified forms of service delivery in 91 per cent of cases for services supplied to foreign markets (versus 88 per cent for the French market). Standardisation is much more unusual: only 27 per cent of companies introduced greater degrees of standardisation (versus 31 per cent for the French market). On the contrary, nearly three-quarters developed more customised services. For the companies in our sample, internationalisation has had two main consequences. First a search for greater internal efficiency, for example, improvements in procedures and by the adoption of quality certificates (41 per cent of firms had obtained a recognised quality standard, 52 per cent had obtained ISO specifications). Secondly, an attempt to match the requirements of foreign clients by adapting services and extending the types of services provided. Such strategies are too common in our sample to be a simple random effect.

CONCLUSION

The service sector has entered a new stage of internationalisation. Recent international agreements as well as increasing economic integration both in Europe and North America will liberalise service trade and will create favourable conditions for new foreign direct investment. New sectors and new firms will probably be developed abroad and we can foresee a growth in the number of foreign service companies operating in France.

This study explores a dynamic process and its findings form a useful reference point for future research. The Haute-Garonne administrative district contains a dynamic and relatively diversified group of internationalised service companies. This service complex is still in an embryonic state but important developments can be anticipated. The three sectors that form the basis of this study are extremely active internationally. Two of them are already well known as being important in the Toulouse region: technical consultancy (including engineering and software) and logistics. The emergence of the third sector (business-management consultancy) at the international level was a less expected finding. This confirms the push towards international markets that is and has occurred in the business service sector.

REFERENCES

Gadrey, J. and Moulaert, F. (1992), 'La question fondamentale des firmes de conseil: le positionnement du métier', in J. Gadrey, C. Gallouj, F. Gallouj, F. Martinelli, F. Moulaert and P. Tordoir (eds), *Manager le conseil*, Paris: Ediscience.

Heskett, James L. (1995), 'Strategic Services Management: examining and understanding it', in J.W. Glynn and G.J. Barnes (eds), *Understanding Services Management*, Chichester: Wiley.

Huault, Isabelle (1998), *Le management international*, Paris: Éditions La Découverte.

Lindahl, D.P. and Beyers, William B. (1999), 'The creation of competitive advantage by producer service establishments', *Economic Geography*, 1 (75), 1–20.

Lovelock, C. and Lapert, D. (1999), *Marketing des services*, Paris: Publiunion.

Mucchielli, J.L. (1991), 'Alliances stratégiques et firmes multinationales: une nouvelle théorie pour de nouvelles formes de multinationalisation', *Revue d'économie industrielle*, (55), 118–34.

Nyahoho, E. (1993), *Les Échanges Internationaux de Services*, Sainte Foy, Québec: Éditions Saint Martin.

O'Farrell, P.N. and Wood, P.A. (1994), 'International market selection by business service firms: key conceptual and methodological issues', *International Business Review*, 3 (3), 243–64.

Richardson, John B. (1987), 'A Sub-sectoral Approach to Services' Trade Theory', in Giarini O. (ed.), *The Emerging Service Economy*, Oxford: Pergamon.

Tannery, F. (1999), 'Espaces et formules stratégiques de l'entreprise dans les activités de service', *Économies et sociétés*, **5** (33), (série Économie et gestion des services, EGS no 1), 171–96.

Van Dierdonck, R. (1998), 'Managing Services across National Boundaries', in B. Van Loy, R. Van Dierdonck and P. Gemmel (eds), *Services Management: an Integrated Approach*, London: Financial Times, Pitman publishing.

7. The internationalisation of commercial activities: some recent theoretical contributions and empirical evidence

Peter Sjøholt

PART I: THEME AND THEORY

Introduction

Internationalisation includes all economic and socio-cultural interaction that crosses national borders. In the field of economics it includes both traditional international trade and the direct production of commodities in host countries as well as of services. In this chapter internationalisation will be explored through an analysis of the wholesale and retail trades. Like Dawson (1993), the definition of commercial internationalisation used includes international sales operations and the transfer of management ideas and commercial expertise by firms (see Bryson, Chapter 8). The analysis will, by and large, disregard conventional trade and concentrate on the development and operation of store/office networks in foreign countries. This also means that the types of activities that are transferred between counties are not confined to distribution *per se*, but are composed of factor inputs consisting of 'hard' investments as well as the transfer of store concepts, expertise and management systems that may frequently be new to the host country. Transfer regimes may differ by industry as well as by type of investment, management and control system.

The main theoretical-empirical part of this study is an inquiry into the why, how and where dimensions of direct cross-border transfers of commercial services. It will be an analysis of processes rather than an assessment of end products. The analysis will concentrate on the different conditions under which internationalisation operates. First, the motives of managers and their rationale for locating parts of the activity abroad will be explored. Key questions that need to be explored are: How far is the internationalisation strategy determined by purely economic motives and how far is it explained by other factors? What is the role of learning? How is technology in the widest sense an important determinant? And, finally, is leadership commitment and vision an important part of the process ?

The 'how' dimension of the internationalisation process naturally focuses on organisational issues. What are the strategies employed and what assets are at hand in realising cross border development? We will have to disentangle the different modes of entry and their rationale in order to understand the dynamics of organisation.

Absent from many studies of internationalisation is the question of location or the 'where dimension'. This includes factors that influence the choice of location. In this perspective many classical non-economic factors determine the locational outcome, and it is hypothesised that this locational process is not only determined by pure economic factors but is increasingly embedded in cultural processes and institutional settings. To assess this issue, both in theoretical and empirical terms, it is necessary to provide an organisational framework for the study and a conceptual structure for the analysis. First, however, a review of the recent literature on internationalisation is required to develop the context for this study.

Internationalisation: Some Recent Trends

Research on internationalisation was for a long time confined to manufacturing industry and its associated activities. The reason for this was that manufacturing dominated international exchange and investment. During the last two decades, however, the value of cross-border trade in services has increased substantially. For a long time cross-border trade has been a feature of the transport and tourism sectors, but it is only relatively recently that advanced producer and financial services have become strongly involved in international exchange.

Direct transfers of service activities across borders have become increasingly commonplace. Partly, this is a response to the increasingly high-tech character of goods with a requirement for follow-up, repair and maintenance and consultancy. In most cases the supplier of the product provides these service activities. Belgian research has shown that 23 per cent of the value of an exported commodity consists of service activities (Segebarth, 1990). Increasingly services have come to play a major role in the internationalisation process through direct marketing. Although partly being associated with the export of merchandise, the internationalisation of commercial activities is the consequence of the identification of market opportunities.

The importance and growth profile of services in international exchange is a matter of some controversy. This is partly due to the fact that some services are not included in international statistics because they are internal company

Table 7.1   World trade in services 1988–98 (billion US dollars)

	1988	1990	1992	1994	1996	1998
No.	600	783	923	1 038	1 271	1 318
%	17.3	18.5	19.7	19.6	19.2	19.6

Source: WTO Annual Report (1999).

transactions, and partly due to statistical errors, because it is more difficult to estimate value and value added for service activities. According to the WTO trade in services accounts for a small proportion of total world trade; in 1998 it only accounted for 17.3 per cent of world trade and this had only increased to 19.6 per cent by 1998 (Table 7.1).

This means that the growth in the value of service trade is only slightly above that of commodities and a relative stagnation in service trade occurred towards the end of the last decade. Growth has also been rather uneven, both between world regions and by sub-sector. Sectorally the broad group 'other services', including most services apart from transport and travel (tourism), expanded dramatically during the last decade.

When foreign direct investment (FDI) is included in the analysis trade in services has gradually outperformed that of commodities. By the mid 1980s the stock of direct investment in services in the leading six OECD countries scarcely amounted to 40 per cent of total investment. However, by the middle of the last decade it surpassed 50 per cent and in Japan reached 65 per cent. Although the number of host countries has multiplied investment is still concentrated in a limited number of countries, the lion's share going to a few large OECD economies. This growth reflects the increasing value and importance of services in the production process. A cross-border presence is required as a consequence of the inherent intangible and immaterial content of services (Gadrey, 1990). Moreover, socio-economic, institutional and cultural differences between nation-states require a permanent organised presence in host countries. Opportunities for transnational firms to undertake FDI have increased due to deregulation and liberalisation, easier communication and reductions in the cost of information. These investments grew particularly rapidly in the late 1980s, slowed considerably during the recession of the early 1990s and started to grow again from 1994.

Commercial activities (wholesale and retail trade) are difficult to measure. Wholesaling is, as emphasised by Dunning (1993a), often supplied by manufacturing firms and is frequently counted as a manufacturing activity. With this in mind, wholesale trade and trade-related services are amongst the most important cross-border activities. Overseas retail activities, on the other hand, are rather insignificant in value when compared with wholesaling and many other types of service activities. Incandela et al. (1999) note that as late as 1996 foreign subsidiaries of the worlds' top five retailing corporations accounted for only 12 per cent of total sales. This contrasts with, for example, banking, which obtains 48 per cent of turnover from foreign activity. There may be many reasons for this discrepancy. To these we now turn for a more systematic analysis.

Theoretical issues

Nilsson (1996) and Edvardsson et al. (1993) both suggest that internationalisation is a unique phenomenon with the latter claiming that: '[I]t is not possible to state general principles, which apply in each particular case'. However, statements like this do prevent a search for more general principles or at least systems of explanation to understand the process of transborder transfer. It is questionable whether a general explanation can be developed that will be able to highlight all types of foreign investment and economic activities. There is evidence to suggest, for instance, that the foreign business operations of manufacturing and service activities have different motivations and development paths.

General explanation systems, however, have not lost their appeal. Among these the so-called eclectic paradigm has gained wide acceptance as a frame of reference for understanding why transborder investment takes place, why it succeeds or fails, how this transfer is taking place and which locations transnational investors prefer. The paradigm is termed eclectic because it has its roots in several theoretical approaches, of which four are particularly important: the theory of the firm, trade theory, organisation theory and location theory. A fully-fledged eclectic theoretical system is ascribed to Dunning (Dunning 1977, Dunning and McQueen, 1982; Dunning and Norman 1983; Dunning 1993a, 1993b). It is founded on the theories of Coase (1937) and Hymer (1960) and there are parallel contributions by Swedenborg (1979), Lall (1980), Kogut (1985) and Porter (1990). Some of these are directly based on manufacturing industry. Dunning (1993a) explicitly extends the theoretical application of the paradigm to international service transfer.

Elements of strategic thinking have been latterly added to this theoretical edifice, the essence of which centres around three dimensions, each one abbreviated to a single letter, the so-called OLI configuration. O stands for ownership qualities and advantages, L for locational variables and I for internalisation advantages, explaining the why, where and how dimensions respectively. The point of departure for an internationalisation decision and the rationale of its subsequent implementation are the competitive advantage of the transnational firm *vis-à-vis* indigenous enterprises, derived from qualities or advantages possessed by the enterprise in question (ownership advantages). Competitive advantages are furthermore dependent on particular conditions of the location to which the transfer of activities is to take place and on the way in which the activity is internally or externally organised by the company. A satisfactory understanding of success or firm failure and of the configuration resulting from the process can only be gained by a combined synthesis of all three dimensions, as the factors are interrelated. A full understanding of the process is only possible by including strategic behaviour and learning into the analysis. Only then can the dynamics of the process be appreciated.

The eclectic paradigm has often been criticised for producing an overtly static analysis. It gives, however, a good frame of reference for the various directions of international movements with the possible exception of aspects of the why explanation. On the other hand, some of the inherent capabilities of firms can provide an answer to this question and it is to a discussion of the why dimension that we now turn.

The ownership advantages – why internationalise

According to Treadgold and Davies (1988) international commercial transfer has multiple motivations. Yet the search for growth was still found to be the most important driving force. This is linked to the classical need for the development of economies of scale both to overcome competitive constraints and remain competitive in the market. This depends on firm-specific ownership advantages. Looming large amongst these is access to capital and particularly surplus capital that can be invested to increase advantages and concomitantly harvest higher dividends abroad than at home (Dawson, 1993).

Motive forces like these, surfacing in commercial enterprises particularly from the early 1980s, reflect an offensive strategy, proactive as opposed to reactive. Many earlier explanations for commercial internationalisation emphasised reactive motives by highlighting home market restrictions as the main driving force. An example might be an excessive regulatory environment that restricts new organisational forms or the impact of strict planning control (Burt, 1986). The market might also act as a restrictive constraint in its own right owing to size and saturation (Laujalainen, 1991).

What is most interesting is the observation that perceptions of opportunity seem to become crucial variables in understanding the process. Thus, Alexander (1990) notes that perceived lucrative opportunities in unfilled niches is the main explanation for establishing businesses abroad. These perceptions are associated with factors that are internal to the firm (ownership advantages), although external factors are still important. Amongst these factors growing deregulation in most Western economies has paved the way for increased cross border activity.

Among internal company advantages a shift has occurred to 'softer' human capital variables. To these belong broader global visions by leaders, strong beliefs in own brands and concepts, akin to what Nyström (1979) calls intended creativity and vision, juxtaposed with realised strategy. It is not only the market *per se* but the above mentioned factors and other leadership qualities of internationalising firms that are important. Only when underdeveloped markets are identified as suitable for the introduction of new organisational patterns, business concepts and products will the process of internationalisation begin. Conversely, lack of resources and a managerial culture not adapted to the requirements of the global scene can be an impediment to the international transfer of activities (Salmon and Tordjman 1989). Alexander (1990) found cultural variables particularly important for explaining an absence of international motivation and failures in business operations abroad.

Increasingly, success springs from competitive advantages linked to dynamic variables, for example the capability of creating new assets and upgrading existing organisational skills. Dicken (1998) emphasises the ability to manage technology transfer as a crucial process variable and an ability to generate brand loyalty as an important product variable. The latter capability is also strongly underlined by Dunning (1993a) who lists creation of a successful image and a consistent reputation along with product differentiation as the most important factors in a successful internationalisation process. Economies of scope are in this context as important as the earlier emphasised scale factors, particularly in commercial asset transfer. To these immaterial motives for investing abroad should be added the desire to have access to new management ideas obtained from information, knowledge and competence derived from subsidiaries and other networks in foreign countries; Kacker (1985) terms this skill learning in a host country.

Internalisation advantages – how firms internationalise

Entry modes into foreign markets have been the subject of much discussion in the recent past. This discussion developed from classical trade theory that emphasised market solutions with traditional exports being the optimal mode of delivery for the transfer of goods and services. Commercial activities and particularly the wholesale export trade have in the past always been considered as typically tradable and only occasionally organised in the importing country by the direct presence of the firm or through agents. In retail activities, on the other hand, the classical market solution is inadequate, as the retailing enterprise by its very nature has to be present in the host country. Service establishments generally have increasingly taken advantage of producing and distributing in specific foreign markets rather than either directly exporting or licensing production to indigenous enterprises. There are many reasons for this organisational mode. One is simple and self-evident: the firm has specific production advantages that it wants to exploit rather than passing these advantages on to another firm. Apart from this, as strongly emphasised by Dicken, the international scene consists of imperfect markets, and growing imperfection makes for increased internationalisation. First, there is a desire to reduce transaction costs, which in foreign markets are far higher than in the home market. Second, internal production may reduce uncertainty which is also higher in less well known markets and, third, we should not overlook the problem of control, an issue which is particularly acute in emerging markets, witnessed in recent years in parts of the former command economies. All these factors contribute to enhancing the internalisation of foreign commercial activities with the predominant form being direct ownership by the parent firm. These factors combined with competitive motives explain the escalation in mergers and acquisitions of foreign firms. Originally this was confined to manufacturing but increasingly service and commercial activities have been targeted.

An important consideration in the decision concerning the choice of entry mode into a foreign market is the reduction of risk. According to Welch (1992) the ability to cope with risk differs widely and may lie behind the choice of alternative organisational forms. The hierarchical internalised model now partly alternates with and has been partly succeeded by new lower risk models of cross-border transfer. Joint ventures, franchising, alliances and looser networking are some of the organisational forms available. These methods require less capital and in most cases generally reduce exposure to risk. Flexible forms of foreign operations are particularly important as an aid to acquiring and developing knowledge and competence. This is especially important in culturally remote markets.

Many authors highlight the role of alliances in retailing (Dawson and Shaw, 1992; Robinson and Clarke-Hill, 1995) as a mechanism for reinforcing a company's ability to compete in the home market. This benefit may easily be extended to the international market. Some scholars consider alliances as strategic variables that strongly impact upon decision making in the internationalisation process. Kobrin (1997) claims that strategic alliances are the new entry mode and that they replace earlier internationalisation forms to the extent of making traditional entry modes obsolete. This claim has two critiques. Dunning (1997a) briefly points to simplifications in Kobrin's argument. On the other hand building strategic alliances help to understand internationalisation as a learning process, a characteristic already put forward by Hollander in his classic study (1970). The claim has later been reiterated by several researchers, most explicitly by Edvardsson et al. (1993) who stress transborder transfer as a process of learning by doing and experimenting, both proactively and reactively, often bordering on trial and error. This contention is in line with modern theoretical approaches that emphasise 'a learning economy' and 'learning region' as a new paradigm for understanding industrial and distributional processes (Florida, 1995; Morgan, 1995).

Location-specific advantages – where internationalisation is likely

Earlier studies of international investment considered that specific foreign endowments and resources were external to the firm and not variables to be explained. One advantage of the eclectic paradigm is that it internalises into the analysis the ways in which foreign assets can be turned to the advantage of the firm or negative factors avoided. Only by including these factors is it possible to understand the final location of foreign activities. For untradeable services, of which both wholesaling and retailing are characteristic, these are paramount factors. Among the variables that can be utilised to the advantage of the service firm are market conditions (size and growth) and particularly unrealised growth in market segments. These conditions may differ between countries as well as regionally within countries, the latter differences frequently being greater than the former (Dunning 1993a).

In addition to different market variables there are different socio–cultural–political environmental idiosyncrasies, which may both enhance and restrict overseas expansion. According to Dunning (1997b) uniqueness and quality of location-bound assets and the way firms are able to coordinate them with their own core advantages will increasingly be part of the competitive advantage of countries and that this will ease the transfer of service activities. Amongst positive endowments are infrastructural investments including adequate premises, good social and cultural services and the availability of specialised legal, financial and consultancy services. Explicitly codified codes of conduct and cultural proximity will always make business transfer easier and often be decisive for the locational decision. Previous research places considerable weight on internationalisation as an incremental experiential process (Johansson and Vahlne, 1977). This often implies a stepwise geographical approach to locational decisions. Operating knowledge is trans-ferred incrementally to new locations, by carefully venturing into institution-ally, politically and culturally similar countries, mainly those that match familiar concepts, knowledge and control systems in the home environment. This type of reduced cultural distance is conducive to internationalisation, particularly in its initial stage (see Wiedersheim-Paul et al., 1975). Only later, during a consolidation stage, will the incremental ad hoc diffusion strategy be followed by more formalised planning based on systematic search (Millington and Bayliss, 1990). Another interesting hypothesis is that of multi-cultural learning through internationalisation, where concepts and service products can be transferred from one overseas location to another and represent an innova-tion, which gives locational advantages in the new market (Sundbo, 1992).

Locational variables can also work to the disadvantage of international investment and operate to constrain operations. These may be both socio-economic and political factors that are strongly contextual in nature. One of the important factors is unstable and uncertain institutional conditions (Aydin and Kacker, 1990) and restrictions on economic transactions, for example difficulties in repatriating dividends and even royalty payments. To this can be added bureaucratisation and outright fraud and corruption. Adverse environmental variables are often linked to cultural distance and may according to Anderson and Gatignon (1986) lead to conflicts in ethical outlook and in communicating with a foreign business network. The latter problem may create difficulties in understanding the particular business milieu as well as in appealing to local demand. All these adverse environmental conditions may, in turn, reinforce perceived risks in venturing abroad.

From Theory to Empirical Evidence: Some Propositions

The role of the wholesale/retail complex in international business transfer has generally been subject to less systematic research than conventional trade relations and export/import performance. The literature on the commercial sector is limited especially when compared to studies of the internationalisation and globalisation of manufacturing industry and increasingly compared to studies of advanced producer services.

A pioneering study was published in the 1970s (Hollander, 1970) but it has taken a long time for this work to be followed by systematic theoretical-empirical investigations. Most research into the internationalisation of commercial services has focussed on retailing. Retailing has generally been explored as a function that is independent of other economic activities. In contrast most of the research on wholesaling has explored this sector as a sub-sector that is dependent on the manufacturing industry.

Many factors that explain internationalisation are common to most economic activities. Internal (O) variables such as the quest for growth and return to scale with an associated requirement for venture capital are ubiquitous. Another common factor is the requirement for a strong position on the home market that predates the transfer of operations to a foreign country. A factor that is also pretty universal is the desire to achieve maximum control and reduce risks. Most types of activities likewise will have to adapt to environmental conditions in a fairly uniform manner. This said, commercial enterprises have idiosyncratic qualities, which determine why, how and where activities will be located. Although economies of scale may be important, particularly for competitive purposes, economies of scope and the ability to customise operations are becoming extremely important. In the same way the search for market niches rather than the expansion of existing markets seems to be significant and is a feature that distinguishes these activities from manufacturing companies (Alexander, 1990). The mode of entry appears to depend on the context. Control without direct ownership is an option that is becoming more and more widespread and may reduce the requirement for financial capital and contribute to spreading risks. In this respect commercial enterprises may be more flexible than most industrial and transport enterprises. Alliances and networks seem to be easy to establish in local areas, facilitating the introduction of standard concepts and operations, which can be reconciled with local consumer tastes and ways of life.

In terms of geography a careful incremental search precedes internationalisation, which, more often than not, means venturing into culturally familiar environments. Cultural proximity more than geographical distance continues to be the hallmark of the diffusion process. This, however, is being increasingly replaced by systematic search, based on opportunities rather than familiarity, as more information and experience are acquired.

In summary the following propositions can be formulated:

- Motivations for venturing abroad are conditioned by market opportunities more than by market saturation. Internationalisation is also dependent on particular qualities that are internal to the firm.
- The mode of entry into a foreign market may assume different forms dependent on the possibilities for exercising control.
- Initially, the geography of diffusion is rather limited, but there is a tendency for it to expand into markets where local competition can be overcome.

Success in the operation of commercial activities abroad is dependent on:

- A firm footing and developed edge competence in the home market.
- Access to venture capital.
- Flexibility and an ability to make adjustments to organisational forms.
- Familiarity with the host environment and cultural fabric.

Problems will particularly arise when:

- The market is risky and subject to uncertainty.
- The external socio-economic and political framework in the host country induces uncertainty and restricts operations.
- Cultural barriers are difficult to overcome.

PART II: EMPIRICAL EVIDENCE

Some General Characteristics of Scandinavian Internationalisation

The economies of the Nordic countries are characterised by a well-developed division of labour, specialisation and high productivity. Sweden has always been the largest economy, but on a per capita basis some convergence has taken place between countries particularly since the early 1990s. Apart from this general picture there are many structural dissimilarities. Sweden has been, and still is, the leader in finished manufacturing products with a strong engineering industry, notably in cars and machinery. Denmark, besides being an important exporter of agricultural products, is strong in R&D-based biotechnology and textiles. Finland and Norway are heavily dependent on natural resources, with the highest degree of refining in the former country, today supplemented by IT and telecommunications. Norway's industrial structure is largely based on fish, petroleum and electrochemical–electrometallurgical processing. All countries are strong in services. All the economies are extremely open with a high export/import rate. This is the context in which the development of direct overseas investment must be understood; until recently Sweden was the uncontested leader in this field but the emphasis was on manufacturing rather than service-related overseas investments.

Investments into wholesaling, which for a long time were an extension of manufacturing, were motivated by a desire to facilitate and increase sales by adjusting the distribution to cover unfamiliar market systems, organisational patterns and political institutions. Many Swedish companies began to trade in finished products, partly producer goods for the machine and car industries and partly consumer goods, of which cars and accessories make up the bulk of the sales. Statistically the value is difficult to establish as these activities are often interwoven with industrial statistics. Sweden also has the longest tradition of internationalisation in the retail sector. This was on a smaller scale and mainly consisted of textile, clothing and furniture outlets.

Compared to the size of the economies the total amount of Nordic countries FDI does not, at present, differ significantly from other West European countries. In 1997, a little more than 10 billion dollars were invested from Sweden and about 4 billion from each of the other countries, with Norway being the largest investor. Apart from Denmark, direct investment in the commercial sector is rather modest. Finland and Sweden even experienced years of negative growth or a withdrawal of investment. We should then be aware that a substantial part of commercial investment has been channelled through other industrial sectors. This also applies to Norway, whose FDI is more recent in origin and mainly has consisted of natural resource products with low value added. During the last 25 years wholesale commodities were mainly fish products supplemented by petroleum products. These two subsectors represent the bulk of wholesale business located abroad, most of it in western Europe but in the case of fish also the US and the Far East. One wholesaling establishment operates in 13 countries all over the world catering to different food cultures. Typically, large companies, particularly in the food sector make these investments. This means that there is a close corre-spondence between the structure of Norwegian exports and foreign commer-cial investment. Only in recent years has there been some diversification, as atypical and footloose wholesale businesses have internationalised on a rather modest scale. In retailing petroleum products have for a long time been marketed by Norwegian companies that have located abroad, partly through greenfield investments, partly effected through mergers with or takeovers of gasoline stations previously operated by international petroleum giants. Such direct foreign operations have, during the 1990s, been followed by grocery chains that have increasingly opened stores on a North and East-Central European basis. This strategy has followed in the wake of rapid concentration and integration in the home market. The value of wholesaling and the retail distribution of petroleum products can be hidden by the inclusion of these operations into non-commercial (manufacturing) statistics. This confusion does not exist in the case of commercial investments that in the late 1990s never surpassed 5 per cent of total investments.

A Note on Research Methodology

The objective of this study is to review the state-of-the-art of research into internationalisation and to uncover the driving forces of Scandinavian (largely Norwegian) direct commercial engagements abroad and to place this research in a comparative framework. With this objective in mind the required method-ology is obvious. The study must be based on direct information obtained from the companies involved in the process. Given the relatively few corporations that have ventured abroad, particularly in Norway, a broad quantitative analy-sis was not possible and the empirical material was acquired from micro in-depth qualitative interviews with ten firms. The firms are listed in the appendix. These firms operate in two sectors; wholesaling and retailing. These sectors where chosen for two reasons; first, increasingly retail and wholesale firms are merging both in terms of ownership and operations and, second, strategies to transcend borders and modes of entry are becoming increasingly similar.

Semi-structured face-to-face interviews were held with managers in charge of international investments and strategic operations. A questionnaire was formulated and used in the interviews, but ample room was given for a free exchange of opinions, particularly on strategic and control issues. This is not a representative sample of companies and as such it is impossible to formulate general statements. Company motivations and the assessment of positive and restrictive factors were assigned scores by respondents and average scores based on ranked importance have been calculated (1 being most important). The limited number of companies in this sample implies that the findings ought to be considered as indications of the process and should be interpreted with utmost care. The study is explorative in character and requires a follow-up investigation. With these reservations in mind this pioneering study should be of some interest and importance.

An Empirical Analysis of Scandinavian – Mainly Norwegian – Internationalisation

The O dimension: driving forces in the process

Internationalisation is the result of many factors. Partly it is explained by factors that are unique to particular business enterprises but it is also partly driven by more general factors. It is the latter we will try to uncover in the following section drawing upon the interview material. The general impression from the respondents is that 'hard' economic factors, or macro market motives, are still important in initiating a diffusion process. According to Table 7.2, general growth takes precedence over all other motives given by respondents as an explanation for developing an international presence. More than half of respondents ranked this variable as their most important motivation for developing internationally. Entrepreneurs also ranked expectations of a growing market highly as well as economies of scale. The acquisition of economies of scale can also improve a company's competitive position in the home market. Important variables are also the leadership of the firm, for example vision and a commitment to internationalisation and a firm belief in the business concept that is being transferred abroad.

Together with perceived advantages in the host country like niche demand and encouragement from foreign business all the motives mentioned above reflect a proactive attitude amongst leaders venturing into foreign markets and

Table 7.2 Motives behind the internationalisation of Norwegian companies (average scores by rank order of importance)

Quest for company growth	2.9
Expectations of a growing foreign market	3.4
Scale benefits from internationalisation	3.4
Belief in success of business concept	3.5
Advantages of niche demand	4.0
Encouragement from foreign firms	4.2
Saturation of home market	4.3
Consolidation	7.0
Competition on home market	Insignificant
Encouragement from foreign authorities	Insignificant

investing some of their financial, organisational and human capital there. Compared to these proactive motives defensive driving forces are given a low rating or were considered as insignificant. Both saturation of the home market, a widely held reason for internationalising commercial activities, and competition on the domestic scene obtain lower scores than all the preceding proactive motivations. This finding suggests that pull rather than push forces are the driving forces behind the present internationalisation process being experienced by Scandinavian companies.

Proactive attitudes held by international entrepreneurs are also revealed in responses given to questions concerning the organisation of the search process and the strategies developed to guide this process. Even though there are exceptions to systematic search and assessment of potential markets, the majority of companies had undertaken a search process and this proactive approach had increased over time. A good example is the case of a Swedish multinational textile and clothing distributor. This firm's early locational decisions were made on an ad hoc basis. Later and current search processes are undertaken systematically. Certainly, there are exceptions to companies drawing upon systematic research to guide their decisions. The company with the greatest experience of internationalisation would not have entered Russia if it had listened to its advisers. A further example of proactive motivation is found in the way companies take the initiative in developing internationally as well as in the way the follow-up process is organised. More often than not, the process originates from the company's top management and responsibility for further action is vested in the higher organisational and strategic level instead of being delegated to other departments, for example marketing.

Organisational and strategic issues: how firms internationalise

Most of the firms with direct international operations have developed foreign operations through subsidiaries. In some cases these have been greenfield investments, but in the majority of cases and particularly among the larger companies, mergers and acquisitions have been the dominant modes of entry into the host country. The dependence on this form of extreme internalisation implied by this entry mode is explained by two factors. First, companies copy the mode of operation used in their home market. Second, the majority of takeovers are of companies that were owner managed and related to this is the desire to establish and maintain direct control over their foreign business. Most of the firms are organised hierarchically. Control practices are moderately centralised, though, often on a differentiated basis. This means that daily operations are left to local, rather decentralised systems, and management and strategic decision making is highly centralised and based on close control constructed around auditing systems. By and large, recruitment of personnel takes place locally, but there seems to be continuous movement of key personnel between the home base and subsidiaries. This mixed model is partly explained by learning processes, but is mainly a reflection of a desire to combat uncertainty and maintain strict control.

Examples of other entry modes and of changes in organisational models over time were also identified. Even large firms have introduced franchising. This is an entry mode followed by the most widely internationalised retail chain as well as by the Norsk Hydro's gasoline station network in Denmark. It is important to note, however, that in these cases franchising implies a strong commitment to the parent organisation and tight control measures. The motivation for developing franchising is tied up with the realisation that franchisees have a greater commitment to developing their business than an only-owned subsidiary and at the same time net benefits accrue to the parent company. Royalty advantages through increased efficiency and advantages of competition can outweigh what is lost in direct income. The literature notes that franchising is a delivery mode that saves capital. This explanation was not, however, explicitly identified as a reason for developing a franchise network.

Some smaller companies have also experimented with franchising, joint ventures and licensing agreements. These techniques are mainly associated with careful, incremental entry into insecure markets, for example the emerging market economies of Central-Eastern Europe. These organisational forms have been more unstable in this part of the world. In some countries franchise and joint ventures have been closed, the latter partly because of a loss of trust in the partner company. In one particular case outright fraud forced the Norwegian firm to withdraw from the relationship.

Alliances and networks have, on the whole, played a minor role in the transfer of activities to foreign countries. Most corporations developed these forms to supplement firmly established foreign activity and mainly to satisfy specific purchasing or marketing requirements. For a couple of enterprises this has meant co-operation by developing common brands that are introduced for competitive purposes and which provide price benefits. On the whole, networking seems to have been most extensively developed by the true globalisers, particularly as solutions to cultural and institutional constraints.

Companies are beginning to realise that commercial operations need to be more closely adjusted to match local conditions without loosening or giving up the particular concept on which the activity is constructed. Market segmentation is becoming important as is the balance between local and central control; all these motives and strategies appear to have become reinforced over time. This means that increasingly greater weight is given to 'soft' as opposed to 'hard' investments. Corporations that have moved into the former planned undeveloped service economies of Eastern Europe particularly advocate this strategy.

Locational advantages: where firms internationalise
The locational decision made by the interviewed companies is one of cautious, incremental engagement with foreign markets. All but one company started their foreign operations in Scandinavia and the majority of firms were content to remain in this restricted market for a long period of time. For some of the firms this is still the only market, and is, in principle, considered as an enlargement of the home market. For most of the firms, however, investment into new sales points has transcended these regional boundaries. It is hard to find any systematic differences between types of enterprises and their diffusion pattern. It seems, though, that those who have a background in strongly developed core

Source: IKEA (1988).

Figure 7.1   Worldwide location of IKEA stores as of 1999

activities and with experience of internationalisation over a fairly long period of time have been the most enthusiastic to develop foreign markets. Nevertheless, only two companies in the sample can be described as true internationalisers, those that operate transcontinentally. The distribution of outlets of a furniture and outfit chain (IKEA) is shown in Figure 7.1. In this case location has not been as much determined by geographical proximity and cultural familiarity as by the centres of economic gravity and expanding markets. Common to the global companies is a particular, if not unique, concept of distribution, whether this is self-service and self-assembly of furniture or the supply of specially modified frozen food to match the requirements of culturally distinct market segments.

Only four of the enterprises have entered Western Europe apart from Scandinavia. More important investment locations are the former planned economies of Central and Eastern Europe. More than a half of the companies have established some activities in this region, some since the early 1990s, others only recently. Most of these are retail businesses, but wholesalers have also transferred commercial activities into these new markets, partly in conjunction with their own production. Norwegian firms have been involved in many countries, but have particularly concentrated on the Baltic States, Poland and the Czech Republic. None of the enterprises have, like the Danes, ventured extensively into East Germany; only one of the gasoline distributors has established a network in this country.

The background to these locational preferences is somewhat varied. The Nordic market was penetrated in the early stages of internationalisation mainly due to cultural and institutional similarities and because competition in these markets could be overcome more easily than in larger economies. Finally, there has been a long tradition of export and import trade with this region. Competitive motives also explain why Ireland was chosen as a host country for petroleum distribution through a major acquisition. The emphasis on Central-Eastern Europe must be seen in a rather wide context. There are no Norwegian export traditions to build on. Some companies have entered this market by free riding on the back of established alliance partnerships. Apart from these the concentration of foreign activity in Central-Eastern Europe must be considered as a proactive grasp of opportunities in undeveloped markets. These are expected to grow at unprecedented rates and early entry into these countries might result in the foreign operator developing a leading position in the market. Petroleum companies particularly stressed this point. Two of these are firmly established in many of these countries and are introducing new sales concepts apart from the sale of fuel.

Enabling and restrictive factors in the internationalisation process

Company managers rate macro-market factors highly when deciding to develop a foreign market (Table 7.3). Access to sufficient financial capital is the most important variable. This may seem to be a surprising finding as the international transfer of services has been identified in many studies as being particularly dependent on human capital. It should be noted, however, that the majority of enterprises in the sample require substantial physical installations to be constructed in the foreign country. These buildings are usually owner-operated and increasingly associated with takeovers and acquisitions. Norwegian investment abroad is difficult to quantify but the small numbers of companies in the sample have invested billions of NOK abroad. This is especially the case where commercial activities are combined with production. In this sense the sample as a whole may be unusual and the results should be assessed taking this into consideration.

Not surprisingly, firmly established capabilities on the home market are considered to be important when trying to enter and develop in a foreign marketplace. Conversely, the respondents considered that an under-exploited growing foreign market is an important factor in developing a firm and lasting international presence.

Human and organisational variables are also important for the successful transfer of commercial activities. This emphasis on human capital complements the importance of financial capital identified earlier (Table 7.3). The existence of an internationally minded leadership with international ambitions, and the development of stable and well-functioning networks in the host country, are particularly valuable assets for corporations intending to conduct operations from a foreign location. Experience in international relations and the size of the enterprise are less important factors. Surprisingly familiarity with the culture of the host environment obtained the lowest weighting. This may be explained by the fact that initially the Nordic countries were the main foreign markets targeted for expansion and many enterprises considered this to be an extension of the home market.

Table 7.3   Positive factors identified by Norwegian companies for locating activities abroad (average scores)

Access to sufficient financial capital	2.3
Edge competence in home market	3.3
Well-adjusted external network	3.5
Leadership with international ambitions	3.5
Untried, growing external market	3.6
Size of company	4.6
Leadership with international experience	5.0
Familiarity with culture in host country	5.7

Table 7.4   *Factors that constrain the internationalisation of Norwegian companies (average scores)*

General market uncertainty	2.9
High-risk markets	3.3
Insecure conditions in host country	3.5
Bureaucracy	5.8
Competition	5.9
Currency control	6.2
Lack of knowledge of local environment	6.2
Language problems	7.3
Control problems	7.8
Cultural problems generally	7.9

Ease of communication is undoubtedly a positive factor and is rated highly by respondents. Use of information technology has also become a prerequisite amongst the interviewed firms. More efficiency and easier control are amongst the most conspicuous benefits derived from IT systems. The degree of sophistication varies. Apart from some large commercial organisations the companies are not particularly proactive in switching to advanced systems. This is demonstrated by the low score given to the use of the internet and the fact that e-mail has only recently been adopted as a communication device. This finding supports that of Dawson (1994) who shows that European retail businesses are slow to accept IT developments.

When assessing constraints on internationalisation respondents emphasised macro market conditions (see Table 7.4). Market uncertainty and high-risk markets are, on average, ranked highest and at the same time unanimously by the respondents. Environmental variables, for example, can alter rapidly. Thus, bureaucracy as a constraint on the establishment process and the control of foreign exchange are rated fairly highly as constraining variables. Factors rooted in internationalising businesses themselves like lack of knowledge of foreign markets and environment and unfamiliarity with business culture and culture generally are recognised as factors that restrict the development of foreign business. Companies operating in emerging market economies identified similar negative factors; corruption and fraud are identified as common in these countries and may restrict business operations.

Discussion

Saturation of home markets and the subsequent spatial diffusion of organisational forms and location have been emphasised, both theoretically and empirically, as characteristics of commercial internationalisation (Johansson and

Vahlne, 1977; Laujalainen, 1991). Certainly, Laujalainen (1991) had to moderate the saturation hypothesis, but still identifies a sequential location pattern as an internationalisation characteristic. In the present study the saturation claim is also given little support. Simultaneously, neither a development towards increasingly committed organisational models nor a gradual extension of locations can be verified although the majority of firms started their international activities in other Scandinavian countries and only incrementally spread outwards from this location.

The analyses of international transfers of commercial activities have identified market conditions as especially important. Both pull and push forces have been identified as important in this context. Arbos (1985) and Alexander (1990) found that restrictions on the home market (market saturation – push forces and expectations of opportunities in foreign markets – pull forces) often work in tandem. To some extent this was also found in the sample companies. However, the general impression is that pull motives reign supreme and that push motives have low ratings. The main reason for expanding abroad, besides a general quest for growth, is the possibility of developing unexploited market niches, particularly in countries and regions judged to have clear demand potential. This, in turn, is dependent on the ability of the business leaders to conduct operations with new and consistent concepts. This finding clearly matches that of Alexander (1990) in his analysis of UK retailers that have developed international operations. It also substantiates the finding by Williams (1992) who interviewed a similar sample of British enterprises. Conversely, incentive factors provided by the host country (special benefits) to encourage FDI were found to be of negligible importance, a finding which is supported by Alexander's study.

In Kacker's analysis (1985) a feedback loop of skills obtained from the learning process that results from working in the host country was emphasised as an important motive of internationalisation. The present study to some extent corroborates this claim. This was the primary motivation given by the Norwegian wholesale company with the most widespread international operations.

None of the comparable studies explored in this chapter highlight the importance of developed capability in the home market as an important factor in the internationalisation process. The results of the present inquiry clearly highlight the importance of this factor and consequently substantiate the proposition developed in the literature review concerning the home market as one of the most important explanatory variables for the successful transfer of commercial activities to foreign markets.

Respondents also identified access to venture capital as a crucial factor. It was rated particularly highly by larger firms in activities that involve natural resources and is a reflection of a commercial structure that may be specific to

Norway. Having said this, however, we should add that softer investments are shown to be also clearly conducive to success. This supports the work of Salmon and Tordjman (1989) who consider that really successful internation-alists are those who simultaneously maintain identity and control as well as trying to make adjustments to unfamiliar environments with particular prefer-ences and tastes, regulations and constraints. The former contention is strongly supported by the case study material explored in this chapter. The latter claims are not so obviously verified by the material. Neither is the proposition concerning the successful development of an international market being dependent on the flexibility of organisational forms. This contention was not supported by the case studies. This is also the case concerning the direct response to the claims of familiarity with the host environment and the cultural fabric as necessary prerequisites for success and the contention that cultural barriers are particularly restrictive. Care must be taken over the statement that institutional and cultural factors are important constraints. Several of the firms provided indirect indications of the importance of these factors. Both the increasingly widespread recruitment of managerial staff from the host country, the sharing of control functions and the conscious development of networking with external business groups are evidence of an unprecedented emphasis on 'softer' management practices and, eventually, on more country-specific cultural factors.

CONCLUDING REMARKS

In his analysis of international retail transfer Treadgold (1988) distinguished between four types of actors: cautious internationalists, emboldened interna-tionalists, aggressive internationalists and world power. Few, if any, of the firms analysed in this chapter, belong to the last mentioned category, the proponents of which are characterised by strong team leadership. World power companies are ardent networkers that combine centralised control with adap-tation to the local cultural environment. In the present investigation 'hard' economic considerations and macro market variables were identified by respondents as being very important factors. This was reflected in the consis-tent emphasis placed on growth as a driving force and the need for financial capital as the most conspicuous requirement for the internationalisation process. This must be seen in the context of the particular structure of Norwegian internationalisation; the majority of firms being strongly rooted in natural resource based commercial sectors. The particular structure of the Norwegian economy may reduce the generality of this study.

During the interviews managers stressed the importance of developing organisational skills and of giving more weight to human capital as being of prime importance when developing foreign operations. Emphasis was also placed on networking. Easier access to what are frequently intangible country specific assets also seems to be a growing requirement for the successful transfer of activities and of organisational forms. However, more research is needed in order to rank motivations for internationalisation and to develop greater understanding of the process. This research should, above all, be comparative. Only then will it be possible to make inferences.

REFERENCES

Alexander, N. (1990). 'Retailers and international markets: motives for expansion', *International Marketing Review*, **7** (4), 75–85.

Anderson, E. and Gatignon, H. (1986), 'Modes of foreign entry: a transaction cost analysis and propositions', *Journal of International Business Studies*, 17:3, 1–27.

Arbos, J. (1985), 'The folksy theories that inspire life-style merchant IKEA', *International Management*, **40** (11).

Aydin, N. and Kacker, M. (1990), 'International Outlook of US-Based Franchisers', *International Marketing Review*, **7** (2), 43–53.

Burt, S. (1986), 'The Carrefour Group – the first 25 years', *International Journal of Retailing*, **1** (3), 54–78.

Coase, Ronald H. (1937), 'The nature of the firm', *Economica*, **4**, 386–405.

Dawson, J.A. (1993), 'The Internationalization of Retailing', in Rosemary F. Bromley and Colin J. Thomas (eds), *Retail Change: Contemporary Issues*, London: Taylor and Frances.

Dawson, J.A. (1994), 'Application of information management in European retailing', *The International Review of Retail, Distribution and Consumer Research*, **4** (2), 219–38.

Dawson, J.A. and Shaw, S.A. (1992), 'Strategic and tactical issues in the development of retail alliances', *EMAC Proceeding Aarhus*, 1275–8.

Dicken, P. (1998), *Global Shift*, London: Paul Chapman, Third Edition.

Dunning, John H. (1993a), *The Globalisation of Business*, London and New York: Routledge.

Dunning, John H. (1993b), *The Theory of Transnational Corporations*, London and New York: Routledge.

Dunning, John H. (1997a), 'Introduction', in John H. Dunning (ed.), *Governments, Globalization and International Business,* New York: Oxford University Press, pp. 1–28.

Dunning, John H. (1997b), 'A Business Analytic Approach', in John H. Dunning (ed.), *Governments, Globalization and International Business*, New York: Oxford University Press, pp. 114–29.

Dunning, John H. (1977), 'Trade, Location of Economic Activity and the MNE: a search for an eclectic approach', in Bertil Ohlin et al. (eds), *The International Allocation of Economic Activity,* London: Holmes and Meier, pp. 395–418.

Dunning, John H. and McQueen, M. (1982), 'The Eclectic Theory of Multinational Enterprise and the International Hotel Industry', in Alan M. Rugman (ed.), *New Theories of the Multinational Enterprise,* New York: St. Martin's Press, pp. 79–106.

Dunning, J.H. and Norman, G. (1983), 'The theory of the multinational enterprise: an application to multinational office location', *Environment and Planning*, **15**, 675–92.

Edvardsson, B., Edvinsson, L. and Nyström, H. (1993), 'Internationalisation in service companies', *The Service Industries Journal*, **13** (1), 80–97.

Florida, R. (1995), 'Toward the learning region', *Futures*, **27**, 527–36.

Gadrey, Jean (1990), 'L'Internationalisation des services personnels et collectifs et le développement en Europe de l'oust et de l'est', *Seminaire sur les services personnels et collectifs*, UN Commission for Europe.

Hollander, Stanley C. (1970), *Multinational Retailing*, MI: Michigan State University.

Hymer, Stephen H. (1960), *The International Operations of National Firms: a Study of Direct Investment*, Cambridge MA: MIT.

IKEA (1998), *Facts and Figures*, Humlebaek, PR & Communications, IKEA International A/S.

Incandela, D., McLaughlin, K.L. and C. Smith Shi (1999), 'Retailers to the world', *McKinsey Quarterly*, (3), 84–97.

Johansson, J. and Vahlne, J. (1977), 'The internationalization process of the firm: a model of knowledge-development and increasing foreign commitments', *Journal of International Business Studies*, **8**, Spring, 23–32.

Kacker, Madhav (1985), *Transatlantic Trends in Retailing: Takeovers and Know-How*, London: Quorum.

Kobrin, Stephen J. (1997), 'The Architecture of Globalization: State Sovereignty in a Networked Global Economy', in John H. Dunning (ed.), *Governments, Globalisation and International Business*, Oxford: Oxford University Press.

Kogut, B. (1985), 'Designing global strategies: corporate and competitive value added chain', *Sloan Management Review*, **26**, 15–28.

Lall, S. (1980), 'Monopolistic advantages and foreign involvement by US manufacturing industry', *Oxford Economic Papers*, **32**, 102–22.

Laujalainen, R. (1991), 'International expansion of an apparel retailer. Hennes & Mauritz of Sweden', *Zeitschrift für Wirtschaftsgeographie*, **35** (1), 1–15.

Millington, A.I. and Bayliss, L.B. (1990), 'The process of internationalisation: UK companies in the EC', *Management International Review*, **30**.

Morgan, K. (1995), *The Learning Region; Institutions, Innovation and Regional Renewal*, Cardiff: Dept. of City and Regional Planning, University of Wales.

Nilsson, Jan-Evert (1996), 'Introduction: The Internationalization Process', in Jan-Evert Nilsson, Peter Dicken and Jamie Peck (eds), *The Internationalization Process: European Firms in Global Competition*, London: Paul Chapman Publishing Ltd, pp. 1–12.

Nyström, Harry (1979), *Creativity and Innovation*, Chichester: John Wiley & Sons.

Porter, Michael E. (1990), *The Competitive Advantage of Nations*, New York: The Free Press.

Robinson, T. and Clarke-Hill, C.M. (1995), 'International alliances in European retailing', *The International Review of Retail Distribution and Consumer Research*, **5** (2), 167–84.

Salmon, W.J. and Tordjman, A. (1989), 'The internationalisation of retailing', *International Journal of Retailing*, **42** (2), 3–16.

Segebarth, K. (1990), 'Some aspects of the international trade in services: An empirical approach', *Service Industries Journal*, **10** (2).

Sundbo, Jon (1992), 'Drivkræfter bag servicevirksomheders internationalisering' (Driving forces behind the internationalisation of service activities), in Sven Illeris and Peter Sjøholt (eds), *Internationalisering af Service og Regional Udvikling i Norden*, Copenhagen: NordREFO 1992:5.

Swedenborg, Birgitta (1979), *The Multinational Operations of Swedish Firms: An Analysis of Determinants and Effects,* Stockholm: Industriens Utredningsinstitut.
Treadgold, Alan D. (1988), 'Retailing without frontiers', *Retail and Distribution Management,* **16** (6), 8–12.
Treadgold, Alan D. and Davies, Ross L. (1988), *The Internationalisation of Retailing,* Harlow: Longman.
Welch, L.S. (1992), 'Internationalisation by Australian franchisors', *Asian Pacific Journal of Management,* **7** (2), 101–21.
Williams, D.E. (1992), 'Retailer internationalization. An empirical inquiry', *European Journal of Marketing,* **26** (8/9), 8–24.
Wiedersheim-Paul, Finn, Welch, Lawrence S. and Olsson, H.C. (1975), 'Before the Export Order: A Behavioural Model', University of Queensland Dept. of Economics Working Paper No. 10.
WTO (1999), *WTO Annual Report,* Geneva: WTO.

APPENDIX: COMPANIES IN THE SAMPLE

Frionor A/S/ Norway Seafoods ASA. Seafood wholesaling. Oslo

Hennes & Mauritz. Norge. Textile and cosmetics chain. Oslo

IKEA International A/S. Furniture and home furnishings, Humlebæk, Denmark

NKL (The Norwegian Consumer Co-operative Association) Consumer goods. Oslo

Norsk Hydro. Petroleum marketing division. Oslo

Rieber & Søn ASA. Food production and wholesaling. Bergen

Statoil Marketing International. Marketing of Oil Products. Copenhagen

The Hakon Group. Retail and Wholesale Groceries. Oslo

The Reitan Group. REMA Norge 1000. Retail Grocery. International Division. Oslo

Tybring-Gjedde. Non-food consumer goods wholesalers. Oslo

8. 'Trading' business knowledge between countries: consultants and the diffusion of management knowledge

John R. Bryson

The management knowledge . . . of the US . . . like Coca Cola and Levi jeans . . . is exported worldwide. (Jacques, 1996: 6)

Service trade involves more than just the trade of a product or a service, but in the case of business services or those services provided to other companies, it involves the transfer or diffusion of information and knowledge. Trade in business knowledge(s) is becoming more important to the extent that American management consultancy companies are beginning to patent management systems and business ideas. Management ideas are big business; the world market for management consultancy is worth approximately $50 billion and 50 per cent of the consultancy industry is based in the United States (O'Shea and Madigan, 1997: 17). As business becomes more international the importance of the management consultancy industry has increased. The development of multinational companies and international competition has gone hand in hand with an escalation in demand for external advice. A good example of this flow of knowledge can be found in China. The Chinese government used to undertake industrial espionage to acquire access to the latest management ideas and technology. Such espionage still goes on, but it is now supplemented by a flow of information and knowledge provided by management consultants. Most of the big American consultancy companies (Andersen Consulting, McKinsey, Boston Consultancy Group, A.T. Kearney and Bain) have established offices in China and Chinese companies employ consultants to obtain information and knowledge that consultants acquire whilst working with other clients.

Transformations in business practices, major alterations in company organisation, in fact the laying down of new economic geographies can all be attributed to the activities of management consultants and their role in the global diffusion of business knowledges. Changes in business organisation and the geography of production can be conceptualised as being the product of three related processes. First, economic change requires exposure to flows of knowledge either in the form of the direct or indirect movement of ideas between companies and places. Second, central to this process are the activities of key individuals, managers and consultants as well as a series of texts, for example newspapers, the business press and manuals of best practice produced by professional associations. The growing importance of strategic alliances between companies has increased the diffusion of knowledge and information between partners, but a more important pressure behind the diffusion of management ideas is the ongoing globalisation of the key business professions of accountancy and the related industry of management consultancy. It is important to remember that management consultancy cannot be classified as a profession as barriers to practice have yet to be rigorously enforced. Third, some of the most recent attempts to explain the spatial reorganisation of production note that there has been a blurring of the organisational boundary of the business enterprise (Bryson, 1997).

Thus, the trend towards outsourcing and externalisation has created a situation in which the knowledge or information required to manage an enterprise is controlled and owned by other companies. This is not a new trend. There has always been a division of managerial knowledges and this has, in many instances, been a spatial division of managerial knowledges. To understand the restructuring of economic activity involves identifying the sources and locations of the ideas that are driving alterations in the geography of production and the internal organisation of business enterprises. The latter may not appear to be the concern of the economic geographer, but there are important differences in the way in which ideas are localised into the cultural environment of a country (see Guillen, 1994 and Jacques, 1996 on this point) or business enterprise (Schoenberger, 1994, 1997). Thus, an analysis of the production of management knowledge and its diffusion by management consultants must be situated in an understanding of the ways in which knowledge is consumed by business organisations and institutions.

This chapter explores the spread of two influential management ideas – the work of Frederick Winslow Taylor (1856–1915), the father of Scientific Management, and one of the minds to influence the development of Fordism, and the work of W.E. Deming on quality management or continuous improvement. Taylor's name is well known within economic geography, but usually only as a signpost to indicate that the nature of capitalist activity was altering and that something known as 'Taylorism' (Knox and Agnew, 1994: 184; Dicken, 1992: 116) had occurred. There have been numerous individuals like Taylor who have had a significant impact on the geography of economic activities, but like Taylor they are unknown to economic geographers. F.W. Taylor's role as management consultant and guru is explored in the understanding that such an historical project will provide an important insight into the spread and adoption of management ideas in the twenty-first century. Key questions which urgently need to be addressed are, for example, what was the role of knowledge and information during earlier periods of capitalism?, how have some of the key business services evolved to meet the changing needs of their clients? and finally why do some management models become adopted internationally?

CONSULTANTS AND THE SOCIOLOGY OF KNOWLEDGE

Management consultancy is a knowledge industry that is founded upon the transfer of management models, theories and procedures that are created in universities, large consultancy companies or within client organisations. This type of knowledge flow is complex and dynamic but it is usually the result of active and passive relationships between a series of social actors. Such knowledge flows can be identified and understood using Actor-Network Theory (ANT) or a sociology of translation (Latour, 1987). The most important paper to explore management consultants using a sociology of translation is that written by Bloomfield and Best (1992) informed by Callon's seminal paper on the fisherman of St Brieuc Bay (1986). They argue that management theories and solutions provided by management consultants can be 'viewed as a process of "translation" or "problematisation" in which solutions are not simply matched to problems; rather, problems are redefined (translated) in terms of existing "solutions", (Bloomfield and Best, 1992: 535–6).

'Translation' is a process, strategy or method by which actors (individuals, organisations) attempt to enrol others into a network. It is via this process that 'the identity of actors, the possibility of interaction and the margins of manoeuvre are negotiated and delimited' (Callon, 1986: 203). Problematisation is a specific form of translation in which actors construct and reconstruct the boundaries of a problem. Drawing upon Callon (1986), Bloomfield and Best argue that consultancy involves two aspects of Callon's problematisation. First, 'one actor can make itself indispensable to another by translating a problem of the latter in terms of a solution owned or within the orbit of the former' (Bloomfield and Best, 1992: 541). Thus, a consultant can persuade a client that a problem with productivity and profitability can only be addressed by using a particular consultancy specific or even copyrighted solution. The secret of good consultancy is to redefine a problem so that it matches a readily available solution.

Second, problematisation involves an active process of identity construction and repositioning by different actors. In the case of management consultancy and management theorists this involves the establishment of a consultant as 'an obligatory passage point' (Bloomfield and Best, 1994: 541). Consultants define themselves as experts possessing specialist knowledge while the client role is constructed as one of dependency. Problematisation occurs both before and during any consultancy assignment and is central to some of the most important aspects of knowledge work: work as role-play, performance and display. In the case of knowledge work the display involves an individual or company convincing others that they alone can supply or have access to a particular form of information or knowledge.

Both processes of translation and problematisation suggest that flows of knowledge supplied by consultants will make client companies increasingly operate in the same way. DiMaggio and Powell (1983) develop the concept of *isomorphism* to explain this type of organisational homogeneity. Isomorphism is 'a constraining process that forces one unit in a population to resemble other units that face the same set of environmental conditions' (1983: 149). DiMaggio and Powell identify three isomorphic processes that force organisations to become similar: coercive isomorphism; mimetic isomorphism and normative isomorphism. First, *coercive isomorphism* results from relationships in an industrial sector between the 'totality of actors' (suppliers, producers, consumers, regulators) and their relational networks. The organisational field produces coercive isomorphism by tacitly or explicitly imposing on individual companies a set of organisational practices and regulatory structures. Secondly, *mimetic isomorphism* results from uncertainty that encourages organisations to model themselves on others. Copying is an inexpensive strategy in comparison to the development of novel solutions. Models are either traded formally or informally via untraded interdependencies (Bryson, 1997) and they are obtained via employee transfers, management consultancy firms, trade associations or in published form in both the business press and in management textbooks (Guillen, 1994). Thirdly, *normative isomorphism* results from increasing professionalism. Professional associations impose upon their members a limited range of expertise and knowledge that define the nature of their work. DiMaggio and Powell (1983) highlight the role of universities and professional training organisations in the production of professional expertise. This education produces individuals with interchangeable expertise and knowledge. Hanlon (1994) highlights the relationship between the university background of graduates entering accountancy training with their social background. The majority of accountants have no need for a university education, but university graduates 'will be more middle class, professional in outlook and appearance, and therefore less difficult' (Hanlon, 1994: 115). This type of filtering encourages the development of normative isomorphism as individuals will acquire the same models of behaviour and thought. Related to this process is the development of professional networks that operate independently of employee organisations. In this case, expertise and knowledge becomes divorced from client organisations and becomes owned by the profession. This exchange of ideas and models of management results in the increasing similarity of capitalist organisations. This type of isomorphism is increasingly derived from the globalisation and the shared nature of forms of management knowledge spread through the agency of business service professionals.

There are some problems with the concept of isomorphism. Companies may acquire the same management knowledge, but implement or understand it in different ways. The consumption of management knowledge rests upon perceptions held by potential consumers of the knowledge (management theory, recipe or fad) and of the knowledge producer and supplier. Perceived expertise and a visible reputation may be more important than actual expertise. The dialectical relationship between knowledge and reputation is a fundamental part of the flow of knowledge into and between companies. It is also fundamental to understanding the consumption of knowledge in general. Knowledge consumption is a social and political process that draws heavily upon the projected, and maybe not actual, life histories of the knowledge producers or distributors. Knowledge is usually contained in language and words, but the same word develops a different meaning with use. Managers in different companies acquire the same fashionable terminologies and buzzwords, but apply them to explore different issues and problems. Over time the buzzwords become discredited with too many conflicting meanings and new terms need to be developed. These cycles of language construction can 'become too short [so that] managers experience a dizzying whirlwind of words which blows through the company at gale force, almost unconnected to action' (Nohria and Eccles, 1998: 291). Old words cannot be recovered as they are associated with old management knowledges and fashions, and more importantly the employment of consultants and the movement of managers between companies shifts word meanings around 'reframing the way people see things, and these new words may open new spaces of action' (Nohria and Eccles, 1998: 291). Consuming fashionable business knowledge, however, can lead to employee disillusionment as new words are created that describe old or well-known concepts. A similar type of disillusionment with new business knowledge is associated with rapid diffusion. The competitive advantage associated with a new management idea is undermined as soon as it becomes commonplace.

THE RISE OF SCIENTIFIC MANAGEMENT

The recent history of economic geography has been associated with attempts to explore the crisis of Fordism and the development of Post-Fordism (Amin, 1994). This literature ignores the role played by key individuals and networks of individuals in creating organisational and management models which ultimately impact on the spatial organisation of production. Alterations in the economic system are the result of a whole series of unrelated and related changes made by independent private and public sector organisations. Central to these alterations are the activities of management gurus and management consultants. The other actors in the process are the media and trade and professional associations that simplify, popularise and spread management ideas. It is these organisations which can create a climate of change not as a result of necessity but as the consequence of media created fashions. Fordism in the geographical literature is closely associated with the work of F.W. Taylor, an American consulting engineer who was both a management guru and management consultant. It is these aspects of Taylor's career that are neglected in the geographical literature. To understand the history of Fordism requires an understanding of the ways in which Taylor's ideas were created and spread amongst business organisations, both in the US and Europe. Three issues need to be examined: Taylor's theory of scientific management, Taylor as management guru and consultant and the spatial diffusion and translation of Taylor's management theory.

Taylor's contribution to management theory was both a set of techniques and an ideology. It is the techniques that have been explored in geography (Cooke and Morgan, 1998: 47–53). The ideology of Taylorism concerns a search for efficiency; for the best way of undertaking a task. It was this ideology which spread throughout the US, encouraging manufacturers to experiment with alternative working practices. Taylor provided American capitalism with a theory of management which was absent from Europe until the 1920s and from some countries until the 1940s. As a management guru it is this ideology which is most important as it provided opportunities for a whole series of management consultants to adopt some of Taylor's ideas. These consultants modified Taylor's ideas to make them more acceptable to client companies. It is, thus, correct to identify Taylor's ideological impact on American capitalism, but incorrect to identify a single set of techniques; there was not just one type of Taylorism, but a whole series of different types which were created by Taylor's 'band of disciples' or Taylorites.

Taylor's contribution to management theory rests on the combination of four related principles (Braverman, 1974: 85–123; Guillen, 1994). First, time and motion studies demystified skills by standardising work tools, practices and by dividing production processes into their simplest constituent tasks. Second, each task should be undertaken by employees best suited to the task: by the cheapest worker. Third, foremen (sic) and an incentive system based on differential rates ensure that the 'scientifically determined' task is matched to the right employee. Finally, the execution of work is separated from its conception. Tacit knowledge is identified and codified and transferred from the shop floor to a planning department. Taylor was one of a group developing revised ways of managing shop floor activity, and Taylor acknowledged ideas which he had taken from other peoples' work (Urwick and Brech, 1945: 33).

To understand the development of Taylor's ideas it is necessary to situate them in his life history. Having worked for a number of companies he established himself as a consulting engineer in 1893. In 1898 Taylor gave up consultancy and took up full time employment with the Bethlehem Steel Company. Taylor's work at Bethlehem was to introduce his management principles into the yard and machine shop (Urwick and Brech, 1945). Like his other attempts to apply his theories this failed (Bryson, 2000) and in 1901 Taylor was sacked. At Bethlehem, however, Taylor was able to develop one of his other interests – technological innovation. In 1898 he discovered a method for heat treating tool steel so that machine tools were able to run at unprecedented speeds without any apparent loss of cutting edge. In 1901, at the age of 45, Taylor retired from consultancy to spend the rest of his life promulgating his principals of scientific management.

The development of Taylor's reputation as a management theorist is closely associated with his development of high-speed tool steel. The reception by European engineers of Taylor's first three papers highlights the importance of his high speed steel work. In 1895 Taylor read his first paper to the American Society of Mechanical Engineers (ASME) (Urwick and Brech, 1953: 88–107). This paper on the piece-rate system was only documented by one of the three leading British engineering periodicals. His second paper on *Shop Management* (1903) in which Taylor developed the basis of scientific management was ignored by the European technical press. The development of high-speed steel enhanced Taylor's reputation amongst engineers and finally led to his election in 1905 as President of the ASME. His presidential address entitled *On the Art of Cutting Metals* was published in 1907 and it is this work which established Taylor's reputation in Europe. This paper drew attention to Taylor's earlier work on *Shop Management* which was only now translated into European languages. Taylor's work as an engineer and his development of high-speed steel cannot be separated from the development of his career as a management consultant and guru. His reputation as an innovative engineer gave his management ideas credibility in the eyes of fellow members of the ASME. Nevertheless, in 1910 the ASME decided that a paper submitted by Taylor should be rejected as engineers would not be interested in its content and that it contained nothing new (Haber, 1964: 18). This paper was published in 1911 under the title *The Principles of Scientific Management*. It is this work which played an important role in the development of Fordist production systems.

THE DIFFUSION OF TAYLOR'S SCIENTIFIC MANAGEMENT

As a management consultant Taylor was notoriously ineffective. None of the companies he worked for or with successfully introduced scientific management. According to Nadworny (1955), by 1915, when Taylor died, the scientific managers and their associates had introduced their techniques into 140 establishments. In this analysis only 63 000 employees were identified as working with Taylor's methods. Similarly Nelson (1974: 490) attempted to assess the importance of Taylor's ideas and was only able to identify 48 establishments that had introduced his ideas between 1901 and 1917. Littler (1982) suggests that these studies should not be used to show that Taylorism had a limited influence in the US, but rather that Taylor and his close associates (Taylorites) were only interested in introducing 'pure Taylorism' to manufacturing plants. Even in 1923, the Taylorites were concerned with their failure to widely introduce full Taylorism, and that one reason for this failure was 'the pressure of unfair competition from illegitimate relatives [consultants]' (Nadworny, 1955: 142). In many respects full Taylorism was unpopular as it contained an implicit depiction of the human being as machine (Schon, 1983: 237) and it also had a history of conflict between managers and employees.

To understand the diffusion of Taylor's ideas involves recognition of three points. First, Taylor became the visible figurehead of a widely dispersed movement that was concerned with increasing the efficiency of production in manufacturing plants. Second, most applications of his ideas were achieved through consultancy projects undertaken by Taylor's close circle of disciples and friends. Finally, the wider diffusion of some of Taylor's ideas and their translation into 'user-friendly' management recipes was undertaken by a group of neo-Taylorists that were not concerned with promulgating pure Taylorism.

During the time he spent working on the shopfloor Taylor developed a group of close followers many of whom became consultants using Taylor's theory of scientific management. There are two important individuals, Henry Lawrence Gantt (1861–1919) and Frank Bunker Gilbreth (1868–1924). Some commentators even describe Taylor, Gantt and Gilbreth as the 'trinity' of scientific management (Urwick and Brech, 1953: 103). Gantt refined and developed aspects of Taylor's ideas especially in relation to the Gantt chart, a chart designed to permit the pre-planning of production on a daily basis. Frank and Lillian Gilbreth improved the methodology of time-and-motion study by introducing the chroncyclograph, or motion picture camera designed to identify the actions required to undertake any task. The 'disciples' kept in touch with Taylor and discussed cases with him. Gantt and Gilbreth developed scientific management to such an extent that they both argued with Taylor who considered that they moved away from full scientific management to only concentrate on one of the four principles.

In 1911, Taylor's disciples also organised themselves informally into an exclusive club called the Taylor Society. The purpose of this society was to ensure that Taylor's work remained highly visible amongst American managers as well as to coordinate Taylor's followers. Organised labour disliked The Taylor Society as the Society agreed with Taylor that scientific management determined wages, hours and working conditions rather than trade union negotiations. The history of Taylorism is until the late 1930s a history of management in the US and Germany, and of the activities of a group of Taylor disciples and neo-Taylorites. Taylor's ideas were ignored and neglected by British managers for a variety of reasons: the scarcity of engineers; the conservatism of management and the opposition of trade unions. Scientific management was adopted by German manufacturers like Bosch, AEG, Siemens, Krupp and Lowe shortly before or during World War 1 (Guillen, 1994: 119). German companies employed American consultants to transfer Taylor's ideas to Germany.

Taylor's ideas were not well received in Britain. Taylor made a single visit to Europe after developing scientific management. In July 1910 Taylor, Gilbreth and Gantt were amongst the delegates attending a Joint Meeting of the Institute of Mechanical Engineers and the ASME held in the Midland Institute, Birmingham. The subject of the meeting was High- Speed Tools and everyone expected Taylor to speak on this subject. However, when Taylor rose to address the meeting it was on the subject of scientific management and his belief that 'it is possible to double the output of the men and the machines just as they stand now, and I believe the same is true throughout this country' (Taylor, quoted in Urwick and Brech, 1953: 94). In reply to Taylor's six-and-a-half page address the chair of the meeting noted that Taylor's paper 'did not deal with that subject [high speed tools] and he would very much have valued any remarks Dr Taylor might have made on tools and machines' (Urwick and Brech, 1953: 96). From this it appears that Taylor had failed to redefine (problematise) the role of engineers in Britain from a concern with machines to a concern with management issues.

Up to 1910 Scientific Management was an approach to shop floor management that was known to a small circle of American engineers. During the years when Taylor was developing and applying his system directly onto the shop floor he was uninterested in publicity. Like all consultants Taylor, the Taylorites and neo-Taylorites obtained clients by word of mouth and especially by the movement of managers between companies. Two events occurred which led to Scientific Management's problematisation into the only solution to the problems of low productivity, low wages and unemployment. Both events involved the acceptance or translation by the business media of

Scientific Management into the perceived solution for the problems of American industry.

The first event was the Eastern Rate Case (1910–11), a famous court case between the railways and business associations from all over the East Coast. In 1910, the railways raised employees' wages, but immediately asked the Interstate Commerce Commission to endorse an increase in freight charges. Business groups combined together to prevent such an increase and asked Louis D. Brandeis, a popular 'people lawyer' to represent them (Kakar, 1970: 174). Brandeis argued that the railways had not proved their case for an increase in rates and that even if they had proved their case the solution did not lie in increasing the rate, but in introducing scientific management. In court he argued that: 'We will show you . . . that these principles [scientific management] are applicable to practically all departments of all businesses, and that the estimate which has been made that in the railroad operation of this country an economy of one million dollars a day is possible is by no means extravagant' (Kakar, 1970: 176). The 'million dollar a day savings' captured the imagination of the media and Taylor was hunted by the press. Hundreds of newspaper and magazine articles were published and America entered a craze for business efficiency. To Haber the efficiency craze 'hit like a flash flood, at first covering the entire landscape' (1964: 52). Taylor had been provided with a media platform to expound his views, but the media's attempt to problematise Taylor as the management guru did not go unchallenged as engineers resented 'Taylor's virtual monopoly of the subject of management' (Kakar, 1970: 177).

The second event was the decision in 1909 by the Ordnance Department of the United States Army to adopt the Taylor system for use in the manufacturing arsenals at Watertown (Aitken, 1960). The Chief of Ordnance, General William Crozier, was requested by a congressional committee to compare the costs at Watertown with prices paid to private sector firms. This 'benchmarking' led Crozier to Bethleham Steel Works and the Midvale Steel Company. Both companies undercut Watertown and still make a profit and both had employed F.W. Taylor. The decision to employ Taylor at Watertown considerably raised the profile of scientific management. However, the Watertown experience ended badly with a major strike and the decision by the House of Representatives to outlaw time and motion study in the arsenals. This was a direct consequence of trade union lobbying and organised labour's success in removing Taylorism from the arsenal undermined the credibility of Taylor's system.

The key problem with Taylorism is that it rapidly became associated with a series of negative connotations. Employees were concerned with its explicit anti-trade union stance, and employers were reluctant to introduce Taylor's four principles as this involved a complete management overhaul.

Consultancy companies drew upon Taylor's ideas, but developed related systems (neo-Taylorite) that enabled them to uncouple 'scientific management' from the negative stigma associated with Taylorism. During the 1930s scientific management began to spread in the US and Europe as a result of the activities of neo-Taylorite consultants, for example Charles Eugene Bedaux (Littler, 1982: 99–140; Lash and Urry, 1987: 180–81; Bryson, 2000: 172–3). The history of Scientific Management in Britain up to 1940 is largely a history of the Bedaux company. Unlike Taylor, Bedaux was not concerned with justifying his ideas academically, rather he was concerned with selling them to engineers and managers (Littler, 1982: 107). Bedaux was born in France, but between the ages of 20 and 41 lived in the US where he developed his management system. During the 1930s he returned to France where he established a consultancy company that played an important role in introducing a reformulated version of Taylorism to European companies (see Bryson, 2000: 172–3; Downs, 1990: 57; Littler, 1982: 112–15).

W.E. DEMING AND CONTINUOUS IMPROVEMENT: FROM THE US TO JAPAN

Taylor and Bedaux are examples of individuals who were involved in the creation and diffusion of business knowledges during the early years of the last century. However, this process continues today as ideas developed in one country or even company are spread around the world by management consultants, the business press (Mazza, 1998) and MBA programmes. A recent example of this process is *kaizen, or 'continuous improvement'*, and the work of Sid Joynson, a West Yorkshire-based management consultant (Joynson and Forrester, 1995) and recent attempts by the Rover Car Group (Birmingham, UK) to introduce it in a modified form to its suppliers. In 1992, Joynson persuaded the BBC to produce a series of television programmes about his consultancy work. The book that accompanies the series, as well as the documentation and training exercises produced for clients, highlights the ways in which a consultant converts a foreign management idea such as *kaizen* into an operational consultancy technique. The source of the Joynson approach is a series of visits he made to Japan in 1990. It was not necessary for Joynson to travel to Japan to acquire access to this knowledge, as *kaizen* is a well-known set of techniques, but the fact that he worked in Japan provided him with credibility. During these visits he worked with Yoshiki Iwata, a Japanese manufacturing techniques guru, and realised that part of Japan's economic success was based on a system of *kaizen* targeted at all employees. Joynson coupled this with an understanding of Zen Buddhism producing a 'new' (revised) consultancy recipe based around 'intuitive learning' rather than 'intellectual learning' (Joynson and Forrester, 1995: 30). In a manufacturing company the shop floor workers are the experts or in other words the expertise is a result of experience rather than theoretical knowledge. This marriage of a Japanese recipe, management language and philosophy results in a consultancy technique which attempts to transfer the control of the workplace to front-line employees and away from management. The technique involves a training day to introduce employees to the concept of continuous improvement and to show them that they are the experts rather than their managers.

The Japanese process of *kaizen* was originally an American management idea that was transplanted to Japan after World War II. The technique of continuous improvement was originally developed by Walter Shewhart (1931), an American statistician who worked at the Bell Laboratories during the 1920s (Wheeler and Chambers, 1986: 5). Shewhart was concerned with understanding the reasons behind variability in manufactured products and processes. He identified two different types of variation: controlled variation or variation over time to a set pattern, and uncontrolled variation or a pattern of variation which alters over time. Uncontrolled variation indicates a system or process which is inconsistent and unstable and the causes of this variation must be identified and removed in order for the system to work as intended. Shewhart identified a statistical technique to identify uncontrolled variation that was widely used by Bell Systems. W. Edwards Deming worked with Walter Shewhart and developed the concept into a management tool which was used during World War II to overcome variation in the manufacture of war materials. In 1947 Deming visited Japan to assist the Japanese Government prepare for a Census (Wheeler and Chamber, 1986: 8) and during this visit Deming introduced the Japanese to the management recipe of using statistical methods to control manufacturing variation.

Deming returned to Japan in 1949 and met with 21 of Japan's top industrialists. He became the leading figure in the total quality/continuous improvement movement spending much of the 1950s and 1960s acting as a consultant to Japanese companies. Ironically, Deming's ideas were largely ignored in the US during the 1950s, but he became an icon for Japanese management. During the 1950s Deming's recipe was transformed by Kiichiro Toyoda, the then head of Toyota, and his deputy, Taiichi Ohno, into the Toyoto manufacturing system (Shigeo, 1989). This management recipe, commonly described as lean production, converts every employee into a quality control expert. Central to this system is the concept of *kaizen* with its foundations in the writings of Deming. Sid Joynson has translated a Japanese translation of an American management guru's translation of an American statistician's management recipe for removing variation from production processes.

The localisation of global management recipes has been taking place throughout the twentieth century. As soon as multinational companies are formed management knowledge(s) spread between companies and countries. The history of multinational companies as well as corporate restructuring is really a history about the effects of specific forms of management knowledge. What is missing from much of the economic geography of multinational corporations is an understanding of this type of knowledge flow. This type of knowledge flow occurs as a result of many of the types of processes identified as being important in a new industrial space or valleyed economy, for example the movement of people between organisations. The history of the spatial spread of Deming's ideas comes full circle with the establishment in the US of Process Management International (PMI), a consultancy company established to promote the work of Walter Deming. PMI established a company in the United Kingdom that persuaded the Rover Car Company to introduce '*process improvement through variability reduction*' into its factories and supply chain. We thus have a situation in which Deming's management recipes entered the United Kingdom in 1996 via a Japanese translation as well as directly from the US.

CONCLUSION

This chapter may appear to be different from the rest of the chapters in this collection. However, the focus on management knowledge rather than directly on trade is deliberately designed to draw attention to some of the less visible, but nevertheless extremely important, aspects of service trade. The development of multinational organisations, the growing importance of foreign direct investment, the growth in global trade, and the globalisation of the business professions all provide opportunities for the exchange of information and more importantly management knowledge. Some of these represent indirect forms of trade, but direct trade in management knowledge by management consultancy companies is now big business, and it is a business that is growing at an extremely rapid rate. The implications of these processes are that companies are beginning to access similar ways of work and management. It must be remembered, however, that we are not suggesting that global homogeneity of business knowledges and cultures is occurring, but rather that knowledge may flow between countries, and companies but it will be consumed differently. It is also important to note that even within the same country the same management knowledge will be interpreted and implemented in different ways by different companies.

Taylorism introduced order and 'scientific rationality' into business enterprises, but at the same time it challenged the individuality of workers. The human relations movement developed in the late 1920s and 1930s at the Harvard Business School as a reaction against Taylorism (Schon, 1983: 239).

Human relations proponents explored the monotony of work, absenteeism, employee turnover and low morale arguing that all of these reduced productivity (Guillen, 1994: 17–18). The history of the human resource movement mirrors that of Taylorism. To understand the similarities between these two movements is to explore the ways in which knowledge is created and transferred between companies and countries. What ties these movements together is an understanding that in the social sciences of which management science is one as well as within business organisations 'meaning is not discovered; it is imposed' (Gillespie, 1993: 4). This point emphasises the social construction of knowledge in general and of management knowledge in particular. The spread of Taylor and Deming's ideas in the US and overseas and the translation of their ideas by other consultants all depended upon two factors. First the life histories of the individuals involved. Thus, both Taylor and Deming acquired clients as well as disciples as a result of established friendship networks; social relationships bind individuals together and it is through these bindings that knowledge and information flows. Secondly, the business media, or more correctly business journalists, as well as business schools (for example MBA programmes) play an extremely important role in constructing the reputations of management theorists or theories.

To understand the geography of Taylorism or Fordism and of the continuous improvement movement requires an understanding of the social, cultural and political constructions of the knowledge(s) which lie behind these production systems. The same is true for all production systems. The difference between Taylor and Deming and the 1990s global consultancy companies is one of scale. There are more consultants and more competing management theorists and theories. The escalation in the quantity of competing theories has resulted in a transformation in the behaviour of large and multinational corporations which has largely gone unnoticed by economic geographers.

BIBLIOGRAPHY

Amin, A. (ed.) (1994), *Post-Fordism: a reader*, Oxford: Blackwell.
Aitken, H.G.J. (1960), *Taylorism at Watertown Arsenal: Scientific Management in Action: 1908–1915*, Cambridge, MA: Harvard University Press.
Bloomfield, B.P and Best, A. (1994), 'Management consultants: systems development, power and the translation of problems', *The Sociological Review*, **40**, 532–60.
Braverman, H. (1974), *Labour and Monopoly Capitalism: The Degradation of Work in the Twentieth Century*, New York: Monthly Review Press.
Bryson, J.R. (1997), 'Business Service Firms, Service Space and the Management of Change', *Entrepreneurship and Regional Development, 9*, 93–111.
Bryson, J.R. (2000), 'Spreading the Message: Management Consultants and the Shaping of Economic Geographies in Time and Space', in J.R. Bryson, P.W. Daniels, N. Henry and J. Pollard (eds), *Knowledge Space Economy*, London: Routledge, 157–75.

Callon, M. (1986), 'Some Elements of a Sociology of Translation: Domestication of the scallops and the fisherman of St Brieuc Bay', in J. Law (ed.), *Power, Action and Belief*, London: Routledge and Kegan Paul, pp. 196–233.

Chandler, A.D. (1977), *The Visible Hand: The Managerial Revolution in American Business*, Cambridge, MA: Harvard University Press.

Cooke, P. and Morgan, P. (1998), *The Associational Economy: Firms, Regions, and Innovation*, Oxford: Oxford University Press.

Copley, F.B. (1923), *Fredrick W. Taylor, Father of Scientific Management*, 2 Vols, New York: Harper and Brothers.

DiMaggio, P.J. and Powell, W.W. (1983), 'The iron cage revisited: institutional isomorphism and collective rationality in organisational fields', *American Sociological Review*, **48**, 147–60.

Dicken, P. (1992), *Global Shift: The Internalization of Economic Activity*, London: Paul Chapman.

Downs, L. (1990), 'Industrial decline, rationalization and equal pay: the Bedaux strike at Rover automobile company', *Social History*, **15** (1), 45–74.

Drucker, P. (1994), *Management*, Oxford: Butterworth-Heinemann.

Dunbar, R. (1996), *Grooming, Gossip and the Evolution of Language*, London: Faber and Faber.

Ehrenreich, B. and Ehrenreich, J. (1979), 'The Professional–Managerial Class', in P. Walker (ed.), *Between Labour and Capital*, Brighton: Harvester.

Gill, J. and Whittle, S. (1992), 'Management by panacea: accounting for transience', *Journal of Management Studies*, **30** (2), 281–95.

Gillespie, R. (1993), *Manufacturing Knowledge: A History of the Hawthorne Experiments*, Cambridge: Cambridge University Press.

Guillen, M.F. (1994), *Models of Management: Work, Authority and Organisation in a Comparative Perspective*, Chicago: The University of Chicago Press.

Haber, S. (1964), *Efficiency and Uplift: Scientific Management in the Progressive Era 1890–1920*, Chicago: The University of Chicago Press.

Hanlon, G. (1994), *The Commercialisation of Accountancy: Flexible Accumulation and the Transformation of the Service Class*, London: Macmillan.

Jacques, R. (1996), *Manufacturing the Employee: Management Knowledge from the 19th to 21st Centuries*, London: Sage.

Joynson, S. and Forrester, A. (1995), *Sid's Heroes: Uplifting Business Performance and the Human Spirit*, London: BBC Books.

Kakar, S. (1970), *Frederick Taylor: A Study in Personality and Innovation*, Cambridge, MA: Massachusetts Institute of Technology.

Knox, P. and Agnew, J. (1994), *The Geography of the World Economy*, London: Edward Arnold.

Lash, S. and Urry, J. (1987), *The End of Organised Capitalism*, Cambridge: Polity.

Latour, B. (1987), *Science in Action: How to Follow Scientists and Engineers through Society*, Boston: Harvard University Press.

Law, J. (1999), 'After ANT: Complexity, Naming and Topology', in J. Law and J. Hassard (eds), *Actor Network Theory and After*, Oxford: Blackwell, pp. 1–15.

Littler, C.R. (1982), *The Development of the Labour Process in Capitalist Societies*, London: Heinemann Educational Books.

Marglin, S.A. (1990), 'Towards a Decolonization of the Mind', in F.A. Marglin and S.A. Marglin (eds), *Dominating Knowledge: Development, Culture and Resistance*, Oxford: Clarendon Press.

Mazza, J.L. (1998), 'The Popularization of Business Knowledge Diffusion: from academic knowledge to popular culture', in J.L. Alvarez (ed.), *The Diffusion and Consumption of Business knowledge*, London: Macmillan, pp. 164–81.

McLean, A. (1984), 'Myths, Magic, and Gobbledegook, A-rational Aspects of the Consultants Role', in A. Kakabadse and C. Parker (eds), *Power, Politics and Organisations: A Behavioural Science View*, Chichester: John Wiley, pp. 147–67.

Nadworny, M.J. (1955), *Scientific Management and the Unions, 1900–32*, Cambridge, MA: Harvard University Press.

Nelson, D. (1974), 'Scientific Management, systematic management, and labor, 1880–1915', *Business History Review*, **28**, 479–500.

Nohria, N. and Eccles, R.G. (1998), 'Where Does Management Knowledge Come From?', in J.L. Alvarez (ed.), *The Diffusion and Consumption of Business Knowledge*, Hampshire: Macmillan, pp. 278–304.

O'Shea, J. and Madigan, C. (1997), *Dangerous Company: The Consulting Powerhouses and the Businesses they Save and Ruin*, New York: Times Business.

Perkins, H. (1996), *The Third Revolution: Professional Elites in the Modern World*, London: Routledge.

Petttigrew, A. (1985), *The Awakening Giant: Continuity and Change in Imperial Chemicals Industries*, Oxford: Blackwell.

Pollard, S. (1965), *The Genesis of Modern Management: A Study of the Industrial Revolution in Great Britain*, Cambridge, MA: Harvard University Press.

Schoenberger, E. (1994), 'Corporate strategy and corporate strategists: power, identity, and knowledge within the firm', *Environment and Planning A*, **26**, 435–51.

Schoenberger, E. (1997), *The Cultural Crisis of the Firm*, Oxford: Blackwell.

Schon, D.A. (1983), *The Reflective Practitioner: How Professionals Think in Action*, New York: Basic Books.

Shigeo, Shingo (1989), *A Study of the Toyota Production System,* Portland, USA: Productivity Press.

Taylor, F.W. (1934), *The Principles of Scientific Management*, New York: Harper and Brothers.

Thurley, K. and Wirdenuis, H. (1973), *Supervision: A Re-Appraisal*, London: Heinemann.

United Nations (1993), *Management Consulting: A Survey of the Industry and its Largest Firms*, United Nations Conference on Trade and Development.

Urwick, L. and Brech, E.F.L. (1945), *The Making of Scientific Management, Vol 1: Thirteen Pioneers*, London: Management Publications Trust.

Urwick, L. and Brech, E.F.L. (1953), *The Making of Scientific Management, Vol 2: Management in British Industry*, London: Pitman and Sons.

Wheeler, D.J. and Chambers, D.S. (1986), *Understanding Statistical Process Control*, Knoxville, Tennessee: Statistical Process Controls.

PART III

The Liberalisation of Service Trade: the GATS

9. Services trade and globalisation: governmental services and public policy concerns

David Hartridge

Since it came into force in January 1995, the GATS has attracted relatively little public attention, despite the fact that WTO Members have been continuously in negotiation on services trade throughout the period. Even the major successful negotiations on basic telecommunications and financial services, both concluded in 1997, were largely ignored outside specialist circles although the benefits they will bring to consumers worldwide, especially in the case of telecoms, are very evident. This is a familiar picture: there is a structural imbalance in public debate about trade liberalisation because the benefits to consumers of cheaper goods and more efficient and cheaper services are too generalised and widely disseminated to generate vocal public support for the liberalising process. The benefits of protection, on the other hand, emphasise producer interests and are therefore sufficiently attractive to justify a serious effort to dominate public and political debate.

The picture is now changing – not internally, where the GATS remains uncontroversial and there is a remarkably cooperative spirit among delegations, but externally. Since the start of the new round of services negotiations in January 2000 there has been a marked increase in the volume of press comment on the GATS and in the attention paid to it by NGOs. A lot of this is designed to promote debate and controversy, and in principle it is very welcome. No institution financed by taxpayers and no policy pursued by the governments who represent them should be immune from public examination and criticism: and the purposes for which the WTO was created would be better served if there were wider public understanding of the reasons why it is essential to have a stable legal framework for the conduct of international trade relations.

But for any debate to be useful both sides of the argument must be heard, and the growing debate about the GATS has so far been strikingly one-sided. Governments are not coming forward to explain their reasons for pursuing the liberalisation of services markets and industry. The field is consequently left open to commentators who are often frankly hostile to the WTO and whose purpose is to mount a case against further liberalisation in the new round. It is perfectly legitimate to hold such opinions, of course, but much of the argumentation used in advancing them is in my view untenable, in that it misrepresents the objectives of the negotiating governments, the content of the GATS and the implications of further liberalisation for social equity and welfare.

The main burden of recent attacks on the GATS has been that it poses a threat to the maintenance of public services and of proper standards for the regulation of services generally. These two concerns can perhaps be seen as different aspects of a single fear – that by virtue of their commitments under the GATS governments will lose or fatally compromise their right to pursue social policy objectives and protect public interests going well beyond the promotion of international trade. On this basis the GATS has been represented as a 'threat to democracy' – presumably meaning a threat to the policies elected governments wish to pursue, rather than to the right to elect them. The purpose of this chapter is to demonstrate that the fear is unjustified – that the GATS contains powerful safeguards against intrusion on the sovereign right of governments to provide and regulate services as they see fit and that experience so far reveals not the slightest disposition on the part of any government to compromise or concede this right.

It is understandable that the GATS should be seen as potentially intrusive into areas of government policy which have not been regarded until recently as having anything to do with trade. It is a comprehensive agreement, covering all services except those provided in the exercise of governmental authority and the greater part of the air transport sector, and all measures affecting trade in services. The definition of trade in services is also very broad: since the delivery of services across borders is only one of the ways in which they are traded internationally, the Agreement also covers the consumption of services abroad, services supplied through the establishment of a commercial presence in the export market and supply through the temporary movement of natural persons into the export market. This comprehensive reach would probably have made the Agreement unacceptable to a large number of GATT member countries but for the very striking degree of flexibility built into its structure. The most important elements of flexibility are, first, the right of all Members to choose those service sectors or sub-sectors, and the modes of supply, on which they are prepared to guarantee the rights of foreign suppliers and, secondly, to schedule limitations restricting the degree of market access and national treatment provided. The basic principle of progressive liberalisation, which recognises that developing countries are not expected to liberalise at a speed inconsistent with their level of development, is another key to the cessation of the North–South controversy which marked the early discussions of services in the GATT. Among WTO Members services is no longer a divisive issue.

SERVICES SUPPLIED IN THE EXERCISE OF GOVERNMENTAL AUTHORITY

The charge that GATS threatens the ability of governments to maintain services in the public sector has been made in the press in France and Canada, for example, and the representatives of public sector trade unions have expressed concern about it. The main focus of concern has been health and education services, and to a lesser extent other social services, but the same arguments can apply to all services supplied by governments. It has been suggested that negotiations will generate heavy pressure for the privatisation of such services; that the principle of universal coverage – the obligation accepted by most if not all governments to make these services available to all segments of the population – will be undermined; and that the provision of free or subsidised services will be called in to question. Fears have also been expressed about job security in the public sector. The GATS has been said to be 'inimical to public services; they are, at best, a missed commercial opportunity and, at worst, unfair competition or barriers to entry for foreign services and suppliers' (Sinclair, 2000).

The implicit assumption that governments themselves are blind to such dangers, if they exist, or complacent about them – or even in a dishonest conspiracy with big business to betray the interests of their electorates – is very strange. The WTO is nothing but a series of agreements between governments in which they have negotiated and accepted limitations on their otherwise sovereign right to intervene in international trade. Such limitations can only be partial and provisional: no country is obliged to become or to remain a Member of the WTO. But there is virtually universal agreement that economic prosperity and human welfare are advanced by the existence of rules for the conduct of international trade relations which reduce the likelihood of unpredictable and damaging interventions by governments. Nevertheless, no WTO Member, and I would guess no government in the world, is prepared to surrender its right to provide vital social services, or to regulate any service, in the public interest.

The status of governmental services was a key issue in the negotiation of the GATS, since it was important to all participants, but not a controversial one. Article I of the Agreement makes it clear that there is a complete exclusion from GATS coverage of all services 'supplied in the exercise of governmental authority', which are defined as those supplied neither on a commercial basis nor in competition with one or more service suppliers. Such services are not subject to any GATS disciplines – they are simply outside its scope. They will not be subject to negotiation in the new round, commitments in national schedules do not cover them and the general GATS disciplines of MFN treatment and transparency do not apply to them. If any disciplines on the subsidisation of services were to be developed in the current work under Article XV of the GATS, they too would not apply to governmental services – even if financial transfers within the public sector could be regarded as subsidies, which seems most unlikely. The only discipline which now exists in the GATS regarding subsidies is that if a government intends to subsidise national suppliers of a service on which it has made a national treatment commitment, but not to extend the subsidy to foreign suppliers of the same service, it should make that clear in its schedule of commitments as a limitation on national treatment. But even in this context subsidies to governmental services would not have to be scheduled: since they are not covered by the Agreement, no measure affecting them can be a 'measure affecting trade in services' in the sense of Article I.

Perhaps because it was not a controversial issue the Uruguay Round nego-tiators saw no need to refine the definition of governmental services – to make more explicit what is meant by services supplied 'neither on a commercial basis, nor in competition with one or more service suppliers'. If the exclusion of governmental services were now to be made an issue – not by other govern-ments, since the question has never been raised by any Member in the six years of the GATS existence, but by NGOs – it would be worthwhile for Members to make their understanding of the meaning of Article I.3(c) explicit. In my view it would be the general understanding that supply 'not on a commercial basis' means the supply of services on a not-for-profit basis, or in the more elegant French expression, *sans but lucratif.* The fact that charges are made for some services provided by governments – for the issue of a driving licence for example – would not cancel their non-commercial status. It would also be made clear that it is perfectly possible for public services to co-exist with private services in the same sector without calling into question the status of the former as governmental services. In the health and education sectors it is so common for public and private services to co-exist that it is effectively the norm. Governments making commitments to allow foreign provision of such services in their markets do not surrender or qualify their right to provide the same services on a non-commercial basis. The coexistence of governmen-tal and private services in the same industry does not mean that they are in competition in the sense of Article I.3(c) and therefore does not invalidate the exclusion from the GATS of the public sector: it would be absurd to suggest, for example, that the existence of private security companies deprives official police services of their status as governmental services and makes them subject to the GATS.

Some commercial services are of course provided by monopolies, either owned or sanctioned by governments. The right to maintain a monopoly, whether public or private, is not in question. They are not subject to GATS commitments on market access and national treatment, which would be a contradiction in terms, but Article VIII of the Agreement states that their operations are subject to the MFN principle, meaning that they should not discriminate between services and service suppliers of other Members, and that they should not act in a manner that would undermine or contravene the country's specific commitments on other services. If a government decides to introduce a monopoly on the supply of a service on which it has made specific commitments, there is an obligation to notify the intention to grant the monopoly and to negotiate, on request, compensation for the commitments withdrawn. The same provisions apply to exclusive service suppliers, where a government has authorised or established a small number of service suppliers and substantially prevents competition among them in its territory. There is nothing in the GATS which requires or promotes privatisation of any service and no obligation to make commitments on any service. Indeed, Members are free not just to refrain from making commitments but to prohibit foreign supply of health or other services completely, if they so wish.

The exclusion of governmental services from GATS coverage was a political imperative. Virtually all governments – indeed, as far as I know all governments without exception – accept that the supply and the quality of certain vital services such as health and education are among their prime responsibilities. Even in a country as heavily dependent on exports of services as the United Kingdom, for example, I would think it inconceivable that any government could allow the status and financing of the National Health Service, which consistently features among the highest political priorities of the population, to be compromised or undermined by commitments under the GATS.

The Agreement also contains more specific safeguards for social policy objectives. Article XIV says that nothing in the Agreement 'shall be construed to prevent the adoption or enforcement by any Member of measures . . . necessary to protect human, animal or plant life or health'. The need to take action to protect health would override all obligations arising from the Agreement, provided that the measures taken did not discriminate in an arbitrary or unjustifiable way between other Members and were not a disguised restriction on trade in services. The protection of public morals and public order are subject to the same exception provision.

There is nothing in the GATS which limits the freedom of governments to impose universal service obligations on service suppliers, whether national or foreign, in any service, including those on which specific commitments are made. There is no need to schedule such a requirement if it applies to all providers; it is agreed that universal service obligations are not market access limitations. It would be possible to require, as a condition for the establishment of a hospital by a foreign enterprise, for example, that a proportion of the beds, or even all of them, should be available free of charge. Nor would governments be prevented from taxing private patients and using the funds raised to subsidise other, less viable, services. If such conditions were to be imposed only on foreign suppliers or services, however, it would be necessary to specify this as a national treatment limitation.

THE RIGHT TO REGULATE

The GATS is also attacked on the grounds that it will constrain or undermine the right of governments to regulate services. It is said, for example, that 'the GATS is designed to enable trans-national corporations, in collaboration with foreign governments, to attack general, non-discriminatory public interest regulations as unnecessary or burdensome' (Sinclair, 2000). This is conspiracy theory. Other commentators have gone as far as to say that negotiations on services 'may abolish regulation' designed to protect health standards and other public interests, and that the 're-establishment of high standards for health protection and public service' may be made 'all but impossible'.[1] The GATS does contain some disciplines on domestic regulation and there is work under way to develop them further, but these suggestions are absurd.

The preamble to the GATS specifically recognises 'the right of Members to regulate, and to introduce new regulations, on the supply of services within their territories in order to meet national policy objectives and, given asymmetries existing with respect to the degree of development of services regulations in different countries, the particular need of developing countries to exercise this right'. The right to regulate is one of the fundamental premises of the Agreement. Many services, perhaps most, are very closely regulated for excellent reasons, the most important of which, perhaps, is to ensure the quality of the service in order to protect public health and safety and the rights of consumers. The objective of the GATS, and of the new round of negotiations, is to liberalise services trade, not to deregulate services. Market access commitments confer a right to supply subject to whatever domestic regulations are in force and whatever new regulations may be introduced, and they carry no implication that technical standards or any other form of regulation will be modified to facilitate supply by foreigners, (A footnote to Article XVII of the GATS makes it clear that 'specific commitments assumed under this Article shall not be construed to require any Member to compensate for any inherent competitive disadvantages which result from the foreign character of the relevant services or service suppliers'). Like the ring-fencing of governmental services, the right to regulate is of capital importance for all WTO Members.

Nevertheless, Article VI does contain certain disciplines on domestic regulation, which are not regarded as barriers to market access and are not subject to scheduling or to negotiations on market access. The basic requirement is that in sectors where specific commitments are undertaken, measures of general application affecting trade in services should be administered in a reasonable, objective and impartial manner. Members are also required to maintain procedures for the review on request of administrative decisions, and for appropriate remedies where justified. Article VI.4 mandates the development of 'any necessary disciplines' to ensure that measures relating to qualification requirements and procedures, technical standards and licensing requirements do not constitute unnecessary barriers to trade in services. Work under this mandate had been proceeding in the Working Party on Domestic Regulation since 1996, and is still going on. While it is not strictly speaking part of the new round, it will proceed in parallel with the market access negotiations, and it is the fact that this work is going on which has given rise to the charges referred to above.

The WTO is not and will never be a standard-setting organisation. It will not specify the level of qualifications to be required of professionals and it does not limit or try to define the national policy objectives that Members seek to achieve in regulating services. The approach which Members have taken so far in negotiations on domestic regulation, and their results, are probably a fairly accurate guide to the likely outcome of future work. It had been agreed at the end of the Uruguay Round that in the development of disciplines on domestic regulation priority should be given to the accountancy sector, which is a highly regulated but also highly internationalised profession, performing very similar functions and applying similar standards across the world. After three years of discussion Members adopted in December 1998 the text of the 'Disciplines on Domestic Regulation in the Accountancy Sector' which had been developed in the Working Party on Professional Services (since reconstituted as the Working Party on Domestic Regulation) (see appendix). They are not yet in force; in adopting the text the Services Council stated that 'no later than the conclusion of the forthcoming round of services negotiations, the disciplines developed by the WPPS are intended to be integrated into the General Agreement on Trade in Services'. In the same decision the Council determined that the decisions are to be applicable to Members who have entered specific commitments on accountancy in their schedules.

The purpose of the disciplines is to ensure that measures relating to qualification requirements and procedures, technical standards and licensing requirements are *inter alia*:

(a) based on objective and transparent criteria, such as competence and the ability to supply the service;
(b) not more burdensome than necessary to ensure the quality of the service;
(c) in the case of licensing procedures, not in themselves a restriction on the supply of the service.

It will be seen from the text of the disciplines that the concerns of Members in this area were above all procedural; they say little or nothing about the substantive content of the qualifications or standards to be applied in the accountancy profession, but rather focus on the need for transparency, meaning access to information about regulations, standards, examinations and so forth, and on equity in the treatment of foreign applicants for licences and professional qualifications. It is made clear that the disciplines do not concern measures which are subject to scheduling under Articles XVI and XVII of the GATS,[2] which restrict access to the domestic market or limit the application of national treatment to foreign suppliers. The measures in question are therefore in principle non-discriminatory; it is not their purpose to erect barriers to the entry of foreign suppliers into the profession. However, differential treatment of foreign applicants would not be inconsistent with the disciplines so long as there were objective grounds for the difference in treatment. There are no provisions as to the content of technical standards. On these the only requirements are, first, that measures relating to standards should be prepared, adopted and applied only to fulfil a legitimate objective; and, second, that in determining whether a measure taken by a Member affecting standards creates unnecessary barriers to trade in services, account should be taken of internationally recognised standards of relevant international organisations applied by the Member.

The necessity test is the focus of the concerns that have been expressed about the work on domestic regulations. Paragraph 2 of the Accountancy Disciplines requires Members to ensure that 'measures relating to licensing requirements and procedures, technical standards and qualification requirements and procedures are not prepared, adopted or applied with a view to or with the effect of creating unnecessary barriers to trade and accountancy services'. They should be 'not more trade-restrictive than necessary to fulfil a legitimate objective'. Legitimate objectives are '*inter alia*, the protection of consumers (which includes all users of accounting services and the public generally) the quality of the service, professional competence and the integrity of the profession' (the phrase '*inter alia*' indicates that this is an illustrative, not a definitive list).

It would be disingenuous on my part to rely on the text of the Agreement alone as a response to the threats which the anti-GATS campaigners claim to perceive. The more sophisticated among them are concerned about the possibility, as they see it, that the dispute settlement system will be used to undermine national policy objectives by attacking the right to regulate and to maintain proper standards. It is suggested that the system is inherently biased against public services and that stringent application of the necessity test would result in severe limitation of regulatory freedom. These charges must also be addressed. Experience so far suggests that Members will be very cautious in invoking the dispute settlement procedures in services: as of December 2000, we have not seen a single dispute settlement case in which GATS obligations were the primary issue, though a case is pending between the US and Mexico relating to telecommunications. Nor has there been any less formal allegation, in the services council or any other committee, of excessive regulation. Nor has the status of governmental services been called into question by any delegation in any context. Nevertheless we must expect that there will eventually be dispute settlement cases and that some of them will refer to regulation. But the possibility of dispute settlement on specific measures cannot rationally or honestly be presented as a generalised assault on regulation as such. Still less is it a mandate for the WTO to review Members' standards and regulatory regimes and to disallow those found to be unnecessarily restrictive. No such power exists and there are no circumstances in which Members would agree to create it.

The attack on dispute settlement is really an attack on international trade law as such. If it were possible for governments to introduce protectionist measures in committed sectors in the guise of 'domestic regulations', in the knowledge that trading partners would have no right to query the justification for the measure or to argue that the objective could be obtained with less disruption of trade or less discrimination inflicted on foreign suppliers seeking to practice in the market, commitments would be valueless. In those circumstances, having no right to challenge what they saw as discriminatory or unnecessarily restrictive measures within an agreed legal framework, countries with enough economic clout would make their own law. Without provision for dispute settlement trade law quickly relapses into power politics.

As far as the regulation of services is concerned, the negotiation of the 'accountancy disciplines' has made it very obvious how strongly regulators of all Member countries, perhaps above all the most highly developed, assert their prerogatives in setting professional qualifications and technical standards. There is no reason to believe that in developing disciplines for other professions or services governments would be any less circumspect than in the case of accountancy. If the accountancy precedent is followed, any further disciplines on regulation will in any case apply only to services on which commitments have been made.

APPENDIX

The following text has been adopted by the Council for Trade in Services. The disciplines will come into force for those Members which have made commitments on accountancy services at the conclusion of the current round of negotiations under Article XIX.

DISCIPLINES ON DOMESTIC REGULATION
IN THE ACCOUNTANCY SECTOR

I. OBJECTIVES

1. Having regard to the Ministerial Decision on Professional Services, Members have agreed to the following disciplines elaborating upon the provisions of the GATS relating to domestic regulation of the sector. The purpose of these disciplines is to facilitate trade in accountancy services by ensuring that domestic regulations affecting trade in accountancy services meet the requirements of Article VI:4 of the GATS. The disciplines therefore do not address measures subject to scheduling under Articles XVI and XVII of the GATS, which restrict access to the domestic market or limit the application of national treatment to foreign suppliers. Such measures are addressed in the GATS through the negotiation and scheduling of specific commitments.

II. GENERAL PROVISIONS

2. Members shall ensure that measures not subject to scheduling under Articles XVI or XVII of the GATS, relating to licensing requirements and procedures, technical standards and qualification requirements and procedures are not prepared, adopted or applied with a view to or with the effect of creating unnecessary barriers to trade in accountancy services. For this purpose, Members shall ensure that such measures are not more trade-restrictive than necessary to fulfil a legitimate objective. Legitimate objectives are, *inter alia*, the protection of consumers (which includes all users of accounting services and the public generally), the quality of the service, professional competence, and the integrity of the profession.

III. TRANSPARENCY

3. Members shall make publicly available, including through the enquiry and contact points established under Articles III and IV of the GATS, the names and addresses of competent authorities (i.e. governmental or non-governmental entities responsible for the licensing of professionals or firms, or accounting regulations).

4. Members shall make publicly available, or shall ensure that their competent authorities make publicly available, including through the enquiry and contact points:

(a)   where applicable, information describing the activities and professional titles which are regulated or which must comply with specific technical standards;

(b)   requirements and procedures to obtain, renew or retain any licences or professional qualifications and the competent authorities' monitoring arrangements for ensuring compliance;
(c)   information on technical standards; and
(d)   upon request, confirmation that a particular professional or firm is licensed to practise within their jurisdiction.

5.   Members shall inform another Member, upon request, of the rationale behind domestic regulatory measures in the accountancy sector, in relation to legitimate objectives as referred to in paragraph 2.
6.   When introducing measures which significantly affect trade in accountancy services, Members shall endeavour to provide opportunity for comment, and give consideration to such comments, before adoption.
7.   Details of procedures for the review of administrative decisions, as provided for by Article VI:2 of the GATS, shall be made public, including the prescribed time-limits, if any, for requesting such a review.

IV.   LICENSING REQUIREMENTS

8.   Licensing requirements (i.e. the substantive requirements, other than qualification requirements, to be satisfied in order to obtain or renew an authorization to practice) shall be pre-established, publicly available and objective.
 9.   Where residency requirements not subject to scheduling under Article XVII of the GATS exist, Members shall consider whether less trade restrictive means could be employed to achieve the purposes for which these requirements were set, taking into account costs and local conditions.
10.   Where membership of a professional organisation is required, in order to fulfil a legitimate objective in accordance with paragraph 2, Members shall ensure that the terms for membership are reasonable, and do not include conditions or pre-conditions unrelated to the fulfilment of such an objective. Where membership of a professional organization is required as a prior condition for application for a licence (i.e. an authorization to practice), the period of membership imposed before the application may be submitted shall be kept to a minimum.
11.   Members shall ensure that the use of firm names is not restricted, save in fulfilment of a legitimate objective.
12.   Members shall ensure that requirements regarding professional indemnity insurance for foreign applicants take into account any existing insurance coverage, in so far as it covers activities in its territory or the relevant jurisdiction in its territory and is consistent with the legislation of the host Member.
13.   Fees charged by the competent authorities shall reflect the administrative costs involved, and shall not represent an impediment in themselves to practising

the relevant activity. This shall not preclude the recovery of any additional costs of verification of information, processing and examinations. A concessional fee for applicants from developing countries may be considered.

V. LICENSING PROCEDURES

14.   Licensing procedures (i.e. the procedures to be followed for the submission and processing of an application for an authorization to practise) shall be pre-established, publicly available and objective, and shall not in themselves constitute a restriction on the supply of the service.

15.   Application procedures and the related documentation shall be not more burdensome than necessary to ensure that applicants fulfil qualification and licensing requirements. For example, competent authorities shall not require more documents than are strictly necessary for the purpose of licensing, and shall not impose unreasonable requirements regarding the format of documentation. Where minor errors are made in the completion of applications, applicants shall be given the opportunity to correct them. The establishment of the authenticity of documents shall be sought through the least burdensome procedure and, wherever possible, authenticated copies should be accepted in place of original documents.

16.   Members shall ensure that the receipt of an application is acknowledged promptly by the competent authority, and that applicants are informed without undue delay in cases where the application is incomplete. The competent authority shall inform the applicant of the decision concerning the completed application within a reasonable time after receipt, in principle within six months, separate from any periods in respect of qualification procedures referred to below.

17.   On request, an unsuccessful applicant shall be informed of the reasons for rejection of the application. An applicant shall be permitted, within reasonable limits, to resubmit applications for licensing.

18.   A licence, once granted, shall enter into effect immediately, in accordance with the terms and conditions specified therein.

VI. QUALIFICATION REQUIREMENTS

19.   A Member shall ensure that its competent authorities take account of qualifications acquired in the territory of another Member, on the basis of equivalency of education, experience and/or examination requirements.

20.   The scope of examinations and of any other qualification requirements shall be limited to subjects relevant to the activities for which authorization is sought. Qualification requirements may include education, examinations, practical training, experience and language skills.

21.   Members note the role which mutual recognition agreements can play in facilitating the process of verification of qualifications and/or in establishing equivalency of education.

IV.   QUALIFICATION PROCEDURES

22.   Verification of an applicant's qualifications acquired in the territory of another Member shall take place within a reasonable time-frame, in principle within six months and, where applicants' qualifications fall short of requirements, shall result in a decision which identifies additional qualifications, if any, to be acquired by the applicant.
23.   Examinations shall be scheduled at reasonably frequent intervals, in principle at least once a year, and shall be open for all eligible applicants, including foreign and foreign-qualified applicants. Applicants shall be allowed a reasonable period for the submission of applications. Fees charged by the competent authorities shall reflect the administrative costs involved, and shall not represent an impediment in themselves to practising the relevant activity. This shall not preclude the recovery of any additional costs of verification of information, processing and examinations. A concessional fee for applicants from developing countries may be considered.
24.   Residency requirements not subject to scheduling under Article XVII of the GATS shall not be required for sitting examinations.

VIII.   TECHNICAL STANDARDS

25.   Members shall ensure that measures relating to technical standards are prepared, adopted and applied only to fulfil legitimate objectives.
26.   In determining whether a measure is in conformity with the obligations under paragraph 2, account shall be taken of internationally recognized standards of relevant international organizations[3] applied by that Member.

NOTES

1.   Murray Dobbin, *Financial Post* (Canada), 26 June 2000.
2.   The text of GATS Articles XVI and XVII is reproduced in an appendix to this document.
3.   The term 'relevant international organisations' refers to international bodies whose membership is open to the relevant bodies of at least all Members of the WTO.

REFERENCES

Sinclair, S. (2000), *GATS: How the New WTO's 'Services' Negotiations Threaten Democracy*, Canada: Canadian Centre for Policy Alternatives, September.

10. The liberalisation of international trade in services: issues of competence and legitimacy for the GATS – and the impact of its rules on institutions

Julian Arkell

INTRODUCTION

The World Trade Organisation (WTO) entered into force on 1 January 1995, and with it the General Agreement on Trade in Services (GATS). Also incorporated was a revised version of its predecessor treaty, the General Agreement on Tariffs and Trade (GATT) which deals with trade in physical products (merchandise). This chapter explores the challenges posed to national cultural values and institutions by the creation of the GATS, and the putting into practice of its principles of liberalisation. The GATS is designed to take account of societal and institutional imperatives because the effects of its principles of liberalisation deeply impact each economy, affecting many aspects of every day life. The rules, achieved by willing consensus among its Member sovereign nations, condition any regulation that affects transactions involving services between people and firms from different jurisdictions.

GATS IN THE SETTING OF INTERNATIONAL LAW[1]

Rights of Nations

International law provides the foundation upon which the rights of each sovereign state rest. The UN comprises a body of nations bound together through common interests and thus constitutes an international community. The WTO is a treaty among many UN Members intended in principle to be compatible with existing international rules, including the UN Charter in particular.[2]

Personalities of International Organisations

A common necessity binds the international community to a bedrock of legal principles for mediating their relationships, concerning issues of global security and common global or 'spillover' problems – such as health, environmental protection, air and water pollution, civil aviation, transit over the high seas and many other issues, including international trade.

International organisations made up of states and created by treaty, such as the WTO, are not identical, their nature or legal personalities (rights, duties and powers) depend on the needs of the international community – in each case based on the subjective belief that their role is necessary in a certain field of international relationships: in the case of the WTO, trading relationships, where sovereign systems of law are juxtaposed. The state members of any such organisation, with their inherent equality and right of self-determination, are joined in this common interest.

Coherence in the Policies of Relevant International Organisations

This poses real practical problems for the WTO as '[t]here is little connection or "coherence" between the World Bank and the IMF [and the WTO] and even less consideration of connectedness between their mandates and the role of the UN and its key agencies, as well as the contributions of bilateral donor agencies for development' (Fried, 2000). 'Until recently, there has been an obvious approach on the part of some developed countries (and occasionally certain developing countries) to marginalize the United Nations in the international debate on trade issues . . . It is clear that coherence requires participation of the UN system as a whole. Only with the involvement of organisations such as the ILO, UNEP, WIPO, UNESCO etc. will it be possible to ensure that trade initiatives are, and are perceived to be consistent with international consensus' (Ricupero, 2000).

Superior Norms of International Law

There is no central law-making authority lying above the WTO in its specific domain, though in general there are superior rules under the Members' obligations to the UN Charter that may be relevant. The WTO cannot, however, override norms of international law from which no derogation is permissible (that is rules of a *jus cogens* nature[3]). For instance the WTO has no powers in relation to basic human rights, and it cannot enforce one general international law against another, should the one violate the other.

WTO Members have both a duty to submit to the existing body of its charter rules and a right to contribute to their modification and development –

indeed these rules cannot be altered by unilateral declaration by one state, however powerful. The essential basis of international law is common consent where decisions are adopted from emerging consensus.

It seems that given a fair wind the decisions of the WTO dispute settlement mechanism will become an important node in the development of international law, as long as its decisions are consistent and its reasoning accessible, and the panels abide by the general principles of equity and good faith between the parties. Its influence could be considerable. Some say this is already too large and closer political control over such policy developments should be established.

Developing International Law at the GATS

The GATS as an integral part of the WTO is placed at a fascinating conjuncture where some of the faster developments of international law may be possible. Securely grounded in an international organisation by binding international treaty, and operating by consensus in the interests of a wide international community, it is capable of developing specific rules for new situations within the conceptually complete international legal system, such that conflicting situations can be determined as a matter of law.

In the case of the GATS the new procedure to act collectively within the WTO framework and, in effect, as a near-universal permanent international conference, is something not before achieved, and its consensus-based rules will strengthen its treaty status.

The moral basis of such rules are an important factor in creating its legitimacy in relation to the member states' rights and duties and those of their individual citizens. The development of international law depends on the standards of public morality as much as upon economic interests. This will become tested as the GATS begins to require certain standards to be met by national legislative bodies and due process procedures, or even to stipulate that there be uniform internal laws – which will produce juxtapositions of principle and law that are less clear than before and more complex. The issues will be how states apply international law internally, and how conflicts between international law and national rules of law are resolved. The reach of the GATS into national affairs will become much deeper than hitherto, because it lays down rules concerning the treatment of the activities of foreign nationals working abroad, of foreign affiliates, their investments and other related matters. Thus rule making now reaches directly to private conduct.

GATS rules are henceforth of central relevance in trading situations where there is a foreign element in cases before national courts and where questions arise as to the court of jurisdiction and applicable law – the first being a juxtaposition of states and the second of legal systems. The principles observed by those systems are very much at issue in the GATS deliberations.

Already international law recognises that states will choose different legal techniques to implement treaty obligations and that this does not constitute lack of reciprocity – in the EU it is called mutual recognition of equivalence, a practical substitute for impossible degrees of harmonisation. In certain cases, though, treaties may provide for uniformity for some matters of private law. Whichever it happens to be, it is important to realise that failure to implement such treaty obligations cannot be justified in international law on legal, practical or political grounds.

A firm of European lawyers, Stibble Simont Monahan Duhot (2000), in an editorial for its recent report on international trade stated that:

> Whether one likes it or not, the WTO sets forth the most comprehensive set of economic rules in the world (Long, 1985). The scope of the WTO is large. It directly affects national customs and trade regimes, development policies, environmental protection and human health measures. These rules . . . are actively being enforced, if necessary through arbitration before WTO tribunals in Geneva. The strong enforcement of internationally agreed rules is another unique feature of the WTO.[4]

The editorial of their report ends with the thought that 'Sensible international rules and strong institutions are indispensable to keep a globalizing world safely on course'.

ISSUES OF LEGITIMACY THAT ARISE FOR THE GATS

General Issues

Having noted that international law is based on a community of interest, equity and morality, how can the legitimacy of the WTO and GATS in the exercise of their powers be assessed? Issues of legitimacy arise whenever power is exercised.

Governments have policies aimed at dealing with the major problems of social evolution, such as unemployment, inflation, balance of payments deficits and sustainable economic growth. Their political aims are founded on social, cultural and even religious precepts. They have to protect the security of the state from armed aggression and terrorists, to protect the freedom and privacy of the individual, and to protect the natural environment. Many of the problems that service suppliers encounter arise from laws reflecting these proper concerns of elected representatives.

In multilateral trade negotiations governments have to balance the needs of the producers (who are the traders) with those of consumers. Producers should be able to pursue ways to be more cost-effective, to improve their services, and to devise entirely new ones. Consumers should have the ability to choose freely between the offers of producers irrespective of origin. Reaching agreement is difficult because the interests of sovereign nations vary widely as to their beliefs, norms, cultures, customs, the resources of producers and consumers, plans for economic development, and protection of the environment. It is differences in resources (the factor endowments) that create the potential for mutual gain through trade. Success in reaching such agreements depends not only on the legitimacy of the governments, but also on the legitimacy of the factor costs.

Ultimately, however, 'it is a truism that a treaty is only worth what its members make of it. If respect for rules and commitments is eroded, if member countries hesitate to intervene when there is a breach of the legal rule simply to keep open the possibility of circumventing the rule themselves, the means of constraint must lose a great part of their force and effectiveness' (Long, 1985).

Ethics and Equity

This is not the place to get drawn into debates on theology, ethics and morality, though clearly they are relevant in the broadest sense, and ethical dilemmas are at the heart of some trade disputes. Whereas science can largely escape the debate because many claim it to be strictly amoral,[5] economics is not a pure science (perhaps not science at all, even dismal!) and has to deal with the real human conditions and activities. Thus we have to perceive the important notion that the interactions of civil society rest fundamentally on moral relationships or covenants, rather than on market transactions (Tyler, 2000), and not just because many caring activities and other social inputs are usually not monetised. Economics is best equipped to handle monetary values or at least proxies for such accounting, and has in the main (along with science) to side-step human virtues. Its 'laws' and econometric models can be powerful tools to clarify the results of working circumstances, but fallible tools they remain, that cannot quantify, and therefore directly accommodate, moral precepts, ethics and legal rights.

Equity is not a cornerstone of the WTO as it is in common law jurisdictions, and indeed does not explicitly feature, because the WTO is more akin to a commercial contract; one between governments. This sets its bounds: governments contract to abide by the rules they have painstakingly agreed upon in this multilateral context. These rules are intended to govern how they legislate on matters that affect trade and thus the created rights of trading partners. Private actors have no direct locus in these rights[6] – although of course it was their interests that governments had in mind when creating the WTO, as to both producers and consumers.

However, there is possibly a fundamental problem for the WTO, alluded to by Olivier Long, which bears on the central theme of this chapter, and which is more difficult to handle: that 'equality among unequals is inequitable'. Long feels this calls into question the central principles of non-discrimination and reciprocity. This has been underlined by the Secretary General of UNCTAD, Rubens Ricupero, who said 'The parameters for tradeoffs at the national level are different from those at the international level and differences between countries. They are also distorted by the dominant role of the major trading countries in determining the subjects to be traded off multilaterally' (Ricupero, 2000).

The GATS framework is sensitive to such inequalities and deals with this fundamental problem in practice by providing for progressive liberalisation and much flexibility in the application of its disciplines.

Exclusion from Decision Making and Catering for Losers

Fears of domination and exclusion of developing country interests in the context of the WTO Ministerial negotiations were very evident, even exacerbated, during the Seattle meeting. Mechanics to deal with the range of complex, some independent, some interrelated and technical, issues had not been developed to enable the disparate parts to be brought together into a satisfactory whole. The WTO as an institution had not updated itself to enable Ministers and their officials from 135 countries to relate to each other effectively and conclusively.

The extension of the reach of external disciplines into national policy making is fraught with political difficulties, as so often politicians feel they have to respond to short-term imperatives: for example any potential losers from trade liberalisation will be well organised, sometimes powerful, whereas there will be no one focus for the benefits that could accrue to the economy as a whole. It is difficult to cease shielding domestic distortion because of the fear of loss of jobs and foreign dominance, and ways will often be chosen to enact less visible forms of protectionism both internally and internationally.

Fully successful liberalisation under the GATS may entail major domestic regulatory reform, that cannot be achieved on a piecemeal basis, nor in the face of opposition of the regulators – indeed national consensus may be needed among consumers, suppliers, regulators and officials (both economic and trade) that such reforms are in the overall national interest.

Thus it will remain true that external disciplines alone cannot secure, or sustain, a liberal world trading environment. Governments have to demonstrate clearly the crucial link between trade policy and securing domestic gains, through the national efficiency of national enterprises, and thus to general welfare.

Legitimacy and the WTO

Those who doubt the legitimacy of the WTO on grounds of community of interest or in international law will have a hard case to prove. General obligations arising from general principles are often non-controversial. The concern is how such obligations are interpreted and applied in practice. The legitimacy of an internationally constituted treaty such as the WTO will rather depend on its observance of equity and its governance and its efficiency as a law-making body, the workings of its dispute settlement mechanism, and compliance of its Members with those dispute settlement rulings.

The WTO will have to be 'As legitimate as possible in the circumstances, or more legitimate than the next realistic alternative'.[7] The WTO must be authoritative (give the right answers), responsive (to ideas in debate), act with fairness by being consistent and flexible, and be effective – by following through with implementation, and maintaining links with local politics and NGOs as connectors to a decentralised public. At present Ministers responsible for some areas impacted by WTO rules, such as the environment and labour, have no seat at the WTO table.

There is no hierarchy of courts and tribunals on the international plane. Therefore the possibility exists that one or other (the European Court of Justice, for example) might come to a ruling in parallel to the WTO on trade issues, that could undermine WTO rulings. Regional dispute resolution procedures between states in trade matters (direct or indirect) might have the same effect.[8]

The WTO Articles are designed to set out principles to guide the lawmakers of its sovereign Members. Nations considered illegitimate will not be accepted into the WTO and remain outside. Acceding Members have to show their laws are legitimate according to the WTO principles. The WTO itself will only retain legitimacy as long as all its Members consent to its principles and procedures which involves a balance between rich and poor, powerful and weak and the answers to questions such as: Is it fair? Does it work? Do all benefit? Does it abide by the rule of law. Does it stay within its remit?

The very success of its predecessor in the past has attracted great membership growth in the past two decades – a doubling and more. Thus it has been loaded up with much more to do, and many interests want it to do even more. But it will not retain legitimacy if it fails in what it already has to do, or is caused to fail by an overload of further issues. A major current problem is already too heavy a current workload, just when many outside interests are pressing for it to take on additional challenges. The WTO is both underfunded and understaffed to a critical extent in view of its mandate.[9]

As pointed out in a recent consideration of the WTO legitimacy, a criticism of the WTO and the GATT before it was that governments 'negotiated in secret, then reported their agreements to national legislatures and publics' (Keohane and Nye, 2000). However, it has also been suggested that the legitimacy of an international body further increasingly depends on the ability of an organisation to command, at least tacitly, broad political support among electorates and legislatures. The task of assuring legitimacy falls largely to governments, which in the case of the WTO 'have not risen to it very effectively', and that 'a prosperous and stable world requires more, not less, open markets, stronger global rules and institutions' *Financial Times* (2000).

International institutions must somehow aggregate 'a bewildering array of interests in ways that are democratically acceptable' in a setting where 'Rule-making and rule-interpretation in global governance have become pluralised.' Thus there is the need to 'institutionalise channels of contact between international organisations and constituencies within civil society'.[10]

The problem is that 'No one has figured out how to make participatory democracy work at a scale larger than the city state'. Due to the impact of trade on many other wider issues, there is a need to involve politicians who can link specific organisations and policies to a broader range of public issues through electoral accountability. 'The lack of intermediating politicians is the most serious "democratic deficit" of international organisations in general, and the WTO in particular. The problem is how to increase transparency and accountability, while enhancing international cooperation and achieving some degree of policy integration. On the input side, mechanisms for accountability exist, but they are not joined into a coherent system with mutually reinforcing components.'

WTO Legitimacy and Globalisation

People are concerned about the effect of globalisation on their own cultures and historic customs – even their sovereignty as nations – the way workers are treated, the safety of their food, the protection of their local and the global environment, suitable education, health care and entertainment for their children, and many, many other vital aspects of living in the new Millennium. Some of these fears are reasonable, others quite extreme. All are sounding warnings about the dangers of globalisation even as they welcome its benefits as consumers, indeed use the new technology to communicate their fears and organise their cause.

As Kofi Annan, the UN Secretary-General, put it in Seattle, this situation arises from the imbalance caused by 'the gap between the integration of the world economy and the continued parochialism of political and social institutions'.

THE PROVENANCE OF SOME GATS PRINCIPLES AND RULES

The GATT

The GATS owes much to the GATT for the provenance of its central principles and some of its rules. 'Unlike most other international organisations, the GATT embodies legal rights and obligations and conventional commitments', and its Members 'have recourse to these rights through the GATT dispute settlement procedure . . . the founding countries of GATT committed themselves to non-discrimination in their trade relations, so as to ensure equal access to markets and reciprocity in trade concessions. They created a trade system designed to bring stability and transparency to the conditions in which trade takes place and to promote progressive trade liberalisation' (Ricupero, 2000).

The GATT also held 'that the less-developed contracting parties should not be expected, in the course of trade negotiations, to make contributions which are inconsistent with their individual development, financial and trade needs' (Ricupero, 2000). The Preamble of the GATS and its framework makes progressive liberalisation a central theme for international trade in services.

Non-Discrimination and Quantitative Restrictions

A defining GATT principle is 'non-discrimination' as expressed in the concepts of 'most-favoured-nation treatment' and 'national treatment'. Unconditional most-favoured-nation (MFN) treatment ensures that the same level of tariff is applied to a particular class of products irrespective of which foreign country those products were made in (Article I): that is, there is no discrimination between countries.[11] The tariff itself is of course a discrimination against all foreign products compared with the same sort made inside the country.

Under the GATS Most-Favoured-Nation Treatment Article (II) the laws of WTO Members must treat services and services suppliers the same no matter from which country they hail.[12]

National Treatment is the second application of the GATT non-discrimination principle: all foreign goods of a particular sort should be classified and taxed in the same way irrespective of foreign origin, and thereafter treated the same as any equivalent goods produced within the territory. There is no exception possible.

By contrast under the GATS National Treatment Article (XVII), governments can elect either to treat foreign suppliers and services in the same way as nationals, or in a different way, as set out in their schedules of commitments.

The GATT bans quantitative internal regulations (such as quotas by number of items, and percentage shares of a market) and internal maximum price control measures – termed Quantitative Restrictions (QRs) – except on cinema films! (Articles XI and XIII). Perhaps it is easier to attempt a ban on QRs for goods because of the agreed tariff structure. As tariff levels have come down, however, the price competitiveness of foreign products has increased, with the result that, like the classical Hydra, as tariff 'heads' are cut off, many new barrier heads have sprouted up in their place. These other ways of discriminating against imported products are dubbed non-tariff barriers (NTBs): an example would be where certain technical standards have to be met by foreign products.

Under the GATS Market Access Article (XVI), quantitative restrictions on access to the market are also banned outright in principle: but only when governments elect to do so (see Section 4.5).

Transparency

The principle of transparency evolved only recently in the GATT, but is given a key role in the GATS, and is included in its Preamble along with progressive liberalisation.

The GATS Transparency Article (III) requires WTO Members to publish any regulation affecting the operation of the GATS before it comes into force and any international agreements related to trade in services into which they enter. Each year any changes to such laws together with any new ones have to be notified to the Council for Trade in Services (CTS) if they significantly affect GATS specific commitments. Members can also notify the CTS of any such measures taken by a Member considered to affect the operation of the GATS (so-called 'counter-notification').[13] Independent tribunals are called for, and Members must have 'enquiry points' that have promptly to supply information upon request by governments.

Market Access

The private sector pressed hard at the outset of the Uruguay Round for the right of establishment in principle – as is provided for in the EU Internal Market. This was not acceptable to the leading developing countries and in its place the artificial construct of Market Access was devised (by analogy with the border over which goods have to pass), which is not a principle but a legal 'hook' to provide for the description of the limitations, if any, imposed on any firm wishing to establish in the market, to which MFN applies. The GATS Article on Market Access (XVI), as mentioned, prohibits limitations (including 'economic needs tests') on the number of suppliers, the total value of transactions, quantity of output, and total number of foreign workers. Measures that restrict or require specific forms of legal entity and limitations in the participation of foreign capital for foreign direct investment are also prohibited. However, governments can continue to impose such conditions on firms – in sectors where they undertake to allow foreign firms to establish a presence – by inscribing them in their schedules of commitments.

Reciprocity

The WTO and GATS, like the original GATT, rely on a simultaneous set of bilateral negotiations to settle on the degree of liberalisation acceptable to each Member in any sector (the so-called 'request and offer' process). These conditions have then to be extended by right to every Member under the MFN principle.

This is the mercantilist approach where the bargains struck are seen as concessions wrung by Members from each other under pressure. The need for this pressure arises because each country's comparative advantage rests in different sectors and products, and varies over time, and so the win–win of trade is an overall optimisation resulting from larger gains and smaller losses. The losers hit by the subsequent need for structural adjustment will naturally resist. The broader the range of products brought into the negotiation, the greater the chance of each Member being able to gain, having more than offset any losses. Hence the traditional call for 'broad' or 'comprehensive' rounds of negotiations. This applies across the major parts of the economy: commodities, agriculture, manufacturing and services, as well as within each. The outcome is a 'broad reciprocity' as opposed to direct or strict reciprocity, the latter requiring exactly the same treatment for a particular product or service to be meted out by both parties to a bilateral deal.

How the GATS Goes Beyond the GATT

The GATS has to take into account a much wider policy canvas than the GATT. Services can be supplied by firms setting up in markets abroad by means of investment and people working temporarily, whether as employees of foreign affiliates or self-employed. Therefore the GATS rules relate not only to services which are exported across borders,[14] but more importantly also the supply of services by the producers when they are abroad, and thus its rules apply to investment in their foreign affiliates and to personnel working in them abroad. In effect the GATS constitutes the first multilateral investment treaty, even though it does not include some important features of most bilateral investment treaties (or BITs), such as repatriation of capital and expropriation.

The precept of progressive liberalisation enables governments to differentiate between different aspects of economy and between service sectors and adjust the rate and period of liberalisation in view of their structural priorities. Under the principle of progressive liberalisation governments can control the rate at which they open up their markets.

There is also a variety of exceptions to GATS disciplines, a few of which help governments to modulate the sequencing of liberalisation.

Domestic Regulation

The GATS Article on Domestic Regulation (VI) goes much further than the Article on Transparency (III) in its general effect, greatly impacting on the macro-regulatory structure of countries. It conditions any laws related to qualification requirements and procedures, technical standards and licensing requirements which must 'not constitute unnecessary barriers to trade in services'. According to the precedents of the GATT such 'necessary' measures must be the 'least trade restrictive' as is reasonable in the circumstances. This is probably impossible to measure, but a form of benchmarking or comparative assessment of best regulatory practices will have to be developed so as to reduce the transaction costs of business in meeting the requirements. This will call for the regular use of regulatory impact assessment techniques, which for services will have to become more sophisticated.

In addition the measures have to be 'based on objective and transparent criteria, such as competence and the ability to supply the service'[15] and be 'not more burdensome than necessary to ensure the quality of a service'. This implies that the costs imposed on suppliers of conforming should be the least possible.

In addition under Article VI where specific commitments have been undertaken any law 'affecting trade in services' has to be 'administered in a reasonable, objective and impartial manner', applications to be registered for supply have to be promptly dealt with, international standards conformed with and 'adequate procedures to verify the competence of professionals' have to be set up.

Recognition

The regulated professions pose a particular problem for the GATS principle of non-discrimination because it is inherently impossible to apply MFN to the recognition of 'the education or experience obtained, requirements met, or licences or certification granted in a particular country'. GATS therefore mandates that agreements to grant such recognition must not 'constitute a means of discrimination between countries ... or a disguised restriction on trade in services'. Furthermore, recognition 'should be based on multilaterally agreed criteria' and Members 'shall work in cooperation with relevant inter-governmental and non-governmental organisations towards the establishment and adoption of common international standards and criteria for recognition and common international standards for the practise of relevant services trades and professions'.

There are many professional and other institutions in each country that will have to take these GATS disciplines on board and adapt their procedures.

Movement of Workers ('Natural Persons')

Immigration authorities and labour ministries will be put under acute pressures by the growing need in the service sector for personnel to travel abroad to supply services, whether through subsidiaries established abroad or to assist the supply from the home base. The issues raised by the entry of migrant work-ers can have broad political ramifications as the successive referenda in Switzerland testify. Clearly the remit of the GATS is far removed from the issues of mass migration and the acceptance of refugees fleeing persecution and seeking asylum, but the same authorities are involved in controlling the movement of workers who wish to be present only for a year or two, and those who aim to become permanent residents.

Governments have a range of policies and techniques for approving entry terms for each individual, as groups of persons cannot be treated like classes of identical goods products. In some service sectors foreigners are banned from working, in others only enough are permitted entry to satisfy insufficient local supply (as judged under the so-called Economic Needs Tests) (ENTs), and conditions for issuing visas and work permits often include specific requirements about location, sector, occupation and employer.

The GATS disciplines will put pressure on the authorities to review their policies, since quotas and ENTs are prohibited, and to greatly simplify and speed up their procedures for approving and processing visas and work permits. However, the GATS negotiations have yet to address how the precepts of liberalisation can be translated into rules and guidance for these procedures.

Developing Further GATS Framework Disciplines

The GATS has a number of Articles with only vestigial or indicative content where further disciplines have yet to be developed. Although negotiations have in principle been started, on some only desultory progress has so far been made. Most work has been done on Emergency Safeguard Measures which would form a 'safety valve' whereby governments could take emergency corrective action should their liberalisation moves produce unforeseen and damaging effects on locally owned services firms. The issues have proved to be intensely difficult to handle and the final form of any disciplines is not yet clear. The safety valve must not form a loophole for protectionism, and should be carefully restricted, in view of the great flexibility built into the design of the GATS framework itself – particularly for developing countries to liberalise progressively at their own pace.

The Working Party on GATS Rules has found that the direct subsidising of exports of services is not prevalent, though subsidised export credits for construction projects do occur. Domestic subsidies for land transport can be aimed at encouraging the use of public transport to reap environmental benefits or for its provision in thinly populated areas. Subsidies for health and education can promote social stability and mobility, while subsidies to support the arts in general are common.

Competition Policy: a Key Framework Element

There is a wide variation among countries in how governments perceive the need for competition law and what its substance should comprise. Many developing countries do not yet have any competition laws and a former IMF economist has stated that: 'The key is less an issue of ownership than of competition . . . so there is more to it for developing countries than just granting access to their markets: a foreign-owned private monopoly has to be spectacularly efficient in a technical sense if it is to be the best way of providing a service. Rather market access must be tailored and supported by complementary policies in a way that increases competition'.[16]

The existence of basic competition laws and an independent competition authority to enforce them are essential, to ensure fair play between firms, whether foreign or locally owned. The design of competition laws should avoid the need for separate sectoral legislation wherever possible, so as to avoid duplication or different tests and standards.

INTERNATIONAL AND NATIONAL INSTITUTIONS: THE GATS IMPACT ON THE MAJOR SECTORS

The GATS will pose challenges to the overall regulatory structure of countries, and highlight the importance of good governance and the quality of regulation. Greater application of the transparency principle will have a beneficial effect on rule making, as will the carrying out of regulatory impact assessments called for in good governance practice, and implied in the GATS rule requiring that the least trade-restrictive measures be selected.

It will especially throw into clear relief the need for developing countries to be assisted with their capacity building. They will have to devise and enact laws for the regulation of their services infrastructures and set up independent regulatory authorities for the major sectors and a competition authority with sufficient political backing and powers of enforcement. This is a difficult and long haul, which cannot be avoided if such countries wish to attract foreign investment and join the world trading community and thus reap the benefits of increased resources for the attainment of their highest social objectives.

Now we can look ahead to consider in which service sectors the new GATS rules are likely to impact most, and thus which international and national institutions may have to modify their current practices. Not all service sectors, though, have international institutions yet, whether for inter-governmental cooperation or created by the private sector. The major sectors are taken in turn, in the order in which most countries have listed them.

What it is very difficult to foresee is the specific effect on international services trade for any sector in any one country that liberalisation will have (that is due to the removal or modification of regulatory barriers). The principal determinants of trade are the existence of national borders, distance, and differences in currencies, language and historical social links, on which GATS does not touch. Other factors that block liberalisation are internal structural characteristics, state ownership, licensed monopolies, defects in competition policy and so on, and again these are off-bounds for the GATS. There is no doubt that such factors can cause major problems.

Professional and Business Services [1][17]

The regulatory setting for these services divides between a group of mainly professional services that have been highly regulated – or self-regulated – for a very long time, and a wide range of business services mostly with no regulation specific to their activities.

The regulated professions

The regulated professions will feel the impact of GATS rules on their traditional aims and procedures. Some professional associations were founded as long as 150 years ago. In many countries the government directly controls these professions either at the federal or provincial level. Their principal aim is to protect the central interests of consumers such as their health and assets, although in some cases it is true that such codes can be unduly restrictive of competition and even smack of featherbedding. Sociologists also point to the value for societal stability of independent groups of professionals of integrity which are not subject to political party control and commercial interests, and provide crucial inputs for welfare, economic efficiency and innovation. The regulation of the professions therefore poses some of the toughest problems for liberalisation.

Governments and professional associations set standards for education and practical training which are tested by examinations. Practitioners are registered and licensed, and must abide by codes of ethics and behaviour. They are held accountable and can be disciplined or banned from practice.

In the EU it took up to 40 years to devise ways of liberalising the provision of professional services within the Internal Market, and the lessons learned this hard way are relevant to the GATS. Full harmonisation is difficult or impossible, for example, of syllabuses for basic education, professional training and practical experience, and the years spent on each. The most that can be done is to settle on some minimum harmonisation and then agree to recognise the rest as equivalent, even though clearly different.

The only way to assure redress for any damage to the interests of a consumer caused by the negligence of a foreign professional no longer in the jurisdiction, and for the proper disciplining of that person, is by mandatory and continual close cooperation between the competent regulatory authorities – as is now provided for in the EU directive for the legal profession that entered into force this year. Such a solution seems well beyond the reach of the GATS at this juncture.

Not unsurprisingly there is room for many differences of standards, scope and procedure between professions and across countries. These can only be resolved by negotiating mutual recognition agreements (MRAs), involving partial harmonisation and recognition of the equivalence of everything else even though different. A mixture of ex ante and ex post rules and procedures is to be found in the most advanced mutual recognition agreements.

Postal Services [2]

The rate at which governments privatise the basic postal services will largely condition how GATS disciplines will apply to the core services. Privatisation is a sovereign policy decision with which the GATS does not interfere. The public postal monopolies, as successor to the King's Messengers, have been cooperating since 1874 through the Universal Postal Union, which was created by the Treaty of Berne.

Universal service obligations are imposed upon postal services for such matters as the frequency of mail deliveries and pickups, and the number of mailboxes and post offices in rural areas. However, the scope of the monopoly is usually quite tightly circumscribed by reference to the size, shape and cost of letters and parcels. In most countries there is free competition for other items, with many delivery firms competing nationally and a few regionally, though there is only a handful offering global services.

The private express courier firms complain that competition is not fair. The state postal monopoly may internally cross-subsidise its own services which compete with them. There may be burdensome charges on the remailing of letters collected into bulk abroad for onward delivery individually in destination states. The onus here is on the competition authority to assure a level playing field.

The GATS Articles on 'Monopolies and Exclusive Service Providers' (VIII) and 'Business Practices' (IX) impose little in the way of disciplines, but they might be built up in future, and specific rules aimed at reducing anti-competitive behaviour might be agreed sector by sector, as in the case of basic telecommunications.[18]

The inter-modal linkages between private express couriers and the state transport systems can be a source of friction, for instance for the air cargo legs operated by flag airlines, the operation of their own rail wagons on state tracks, and restrictions on the pick up abroad of loads by trucks for the return journey home.

The state postal service may have an old boy's agreement for preferential treatment with the customs authority and the other agencies that check on parcels, not only to collect duties, but for reasons of public safety, decency, human and plant health risks and criminal activities. Postal institutions will progressively be disciplined by GATS rules, and they will be under pressure to eliminate special or preferential treatment in order to achieve a level competitive playing field.

Telecoms

Privatisation is proceeding apace in many countries, but for fixed line voice telephony the most durable monopoly relates to the 'local loop' – the pair of copper wires that go into the premises of organisations and homes. Until access is opened up to competition the sector cannot be fully liberalised.[19] For mobile services – the fastest expanding part – the allocation of scarce frequencies (a public good) is a central issue, and how governments can best capture the monopoly rent potential, such as through the auction of third generation licences which recently netted some European governments sizeable windfalls.

The WTO has developed links with the International Telegraph Union (ITU – formed in 1865) and recognises its technical standards for 'inter-operation', which are set to enable the international systems to function. The ITU also maintains an artificial construct of notional accounting rates for international calls, with the cost of each call split equally, so resulting in a balance of money to be paid by the country making the most calls to the other. The less developed the country is the more it receives in this way due to the higher notional cost charges still in force and because far fewer calls originate there.

Technological change is inducing governments to reconsider this system, which will push down the rates to levels more closely reflecting actual costs of transmission. For developing countries the transition may pose problems for the public exchequer used to gaining from this indirect form of aid.

As GATS rules bite and the sector regulators set specific rules we will hear more about such issues as: universal service obligation, access to networks, inter-connection charges, price setting for better services such as ISDN, resale of bulk capacity, competition with Internet Service Providers, and Applications Service Providers.

To assure fair competition ensues liberalisation, the main GATS tool is the Basic Telecommunications Reference Paper concerning a telecoms regulatory framework. Agreed in April 1996 it consists of a set of principles covering such matters as competition safeguards, interconnection guarantees, transparent licensing processes and the independence of regulators. It includes language on pricing, such as 'cost-oriented rates' and connection 'charges that reflect the cost', and it bans 'anti-competitive cross-subsidisation'. A broad majority of signatories have inserted commitments on these lines, and thus governments have rendered themselves liable to multilateral dispute settlement on substantive and procedural aspects of competition policy.

Audio-Visual Services [2 D]

Broadcasting is regulated due to scarcity of ether frequencies and the need to control content for public morality or religious stability. Advertisers are big users of broadcasting and other media, and thus their advertising agencies as well as the providers of programming content may be regulated. Often the nationality of those who feature in the advertisements is controlled and foreign production firms banned, or restricted to providing a minority of the material in the advertisement. State-controlled agencies which place advertisements in the media and apply monopoly prices with no competition can create unfair situations. Such regulations and practices are, however, disappearing quite fast.

The core issues revolve around the cultural dimensions: subsidies for national film and TV productions, and local content quotas, which presumably will remain exempted from GATS rules, though not the monopolistic practices of cinema chain owners.

Construction and Related Engineering Services [3]

Construction sites are regulated for safety reasons (for example for the risk to operatives, and transport access) and the buildings as constructed are regulated for health, structural, safety and fire precautions and so on. Such laws must not now discriminate against foreign construction firms, foreign labour and foreign building owners. The same goes for regulations pertaining to the import of construction equipment (and often its re-export), and the materials and equipment incorporated into the building, to which undertakings under the General Agreement on Tariffs and Trade may additionally apply.

The most high profile issue is the entry of foreign construction site workers, possibly in large numbers. They pose potential public order and immigration problems and liberalisation is difficult to conceive except for small groups.

The professional aspects of design and supervision of construction may be regulated in many countries.

Distribution [4]

Although the wholesale and retail aspects of distribution are quite distinct, many of regulatory issues arise from similar causes: the need for land and buildings which are controlled by regulations for town and country planning purposes and transport access.

Trade liberalisation will take second place to planning policies based on societal objectives and expressed through land-use zoning and limits on numbers and size of super- and hypermarkets, and wholesale storage and distribution units. However, the regulations deemed necessary should be the least trade restrictive practicable, as required by the GATS.

Environmental Services [6]

Environmental services are involved with local, regional and global environmental problems. Consultancy advice helps governments solve the tough issues posed by pollution, environmental degradation, tourist intensity and so on. Any foreign expertise can be supplied cross-border and is not usually regulated.

The pace of privatisation and the degree of outsourcing affects the operation of water and sewage treatment, and refuse disposal facilities. Land-use issues arise for sites where the processes are carried on. The degree of liberalisation will be subject to environmental standards. The WTO (including the GATS) does not set such standards, but can recognise truly international standards as legitimate and thus not unnecessarily trade distortive.

Financial Services [7]

The financial services sector has a truly unique dimension that faces us with the prospect for potential societal collapse like no other: that is the possibility for rapidly spreading contagion from defaults across the three principal sectors – banking, securities and insurance – and across national boundaries.

There is an overriding need for prudential control of the institutions and their managers to avoid or lessen the damage done by systemic failure at the national and global levels. The necessary standards, norms, and guidelines are being devised, under instruction from Finance Ministers, by the Financial Stability Forum, a recent expansion of cooperation among regulators and supervisors at the global level, in cooperation with the World Bank and IMF. To an extent not yet properly addressed, the WTO should also coordinate its activities here, though this may not be as easy as it sounds for traditional institutional turf reasons.

It is clear that no liberalisation of trade in financial services can proceed without the buy-in of the prudential supervisors, who themselves will have to coordinate their activities ever more closely. Their aim of preventing systemic collapse and promoting liquid markets with full transparency of information must remain paramount.

The GATS Annex on Financial Services, which is binding on all Members, includes a crucial feature usually referred to as the 'prudential carve-out'. This provides that a Member government 'shall not be prevented from taking measures for prudential reasons, including the protection of investors, depositors, policy holders or persons to whom fiduciary duty is owed by a financial services supplier, or to ensure the integrity and stability of the financial system'. The only condition laid on this broad exception is that 'Where such measures do not conform with the provisions of [the GATS] they shall not be used as a means of avoiding the Member's commitments and obligations' under the GATS.

The services negotiators will be wary of attempting to reduce the scope of this carve-out, but it would seem necessary to consider whether financial services regulators and supervisors can adopt and publish clearly stated principles and guidelines, hopefully converging on high, internationally agreed standards, so as to increase transparency.

Health Care and Social Services [8][23]

Governments provide basic health care, usually free (or nearly so) for their citizens. In addition there are privately supplied services which are regulated in the public interest. The balance and extent of the two vary as between countries, with a certain degree of outsourcing on some national agendas, including to foreign firms. This causes the labour unions to resist any reduction in the scale or scope of publicly provided services, due to the fear over loss of jobs and union power, and their concern to prevent the lowering of standards.

In one or two countries even the provision of prison services are to a limited extent privatised, and security regulations and public fears play an even stronger role.

Tourism and Travel-Related [9]

Many countries have prohibitions or restrictions on foreigners acting as guides and hosts within their territory, or on national heritage sites. These bans are related to cultural values, language and history. It does not seem likely that the GATS rules will have much impact on such sensitive cultural matters

Hotels and Restaurants

The regulations related to hotels and restaurants are generally similar to those of retail outlets, but the degree and timescale of liberalisation may have a more urgent dynamic in some districts due to the desire to promote tourism.

Transport – Air, Maritime and Rail [11]

Merchandise trade between countries involves some form of transport, whether by land, sea or air. In the EU, for example, the policy of forging a backbone network of connected routes is of major importance for the operation of the Internal Market. All will be affected by GATS disciplines. The associated flow of information that parallels these activities is carried by the postal, courier and telecoms networks.

Some of the international institutions that may be affected have a long history such as the International Union of Railways, the International Road Federation and International Road Union. The UN International Civil Aviation Organisation for governments and International Air Transport Association for airlines were created more recently.[21] All have been responsible for coordinating the activities of national organisations – often state-owned. Privatisation, re-regulation and deregulation, and resultant liberalisation, of national systems are causing changes to their status and activities.

Government ownership of airlines, airports and air control has been the general pattern for the past half century. Since the 1940s governments have concluded nearly 4000 bilateral agreements and approved schedules and prices for their flag carriers. These fares are proposed by IATA Traffic Conferences in an uncompetitive way that has not always served consumers' interests well. Uncompetitive practices naturally were spawned also for the various ground-based support services such as ground handling, storage, communications, security and so on.

At present most air transport activities are 'carved out' of the GATS leaving behind a small set of peripheral activities,[22] and there can be problems even with those, such as when air lines and travel agents are forced to use national computer reservation systems. Activities that could be subjected to GATS rules might include airline catering and ground handling, and even cargo and charter services, as proposed by some negotiators. IATA is strongly opposed to ceding action on further liberalisation to the GATS. Multilateral liberalisation will depend on the will of governments to dismantle the bilateral agreements in favour of GATS disciplines.

Air transport combines many of the most intense regulatory issues because public safety demands high standards for the pilots, planes, airport equipment and air traffic controllers. Airport landing slots are a crucial scarce public resource especially at peak times. Public safety will always be paramount, and more airport slots cannot be clutched out of thin air.

During the Uruguay Round negotiations on maritime transport in 1993 the EU suggested that the wide range of activities in this sector be grouped into three categories comprising the main transport for freight and passengers between countries across oceans, various auxiliary services,[23] and port services.

Most seaborne trade consists of the carriage of oil, iron ore, coal and grain, for which there is intense competition among fleets which often have specialised ships. On some ocean routes cartel-like action by shipping lines may act to restrict price and service competition and the entry of competitors for general cargo.

The fastest growing trade is in container traffic, although not a large percentage of overall shipping ton-miles. Here too there is plenty of competition. Door to door container service providers are keen on freeing up the various transit legs that constitute multi-modal forms of delivery, which is where the GATS will have to concentrate its efforts.

The liberalisation of cabotage (that is services between the ports of one country), has only been put on the table so far by a few countries.

The ownership and operation of seaports raises key issues because they are still mainly publicly owned.[24] Some have been privatised and the operations and equipment have been handed over to private firms in many more. Dock worker union sensitivities have played a big role in slowing the pace of liberalisation. However, the pressure on them is intense because governments can see that inefficient port services impose a significant cost burden on imports and exports alike, the latter often a high priority for economic development.

The infrastructure of links with seaports for rail and road, and for storage and handling capacity, are crucial, too, and will be impacted by GATS liberalisation commitments. Institutional change may be rather slow and its degree conditioned by spending on infrastructure and the power of the stevedoring unions.

In most countries the railways are publicly owned and governments are the sole providers of investment in their fixed facilities, such as track and signalling. This also goes for much of the rolling stock, though here privately leased or owned equipment is significant in some countries, and the related investment is from private sources. Privatisation is occurring where governments seek to encourage greater investment and competition among services running over their tracks. GATS rules will impinge on this sector to the extent that government monopolies do not prevail.

Electronic Commerce

Electronic commerce is not a sector of itself but relies on the support of many interrelated services and the physical infrastructure for its 'transport'. Much of the latter is still owned by public network operators. However, the broadband Internet backbone structure that transports our vital information is privately owned – in contrast to the road and rail systems. The owners interconnect with each other (often reciprocally carrying traffic for free) and charge telecoms network operators and business users. Domestic consumers get charged indirectly by the telecoms companies.

Anything delivered electronically constitutes a service, and is thus subject to GATS disciplines, even if it can be incorporated into a physical product at a later stage (like a book or CD). There is a whole raft of issues that touch on keeping the Internet open for trade, but many of them fall outside the remit of the GATS. They include privacy, child morality, taxation, encryption, secure payment systems, jurisdiction for redress and so on.

The private sector is keen to ensure that within the bounds of the GATS remit, a 'cluster' of services that support electronic commerce (principally telecoms, financial services and transport) are liberalised in step so as not to hinder its rapid development.

FINAL REFLECTION

An apt quotation on which to end is taken from an article by a senior Canadian negotiator who wrote: 'In sum, today's trade negotiations are about good governance and democratic development: the creation of stable and transparent supervisory structures that ultimately provide a non-corrupt and predictable environment for traders, investors and consumers' (Fried, 2000). Let us hope the GATS will play a central role in 'a system of international governance geared to sustainable growth and sustainable development', as he put it.

NOTES

1. This section draws on 'Oppenheim's International Law – ninth edition, Volume 1, Peace, Introduction and Part I' Edited by Sir Robert Jennings QC and Sir Arthur Watts KCMG QC. I am grateful to Nina Hall for assistance with my commentary on the legal scene.
2. There is no recognised hierarchy of rules of law in international law – with the exception of *jus cogens* (see Section 2.3): the WTO treaty and the UN Treaty are on a par with each other.
3. *Jus cogens* is the only real category of 'superior' rules in that treaty law cannot derogate from them. They include, for instance, anti-slavery, human rights, genocide, and so on.
4. In some legal systems the WTO agreements are 'self-executing': they have the force of domestic law with direct application.
5. Scientists lay great stress on their honesty, of course.
6. The WTO Agreement on Trade Related Intellectual Property Rights 'entrench[es] individual property rights in its preamble . . . And it also provides for the right of a foreign corporation to take action in the host country in order to safeguard those rights. So, it is about as intrusive and as radically different from the GATT as one could imagine' (Ostry, 2000).
7. This quotation and the substance of this paragraph are from Daniel Esty commenting on Keohane and Nye, Harvard, June 2000.
8. The ECJ, or other regional body, would have first to consider whether it was the proper forum, given the WTO treaty. The points in this paragraph and footnote are from Nina Hall, in correspondence.
9. 'Few people seem aware of the fact that the WTO's entire budget is less than the travel expenses of the IMF, and three times smaller than that of the World Wildlife Fund (WWF)' (Ostry, 2000).
10. The quotation here, and in the next paragraph, are from Robert Hudec commenting on a paper by Keohane and Nye, Harvard, June 2000.
11. Before the start of the Uruguay Round, Long (1985) wrote 'In fact, the Quad countries are virtually the only trading partners which are dealt with on an MFN basis'.
12. When the GATS entered into force Members could initially suspend MFN for specified situations – often to exempt specially favourable treatment existing under bilateral treaties. This also applies to acceding new Members.
13. In the GATS the term 'measure' means 'any measure by a Member, whether in the form of a law, regulation, rule, procedure, decision, administrative action, or any other form' Article on Definitions (XXVIII).
14. It also covers services supplied to customers who are outside their national territory when consuming a service.
15. And if altered, must not 'nullify or impair' existing specific commitments.
16. L. Alan Winters, University of Sussex, discussing a paper by Jeffrey A. Frankel at the conference on 'Efficiency, Equity and Legitimacy', Harvard June 2000.
17. The numbers in square brackets for each sector are those given in a classification list devised by the GATT Secretariat in 1991 – the so-called 'GNS W 120' list.
18. These rules are contained in the Basic Telecommunications Reference Paper, to which WTO Members can elect to be bound, in whole or in part.
19. This is of growing importance as ways are found of increasing the 'bandwidth' of the copper wires without the need to replace them.
20. Similar issues arise in the case of Education Services [5].
21. The Convention on International Civil Aviation was signed in Chicago in 1944. The ICAO functioned provisionally from 1945 to 1947, when it came into force and became a specialised agency of the UN linked to the Economic and Social Council. IATA was founded in Havana in 1945 for inter-airline cooperation and now has 230 members from over 130 countries.
22. The Annex on Air Transport Services restricts the application of the GATS to 'measures affecting (a) aircraft repair and maintenance services; (b) the selling and marketing of air transport services; [and] (c) computer reservation system (CRS) services'.
23. Including cargo handling, storage and container stations, freight forwarding, and customs clearance.

24. However, many specialised ports for gas, oil, ores, cement and coal are private and not open for general trade.

REFERENCES

Financial Times (2000), Leader, 24 April.

Fried, J.T. (2000), 'Governance in the Global Age: a Public International Law Perspective' in R.B. Porter and P. Sauvé (eds), *Seattle, the WTO, and the Future of the Multilateral Trading System*, Harvard: The Center for Business and Government, Harvard University.

Hudec, R.E. (2000), 'A comment on Robert O.Keohane and Joseph S. Nye Jr "The club model of multilateral co-operation and the WTO: problems of democratic legitimacy", mimeo UNCTAD Conference, 'Efficiency, Equity and Legitimacy: The Multilateral Trading System at the Millennium', Harvard University, 1–2 June.

Keohane, R.O. and Nye, J.S. (2000), 'The club model of multilateral co-operation and the WTO: problems of democratic legitimacy', mimeo UNCTAD Conference, 'Efficiency, Equity and Legitimacy: The Multilateral Trading System at the Millennium', Harvard University, 1–2 June.

Long, O. (1985), *Law and its limitations in the GATT Multilateral Trade System*, Dordrecht: Martinus Nijhoff Publishers, Kluwer Press.

Ostry, S. (2000), 'Making Sense of it all: a Post-mortem on the Meaning of Seattle', in R.B. Porter and P. Sauvé (eds), *Seattle, the WTO, and the Future of the Multilateral Trading System*, Harvard: The Center for Business and Government, Harvard University.

Ricupero, R. (2000), 'A Development Round: converting rhetoric into substance', mimeo UNCTAD Conference, 'Efficiency, Equity and Legitimacy: The Multilateral Trading System at the Millennium', Harvard University, 1–2 June.

Stibbe Simont Monahan Duhot (2000), *The Stibbe Report*, Vol VIII: 1, Brussels, April. See www.sibbe.com

Tyler, C. (2000), 'The area of moral confusion', *Financial Times Weekend*, 22/23 April 2000.

11. GATS 2000: the issues at stake, an EC perspective

Sergio Balibrea*

The GATS (the General Agreement on Trade in Services) is the first multi-lateral and legally enforceable agreement on trade and establishment in the services sector. It is a breakthrough agreement as it brings services within the scope of the world trading system. At the same time, it provides a framework for future and regular negotiations on the further reduction of barriers to trade in services that have triggered a new round this year. This chapter reviews the state of these service negotiations (GATS 2000 negotiations) and provides my personal opinion from the perspective of the European Community (EC).

THE IMPORTANCE OF SERVICES IN THE ECONOMY

A few facts explain the importance of services in today's economy and, in particular, for the EC. Services are the largest sector in most world economies. In the EC, they account for around two-thirds of Gross Domestic Product (GDP), far ahead of agriculture and goods (for instance, in France: 72 per cent services, 26 per cent industry, 2 per cent agriculture; in Germany: 44 per cent services, 55 per cent industry, 1 per cent agriculture). It should be noted that this proportion is not so different for many developing countries (for instance, in India: 45 per cent services, 30 per cent industry, 25 per cent agriculture; in Brazil: 57 per cent services, 35 per cent industry, 8 per cent agriculture).

At the same time, the importance of services in world trade continually increases: between 1986 and 1996, they expanded at an annual rate of 8.7 per cent, slightly faster than the growth of trade in goods (at 8.1 per cent). The EC is the top world exporter and importer of services, with 25 per cent of world

* Sergio Balibrea is Head of Sector at the European Commission, Directorate General for Trade, Trade in Services Unit, Brussels (E-mail: *sergio.balibrea@cec.eu.int*). The views expressed in this chapter are those of the author and do not necessarily represent the views of the European Commission.

trade in services (while it covers 20 per cent of world trade in goods), compared with 22 per cent in the US and 7 per cent for Japan.

Nevertheless, there is a gap between the importance of services in any given national economy and its weight in terms of international trade. In the EC, for instance, the predominance of services in the economy (two-thirds of total GDP) is not fully reflected in terms of trade (only 25 per cent of EC total exports are made up of services). The same happens in many countries with a strong services industry (in the US, only 23 per cent of all exports are services). As it is in the services industry that the majority of jobs are created, the reduction of such a gap will benefit welfare globally.

One reason for the traditional insufficiency in trade in services worldwide is the absence of a well-structured legal set of international trade rules that could provide legal certainty to traders and consumers. While GATT was created in 1949 to regulate trade in goods, nothing similar existed for trade in services before the Uruguay Round was completed in 1994. The GATS entered into force but there is still a long way to go before traders of services can obtain similar legal coverage to that of traders of goods. This is mainly because the GATS is a rather 'à la carte' agreement, which allows for 'specific' liberalisation commitments applicable only to the extent that a WTO Member has accepted them (see more details below). These individual commitments are insufficiently developed to date and improving them is one of the main objectives of the new services negotiations.

WHAT IS THE GATS?

The GATS is the international agreement regulating trade in services. It has wide-ranging coverage as, (a) it regulates trade in all services sectors, (b) it covers all ways or modes to provide a service, and (c) it covers all types of domestic measures.

(a) The GATS Regulates Trade in all Services Sectors

GATS embrace all commercially 'tradable' services with no services sector excluded (except for some sub-sectors of air transport). The sectors identified so far in the 'standard' WTO classification are: business services (professional services, computer services), communication services (postal, telecommunication), construction, distribution, education, environmental services, financial services, health-related and social services, tourism and travel-related services, recreational, cultural and sporting services, and transport services. In addition, the category 'other' would include new services or services not included above, such as energy.

(b) The GATS Covers all Ways or Modes to Provide a Service

These are mode 1: simple cross-border supply (for example by post, e-mail, telephone); mode 2: supply on the domestic market to a foreign consumer (for example, services provided to a foreign tourist visiting our country); mode 3: supply through the establishment of commercial presence abroad; mode 4: cross-border movement of the person providing the service.

(c) The GATS Covers all Types of Domestic Measures

The GATS covers all types of domestic measures influencing trade in services, from laws to secondary legislation, administrative guidelines and all types of administrative actions. The obligations of the GATS apply – like those of the GATT – to all levels of government, that is to the central, regional and local authorities of each WTO Member.

In its application, the GATS distinguishes between, (a) 'standard' obligations which apply to all WTO Members, and (b) 'specific' liberalisation commitments which apply only if, and to the extent that, a WTO Member has accepted them for itself

(a) 'Standard' Obligations

The most important 'standard' obligation is that of most-favoured-nation (or MFN) treatment. It forbids WTO Members from discriminating in any way between services and services providers from different countries: all should be given equal treatment and granted all trade preferences as provided to any other country. This obligation applies to all sectors, even if a country has not made specific liberalisation commitments (see point (b) below).

Exporters of services also need a transparent economic and legal framework in which to operate on the foreign market. The GATS therefore contains 'standard' obligations to publish all measures related to trade in services and to ensure recourse to appropriate remedies against administrative and court decisions for foreign services suppliers. At the same time, the GATS expressly recognises the national sovereign right to regulate, however qualified and restricted in view of the goal of liberalisation.

Finally, all WTO Members have to participate in the regular rounds of WTO services negotiations to be held every five years with the aim of achieving a progressively higher level of liberalisation (in particular on the 'specific' commitments, see below).

(b) 'Specific' Liberalisation Commitments

Apart from the obligations above, which are binding on all WTO countries, all other GATS commitments (on a sector-by-sector basis) only go as far as each WTO Member has accepted them, usually following a trade negotiation. A country can undertake commitments to open its market to foreign suppliers (market access commitments) and/or to provide similar treatment to that granted to domestic suppliers (national treatment commitments). These commitments are consigned in a 'schedule of specific commitments', different for each WTO Member. There is no binding minimum standard for the number and nature of the sectors to be included. Some countries have included almost all the major sectors in their schedules, whilst other have only opened a minimum number of sectors and to different extents. The current services round will aim at increasing the commitments accepted by WTO Members.

WHY A NEW ROUND OF SERVICES NEGOTIATION?

There are two reasons for launching GATS 2000: a procedural one (this was agreed at the end of the Uruguay Round) and, most importantly, a substantive one (to fill the gaps in the GATS left unresolved by the Uruguay Round).

The Uruguay Round Mandated Agenda

As a result of the Uruguay Round negotiations, WTO Members committed themselves under Article XIX of the GATS to resume negotiations on all services sectors no later than 1 January 2000 – the 'GATS 2000' negotiations. On this basis, all WTO Members are committed to starting a new round of negotiations, with a view to achieving a progressively higher level of liberalisation. These negotiations have to be comprehensive and cover all sectors. They emphasise the need to take into account the interests of all participants on a mutually advantageous basis in order to secure an overall balance of rights and obligations. In particular, this entails that the needs of developing Members be given due consideration.

It is on this legal basis that the 'GATS 2000' negotiations began on 1 January 2000 as mandated by Art. XIX of the GATS.

The Shortcomings of the GATS

Although the basic rules and principles for the liberalisation of trade in services were included in the GATS, many issues were left unresolved. In fact, the main objective in the Uruguay Round was to lay down the principles and the architecture of the services agreement (MFN, transparency, commitments to market access and national treatment). As the work remained inconclusive, both in the sectoral coverage of commitments and on horizontal rules, Members agreed to close the negotiations and set a date for further negotiations on market opening.

Gaps in the Sectoral Coverage of Commitments by WTO Members

During the Uruguay Round there were insufficient negotiations sector by sector. The final outcome appears more a collection of the commitments that countries were ready to undertake than the result of real negotiations. As a result, while the GATS covers all services sectors, only a few WTO Members entered commitments in a comprehensive way.

As of today, only one-third of WTO Members has committed more than 50 per cent of all sectors and sub-sectors. Most WTO Members (two-thirds) have committed less than 50 per cent and, out of these, most WTO Members have committed even less than 15 per cent. These figures include the results of the two successful sectoral negotiations concluded after the Uruguay Round (financial services and basic telecommunications) which makes the remaining work even more obvious. A good example of insufficient commitments is the transport sector. Although this is the largest sector worldwide (25 per cent of trade in services), it has only very patchy coverage by Members, with significant absences among some of these. This is partially due to the failure on maritime transport negotiations, which were suspended in 1996 without any agreement.

As a result, the GATS currently looks very incomplete in terms of individual sectoral commitments and the advantages of the agreement are still more potential than real for many sectors and countries. The gap between the comprehensive coverage of the GATS and the limited commitments undertaken by WTO Members as a whole needs to be narrowed. This is all the more necessary as international trade in services is already much more liberal in reality than what WTO Members have actually committed themselves to under the GATS. There is, therefore, a need to increase the number and quality of commitments across countries, services sectors and modes of supply.

Unfinished Horizontal Rules

The GATS is a young agreement and a number of areas affecting all services sectors need to be considered. As the work could not be completed at the Uruguay Round, it was agreed to continue after it. GATS 2000 should, therefore, tackle the following horizontal areas:

(a) Domestic regulation

The need for regulatory disciplines to underpin market access and national treatment commitments appears increasingly important. It would be worthless to negotiate market access commitments internationally which could then be wiped out by local restrictive regulations, notably on licensing of services suppliers. The disciplines based on Article VI.4 of the GATS should be strengthened. The aim should be to ensure a transparent and predictable regulatory environment that can provide legal certainty and confidence to services suppliers, investors, users and consumers. Domestic regulation should be 'transparent', in particular regarding the public policy objectives of regulations and the procedures leading to their adoption and promulgation. It should also be 'necessary', in the sense that domestic regulations must be adequate and proportional to the objective sought and the least trade restrictive.

(b) Safeguards

Some WTO Members consider that countries should have a mechanism to intervene if emergencies occur which seriously affect their services trade position, notably as a result of a surge of imports. The discussion is difficult as, not only is there no agreement on the need for such an instrument, but also its operation would be very complicated in the case of services. Indeed, not only are statistics patchy, rendering it difficult to measure whether any conditions to trigger the mechanism would be met, but the consequences of a safeguard clause could affect existing foreign investments. Discussions in the WTO have been more substantial since February 2000 but it is far from certain that it will be possible to finish work by the target date of end 2000 and discussions may continue through 2001.

(c) Subsidies

A subsidy arises when a government or other public body confers a financial benefit on a specific producer or group of producers. Under the GATS, trade in services does not benefit from specific subsidies rules. Article XV of the GATS merely provides the right to consult in certain situations and a commitment to negotiate specific rules later. It is not possible just to transpose GATT subsidy rules to the services area as the GATS architecture is very different from that of the GATT. Subsidies may be a substantive subject for discussion in GATS 2000 as work on this issue has seen very little progress so far. It may at least be possible to define those subsidies that are acceptable in all cases and those which should always be prohibited.

(d) Government procurement

At this stage, services that are supplied under government authority are excluded from the liberalisation. This will require more attention as in many services sectors much of the trade is carried out through public procurement procedures and the need for rules compatible and coherent with those negotiated on goods should be examined.

PREPARING AND LAUNCHING GATS 2000 NEGOTIATIONS

Given that there was agreement in principle to resume negotiations on services, a preparatory process was set in motion before the actual launching of the negotiations. Preparations consisted mainly of, first, an information exchange programme, whereby the WTO Secretariat and Members circulated a large number of documents setting out the state of play of liberalisation in all services sectors since the entry into force of the GATS. This was completed in early 1999. Second, an assessment of services trade during 1999. This consisted of several sessions in the WTO during which documents issued by WTO Secretariat and UNCTAD were discussed. Third, the preparation of the negotiating guidelines, that is, a set of principles under which negotiations would be conducted. WTO Members circulated a number of submissions in 1999 showing a remarkable degree of convergence. The consolidation work was easy and, by November 1999, a text was almost ready for adoption. All in all, the preparatory work before Seattle was more than sufficient to launch a successful services round.

As explained above, the resumption of negotiations on services had been agreed at the Uruguay Round. The same had been agreed for agriculture. Both areas formed the so-called 'mandated agenda' for a new round of WTO negotiations.

In October 1999, the EC formally decided to push for the launch of a wider round of trade negotiations in Seattle (at the 3rd Ministerial WTO Conference, from 30 November to 3 December 1999). The round had to be comprehensive and cover not only agriculture and services, but also investment, competition, trade facilitation, tariffs, environment, intellectual property, government procurement and technical barriers to trade. It was argued that a comprehensive trade round offered the best way to take account of the trade interests of the WTO membership as a whole.

Although other WTO Members supported the principle of a comprehensive round, there was no agreement on such a round in Seattle. As a result, only negotiations on services and agriculture were initiated on 1 January 2000. In procedural terms, the main setback for GATS 2000 (aside from the absence of a comprehensive round) was that the negotiating guidelines, notably a calendar and a deadline for negotiations, could not be agreed in Seattle. This remained open to be rubber-stamped during the year 2000.

Nevertheless, as could be expected, the start of negotiation in early 2000 was slow not least because some issues relating to the procedural launch of the negotiations had to be re-discussed at the request of some countries. Also, Seattle obviously had and has an impact. The absence of a comprehensive round has also made the link between services and agriculture more direct, which is not always to the advantage of GATS 2000.

In July 2000, a 'roadmap decision' was agreed at WTO, after long and painful formal and informal discussions. This had the value of being the first agreement on a way forward in the services negotiations and was very positive for confidence-building. Nevertheless, its practical benefits, in relation to the previously agreed mandate to launch GATS 2000, are very limited.

The decisive push to enter into meaningful negotiations could come after an agreement on 'negotiating guidelines'. These would be more precise than the 'roadmap decision' and would notably set deadlines for the negotiation. In this respect, the EC has proposed that countries submit initial proposals or requests for higher levels of liberalisation by December 2000 if possible (and in any case by March 2001 at the latest), and that the date for lodging initial offers is agreed by March 2001. It is not yet clear what could be a realistic deadline to conclude the negotiations. Some consider that negotiations can last for three to five years, to finish between 2003 and 2005. Whatever the date, it is likely that the timing will not be decided by the services dynamic alone but also by other external factors, such as the agriculture negotiations, or the launching in the near future of a wider round of trade negotiations.

Following the adoption of the negotiating guidelines, we would then move to sectoral market access negotiations as soon as possible. This is indeed where the real momentum can be created (the successful telecommunications and financial services negotiations being a case in point), and where the concrete value of any deals may appear to WTO Members. The trigger of these market access negotiations will be the submission of initial requests, possibly at the end of the year 2000, that will be continued by the submission of offers, possibly at the end of 2001. Additionally, rule-making should be conducted in parallel.

Throughout this process, the European Commission will negotiate on behalf of the 15 EU Member States, on the basis of a mandate received in October 1999, which is as follows:

> Negotiations should be comprehensive and bring about a deeper and broader package of improved commitments across services sectors from all WTO Members to market access and national treatment. Current imbalances in commitments across countries and services sectors should be reduced. Negotiations should also aim at strengthening of the GATS disciplines with the aim of ensuring transparent and predictable regulatory environment. Any unfinished business (for instance, safeguards, subsidies, government procurement) should also be absorbed in the negoti-

ations. Other aspects of the functioning of the GATS which have been subject to inconclusive discussion on interpretation or implementation could be reviewed. The participation of developing countries should be facilitated by exploiting fully the opportunities offered by the GATS. For the efficiency of the negotiations and in order to maximise the results while at the same time ensuring coherence of commitments by sectors and by mode of supply, horizontal formulas, when appropriate, should be considered as a useful tool for the negotiations. This would apply across the board to sectors committed, except where expressly indicated.

The EC negotiates as a block *vis-à-vis* third countries. Trade agreements amongst EC countries themselves are exempted from WTO negotiations as the EC forms an area of economic integration formally notified to the WTO.

In overall terms, it is considered that there is a need to increase the number and quality of commitments across countries, services sectors and modes of supply. Therefore, the agenda for the negotiations should be comprehensive and no sector should be excluded *a priori*. Moreover, the negotiations should be open-ended affording the possibility to all WTO Members to raise any issue.

The quality, clarity, transparency and coherence of commitments undertaken should be improved; this will require substantial work on classification. As shown by the negotiations on financial services, classification is important as the right of WTO Members to draft their schedules according to their needs results in inconsistencies in the effective commitments undertaken.

Moreover, for the efficiency of the negotiations, and in order to maximise the results while at the same time ensuring coherence of commitments, the use of some horizontal formulas may be considered as potentially a useful tool for the negotiations. These would apply across the board to sectors committed, except where indicated. The purpose of this exercise would not be to put into question the positive listing approach of the GATS (that is, that only what is expressly indicated is committed), but to achieve economies of scale in the GATS negotiations by addressing certain sets of barriers generally for a multiplicity of sectors. A traditional negotiating approach based on request and offer would also be required.

Regarding autonomous liberalisation, there is an obvious need to reduce the increasing gap between WTO Members' commitments and the level of effective liberalisation. Although it is understood that credit should be given for binding autonomous liberalisation, the objective of the negotiations is clearly further liberalisation.

Looking at individual sectors, some sectors with strong export potential are financial services and telecoms. On financial services, we need more than just binding autonomous liberalisation *vis-à-vis* establishment, and we will have to address cross-border trade. On telecommunications, more countries should make commitments both on market access and regulatory disciplines, as well as consider the elimination of current restrictions and MFN exemptions.

New sectors where not much has been done so far, also need to be addressed, in particular energy, environmental services, construction and distribution. Regarding the transport sector that was subject to unsuccessful negotiations, GATS 2000 should incorporate a larger part of these sectors in the GATS commitments.

It should also be noted that the objective of the forthcoming negotiations is not to dismantle monopolies, provoke privatisation or a general deregulation of the sectors concerned, notably in certain services sectors that are exclusively or partly linked to the State. In particular, attention should be paid to the need to preserve the high standards regarding consumers' safety and protection.

Finally, developing countries have emphasised their concern that the forthcoming negotiations should take better account of their interests. In this context, the benefits that developing and developed countries are gaining from the GATS have now been better analysed. The GATS is particularly relevant to development, as it provides a key opportunity for all countries to attract stable long-term investment and to improve the related infrastructure (transport, telecommunications, financial services, energy) thereby fostering their growth and the competitiveness of their economies as a whole. One challenge of these negotiations will also be to increase the participation of developing countries in the GATS. In real terms, this means obtaining more market access commitments in sectors to their advantage and dealing with their horizontal requests, notably on temporary movement of services suppliers and emergency safeguards. Transitional periods should also be considered, with particular attention to least developed countries. In parallel, developed countries should also take into account suggestions to provide technical assistance necessary to benefit fully from market access liberalisation and to implement the commitments undertaken.

SOME IMPORTANT AREAS COVERED BY THE SERVICES NEGOTIATION

Below is a description of some key issues covered by the GATS 2000 negotiations. The first four are important sectors, while the other four refer to horizontal issues.

Telecommunications

Telecommunications is a key infrastructure needed for overall development and is necessary for any kind of activity and trade in a modern economy. A competitive telecommunications market reduces its cost as an input to other activities and massive investment in this sector is a prerequisite for e-commerce.

Out of the more than 130 WTO Members, 75 have made commitments on at least one telecoms sub-sector but a large number of restrictions remain in many developing countries. The EC's commitments are very liberal: all but two sub-sectors have been committed with restrictions that will soon lapse (the end of the transitional periods for liberalisation will have been reached).

In addition to market access, domestic regulation that promotes competition is needed in the sector, especially where historical monopolies prevailed on the eve of liberalisation. To that end, 62 Members, in some instances with changes, have adopted a reference paper detailing pro-competitive principles for Basic Telecommunications.

On Telecommunications, following the results of the post-Uruguay Round sectoral negotiations, it would now be necessary to achieve full market access across the board for all/most countries, with some flexibility as regards the transition periods, depending on the level of development. All countries should also put the whole reference paper in their additional commitments.

Distribution

The distribution sector is the crucial link between producers and consumers and has a strong influence on consumer welfare, as margins can affect prices considerably. Failures of the distribution sector can lead to a misallocation of resources and increased economic costs. Distribution accounts for a significant part of economic activity from around 8 per cent (Germany or Ireland) to over 20 per cent (Hong Kong or Panama). In many economies, the sector is only second to manufacturing in its contribution to GDP, and ahead of other sectors such as agriculture, mining, transport, telecoms and financial services. Its contribution to employment is usually even greater than that to GDP, reflecting the high labour-intensity of the sector.

Surprisingly, given the importance of this sector, out of the more than 130 WTO Members, only 33 have committed at least one distribution sub-sector. Only health and education have been the subject of fewer commitments. This is a gap to be filled. In addition, out of these 33 WTO Members, some maintain important product exclusions (cars, pharmaceutical and medicals, agricultural goods, food, beverages, tobacco, precious metals) and other restrictions (citizenship and residency requirements, purchase or rental of estate, restrictions on equity holdings, and so on).

Distribution is a highly regulated sector, particularly at local and regional levels (usually for legitimate reasons of urban planning). Nevertheless, authorities may sometimes implement regulation without transparency or predictability and discriminate against foreigners, notably in the granting of authorisations and licences. Work on domestic regulation should correct behaviours that may completely undermine commitments undertaken.

Financial Services

As a result of the GATS financial services negotiations, successfully concluded in December 1997, over a hundred WTO Members have now undertaken commitments in this sector. Almost all of them cover the core services in insurance, banking and securities, and fewer Members have made commitments in areas such as insurance intermediation and the provision and transfer of financial information.

Member's commitments are concentrated on establishment (mode 3). Commitments on cross border provision (mode 1) are much poorer, and are generally limited to transport insurance, reinsurance and advisory and other auxiliary banking and insurance services. The reason for limited cross-border commitments are Members' concerns relating to different prudential and supervisory approaches. Coverage of consumption abroad (mode 2) is in general wider than cross-border (most non-insurance financial services).

There are significant restrictions in developed, but many more in developing, countries such as ceilings on foreign shareholding, economic needs tests to allow new entry, limitations on the form of commercial presence (that is, only through subsidiary, or only via branch), restrictions to geographical expansion or discrimination as to the types of activities that can be carried out, quota systems or even bans on new entrants.

The EC financial services sector is open to third country competition. Establishment in the form of subsidiaries in banking, insurance and securities is subject to no restrictions other than the usual prudential safeguards. Foreign institutions can establish subsidiaries in any EU country and enjoy the 'single EU passport' under national treatment conditions. The establishment of foreign branches is also possible under broadly national treatment conditions in each Member State. The regulatory framework and supervisory practice in the EU are among the most advanced in the world and are currently being further improved through the 'Framework for Action' and its implementing Action Plan. This includes a broad set of measures aimed at improving the functioning of the EU Single Market in financial services.

For financial services, the main objective for GATS 2000 should continue to be the establishment of commercial operations in third countries. The cross-border supply of financial services is increasingly important although we must be aware that the supervisory questions are complex and have to be resolved satisfactorily. Regulatory issues are bound to become one of the key areas of discussion on financial services in the current GATS Round as adequate regulation and supervision are necessary elements for countries to grant a more liberal access to their markets.

Transport Services

Quick, safe and reliable transport services are essential for trade in goods and needed in almost all export sectors. Nevertheless, the Uruguay Round had very limited implications for transport and it is therefore one of the sectors with the greatest potential for improvement in GATS 2000.

Maritime transport

On Maritime transport, a critical mass of commitments was not reached at the Uruguay Round, so most countries withdrew offers, and the MFN obligation does not apply to international maritime transport. A standstill clause was agreed to protect the introduction of new restrictions. Nevertheless, international maritime transport is already quite liberal (much more than air and land transport) and it would be a start to at least bind this existing regime in GATS 2000. In any event, discussions will possibly resume on the basis of the draft model schedule developed at the time of the last negotiations that may accelerate results. The other pillars of maritime transport are auxiliary services, access to port services, and multi-modal operations, which will also be covered by the negotiations. The EU has a very strong position in maritime trade and has traditionally had a leading role in negotiations.

Air transport

Air transport is mostly excluded from the GATS (see below on air transport review) and the areas covered (sales and marketing, computer reservations systems, repair and maintenance of aircrafts) are usually protected by MFN exemptions. Current talks in Geneva, where the WTO is based, are focussed on a review of the excluded areas but, in any event, more and better commitments could be agreed for services already covered by the GATS.

Land transport

On land transport, inherent geographical limitations on cross-border provision resulted in limited commitments at the Uruguay Round, other than for commercial presence for road transport and some maintenance activities. MFN exemptions are common for cross-border provision and a complex set of bilateral and regional agreements is in place, especially for road transport. Rail transport is normally sensitive to market access opening but, within the EU, is now subject to projects for liberalisation.

THE TEMPORARY MOVEMENT OF SERVICES SUPPLIERS (MODE 4)

Following the Annex on 'Movement of Natural Persons' (agreed as part of the Uruguay Round in 1994), on 21 July 1995 the 'Third Protocol to the General Agreement on trade in services' was adopted.

Both the Annex and the Third Protocol focus entirely on the temporary presence of services providers, or mode 4, one of the four possible forms of providing a service under the GATS. This mode applies to measures affecting the temporary stay of natural persons who are either an independent or an employee of a juridical entity. The Marrakech's Annex on 'Movement of Natural Persons' explicitly excludes, from the scope of the GATS, measures regarding citizenship, residence, employment on a permanent basis, visa and immigration policy. The GATS is strictly limited to providing access to natural persons as services providers in the receiving country. The specific service is to be provided for a given length of time, limited, but of a duration not generally specified in the GATS and subject to any conditions inscribed in the concerned country's schedule.

The European Community contributed to the success of the GATS negotiation by offering substantial commitments on the entry and temporary stay of natural persons supplying services. The result is a very substantial coverage touching on:

(a)   all foreign persons working in the EU as employees of a company (excludes the self-employed) without commercial presence (also referred to as a 'contractual services supplier');
(b)   all foreign natural persons on temporary entry in the EU to negotiate for the sale of services;
(c)   senior personnel on temporary entry in the EU for the setting up of a commercial presence;
(d)   intra-corporate transferees of foreign persons in the EU working in a senior position or who possess an 'uncommon' knowledge and a high level of qualification.

Mode 4 is of high interest for developing countries, who expect to 'export' their labour advantage, but also to transnational companies who need to circulate their employees amongst their subsidiaries abroad. While taking into account the exclusions in the Annex and the Third Protocol referred to above, there is still scope to improve existing mode 4 commitments during the negotiations, especially by those WTO Members that still maintain a limited offer in this respect.

In particular, within an increasingly global business environment it is important that companies can temporarily transfer key personnel between subsidiaries and associate companies in different countries. Indeed, clients of services suppliers are increasingly international and require services on a global basis. In many cases, services suppliers increasingly need to bring in individual key staff members supplied from their pool of global personnel. International mobility for training purposes within the company is also essential.

Another objective could be to seek clarification on the definitions of personnel under mode 4 commitments that are neither clear nor consistent. It would be important that as many countries as possible agree on common terms for executives, managers and specialists under intra-company transfers. This would create a more predictable, harmonised and transparent system that would improve implementation.

Also, commitments are often limited by economic needs tests. With the objective to ensure effective application of mode 4 policy any tests should be more transparent and define their application criteria.

DOMESTIC REGULATION

The GATS recognises the sovereign right of Member governments to regulate the supply of services in their territories in order to meet national policy objectives. At the same time, the GATS states the wish of WTO Members for an expansion of trade in services under conditions of transparency and progressive liberalisation.

As a result, while safeguarding the regulatory freedom of Members, the GATS aims at both improving the transparency of domestic services regulations and at ensuring that domestic measures that affect trade in services are administered in a reasonable, objective and impartial manner. It also establishes some general principles essentially linked to the rule of law. Indeed, foreign services suppliers should be able to challenge administrative decisions that affect them, although this possibility should be offered with full respect of the constitutional structure and the nature of the legal system of each country. Also, foreign suppliers should be informed within a reasonable period of time whether their applications for the authorisation to supply a service have been accepted.

For certain specific measures that affect trade in services (qualification requirements and procedures, technical standards and licensing requirements) the Agreement also asks Members to develop the GATS disciplines to ensure that those measures are based on objective and transparent criteria and are aimed at ensuring the quality of the service. In other words, that they do not unnecessarily hamper trade in services. Until such disciplines are developed, these criteria already apply to the sectors for which Members have offered specific liberalising commitments.

After the Uruguay Round, in December 1998, a set of disciplines on domestic regulation in the accountancy sector was agreed. In April 1999, a decision was adopted to develop disciplines applicable to all sectors and also, if appropriate, disciplines for individual sectors or groups of sectors. This work is being carried out in the WTO Working Party on Domestic Regulation, which is now focussing on the following two parallel avenues:

(a)   Disciplines applicable to professional services: consideration of the applicability of the Accountancy Disciplines to other professional services, and the development of some general guidelines.

(b)   Disciplines applicable to all services sectors: the main areas of work being discussed are transparency and necessity. Transparency of domestic regulation refers essentially to the publication of measures, provision of information to other Members and notification obligations to the WTO. On necessity, the discussions are about setting rules to determine whether measures restricting trade are really necessary or not. This is the most sensitive area of current work on domestic regulation and some discretion should be left to Members on their measures to achieve legitimate objectives.

PUBLIC SERVICES AND GATS 2000

'Public services' is not defined in the GATS and is regularly referred to as both the market- and non-market-based services which are of general interest and therefore subject to specific public services obligations. The main objectives of these services are essentially satisfying public needs, the protection of the territory and of the environment, economic and social cohesion, and the protection of consumers. It is important for the society that these services are provided in a form which guarantees continuity, freedom, universality and equality of access. The main goal is to ensure a high quality of services to the whole population at accessible prices.

Although it varies greatly across countries, public services can be rendered in different ways:

(a)   Some of these services are exclusively within the hands of public structures, like the administration of justice and security.

(b)   In some areas the bulk of activities administered by public institutions are complemented with private structures which may offer services like, or close substitutes to, those offered by the public sector (like higher education, hospitals).

(c)   Finally, private companies (sometimes also with public capital) may generally operate in other sectors (like transport, energy, water supply, some professional services) where the public services considerations have lead to the imposition of clear, transparent and objective obligations (fixed prices, universal services, and so on). Companies must follow such obligations when they render these services while for the rest of their activities they are submitted to the market.

The GATS fully preserves Members' sovereign right to regulate economic and non-economic activities within their territory and to guarantee the achievement of legitimate public objectives. It does so mainly in the following ways:

(a)   in Article I, by exempting, from all disciplines, any services which are not offered under market conditions, that is, if they are not supplied on a commercial basis or in competition;

(b)   in Article XIV, noting that nothing in the GATS shall prevent the enforcement of measures necessary to protect, amongst other, public morals, public order, human, animal or plant life or health, data privacy or safety;

(c)   by the GATS architecture, which leaves each WTO Member complete flexibility in deciding the level of opening of their market for foreign suppliers.

(d)   finally, in its Article VI, which, even for areas opened to foreign suppliers, maintains the sovereign right of countries to regulate activities within their territory and to guarantee the achievement of legitimate public objectives. Thus, each WTO Member has the possibility to maintain the quality standards and the social objectives which are at the basis of its system, although this should not be used as an inappropriate barrier to trade (see above point on domestic regulation)

The basic principles of EU policy on public services are set out in the Communication of the European Commission of September 1996 on Services of General Interest. Article 16 of the Amsterdam Treaty confirmed this approach and gave further emphasis to the importance of these services while preserving, at the same time, the application of the relevant provisions on competition and internal market.

The EU has been able to make the GATS commitments in several sensitive sectors, including for example private funded education services and hospital services, without any risk of dismantling their public services policy, by introducing two specific clauses in its GATS commitments:

(a) the existence of public monopolies or of exclusive rights granted to private operators in services considered as 'public utilities' cannot be considered as a violation of its GATS commitments. This allows the existence of exclusive services suppliers (public or private; domestic or foreign) in sectors such as health services, environmental services, transport services;

(b) the subsidisation of a service within the EU public sector cannot be considered as a violation of its commitments. This allows the maintenance of financial support to specific policies and activities (education, health system) which are essential to achieve public policy objectives.

E-COMMERCE

Electronic commerce is an issue of growing importance for international trade. At the beginning its development was focused within each WTO Member's economy but is increasingly benefiting trade between all countries.

On e-commerce, other than the work programme, formally aside from GATS 2000 (see below), the services negotiations should aim at removing all market access restrictions for activities that are prerequisites for conducting an e-commerce transaction (such as telecommunications, software-related, advertising, payment, distribution services). These services constitute the infrastructure of e-commerce and if market access and national treatment are restricted on those sectors, electronic deliveries will be hampered or illegal under WTO rules. For instance, if a country does not allow the cross-border supply of advertising services, it will simply be impossible for portals to provide any service from abroad since their main source of revenue is advertising (including by providing links to others). As far as telecommunications and payment services are concerned, it is also a matter of efficiency of the underlying markets. Additionally, the transaction made up by physical deliveries of electronic orders is a cross-border distribution services (either wholesale or retail).

GATS 2000 should also promote services that could benefit from e-commerce such as financial services, tourism services, and some professional services. Finally, the necessity to develop disciplines on domestic regulation in relation to e-commerce may come up in a not-so-distant future to ensure that all providers worldwide abide by similar rules.

DISCUSSIONS ON SERVICES SEPARATE FROM GATS 2000

Formally separate from GATS 2000 negotiations, other areas related to services are currently being discussed in WTO. Although they are not officially linked to the negotiations, they will definitively impact on GATS 2000 in the following years. The most important ones are:

(a) *MFN exemptions review*   This is the review mandated by the annex on the GATS Article II MFN exemptions: 'The Council for Trade in Services *(the WTO body in charge for services)* shall review all *(MFN)* exemptions granted for a period of more than five years. The first such review shall take place no more than five years after the entry into force of the WTO Agreement' (that is by the year 2000). The annex goes on to indicate that the review 'shall examine whether the conditions which created the need for the exemption still prevail'. It appears clear that, notwithstanding the review, most WTO Members do not have the intention to discuss the possibility to remove their MFN exemptions outside the context of proper services negotiation.

(b) *E-commerce work programme*   The WTO started to address the trade issues raised by electronic commerce through a Work Programme in September 1998. The objective is to clarify how existing rules and commitments apply to e-commerce and whether additional rules may be necessary. Important issues are: the application of all existing WTO rules, the classification of electronic deliveries, the technological neutrality of the GATS and TRIPS agreements (meaning that they apply whatever the means used to provide a service, including e-commerce), domestic regulation, competition and telecommunications issues. The Work Programme was launched with a precise agenda for each of the bodies involved to work upon: the GATS, GATT and TRIPS Councils and the Committee on Trade and Development. These bodies reported on the progress of their work by the autumn of 1999 but the Ministerial Conference in Seattle could not reach any conclusion on this issue because of the failure of the session itself. Discussions continue under the work programme.

(c) *Air transport review*   This is the review mandated by the annex on Air Transport: 'The Council for Trade in Services shall review periodically, and at least every five years, developments in the air transport sector and the operation of this Annex with a view to considering the possible further application of the Agreement in this sector'. The review is necessary as the annex provides for the sole exception to the full coverage of all services activities by the GATS. Indeed, the GATS 'shall not apply to measures affecting traffic rights or services directly related to the exercise of traffic rights'. These activities are instead covered by numerous bilateral agreements. The review aims at considering whether this exception is still justified. Nevertheless, as before, it is difficult to imagine, outside GATS 2000, a different outcome to this review than the existing status quo.

(d) *Review of the understanding on accounting rates in telecommunications*

The objective is to review the political understanding reached at the end of the basic telecommunications negotiations in 1997, according to which application of differential accounting rates would not give rise to action by Members under the WTO dispute settlement.

CONCLUSIONS

The GATS 2000 negotiations, that started in the WTO in January 2000, are the most important negotiations on services since the end of the Uruguay Round in 1994. In turn, services have already become the driving force in today's economies and create the vast amount of the world's employment. The outcome of these negotiations can have a considerable impact on our living standards in the years to come. While the Uruguay Round established the legal framework for international trade in services, it only bound some market access amongst WTO Members. With 50 years' delay in relation to goods, GATS 2000 should now bring the decisive push in the liberalisation of trade in services worldwide. The EC is committed to meaningful and ambitious market access negotiations to the benefit of all countries, services suppliers and citizens of the twenty-first century.

12. An American policy perspective on service trade: the views of the Coalition of Service Industries on the United States negotiating objectives for services at the Seattle WTO

Robert Vastine

The Coalition of Service Industries (CSI) was established in 1982 to create greater public awareness of the major role services companies and their workers play in the American economy. The CSI promotes the expansion of business opportunities abroad for US service companies, advocates an increased focus on liberalisation of trade in services in international trade negotiations and encourages US leadership in obtaining a fair and competitive global marketplace. CSI members include an array of US service industries including the financial, telecommunications, professional, travel, transportation and air cargo, and information technology sectors. Included in the coalition of sectors with which CSI works are energy services, entertainment, retail distribution and educational institutions. CSI has been active in multilateral trade negotiations since before the Uruguay Round and played an aggressive advocacy role in obtaining successful WTO negotiations in telecommunications and financial services. This chapter is an edited version of a CSI statement presented to the United States Senate Finance Committee Subcommittee on International Trade. It provides an account of US interests and objectives in service trade negotiations.

SERVICES 2000 NEGOTIATIONS

The CSI is committed to a comprehensive, highly ambitious new multilateral services negotiation starting in 2000. These negotiations will further expand America's global markets, enabling the service sector to increase its 77 per cent share of US employment, its 79 per cent share of GDP, and its trade surplus of about $80 billion (about 30 per cent of US exports). Foreign companies have a high propensity to consume US services. Were these negotiations to reduce barriers across a wide range of highly protected foreign services markets, they could materially stimulate US trade. The US is very competitive in virtually every category of services trade (see appendix).

It has recently been suggested that US services exports could offset the structural goods deficit. Catherine L. Mann, in a study for the Institute for International Economics suggests that:

> as income in a foreign country grows, its imports of US services tend to rise disproportionately. Successful broad-based negotiations on trade in services will likely increase US exports of services even further, with a positive effect on the trade deficit. The long-term trajectory of the US external balances could be altered significantly by the combination of successful service-sector negotiations and broad-based liberalization and deregulation at home and especially abroad. These together would unleash higher productivity and faster growth at home and abroad, which would narrow the US current account deficit. (Mann, 1999: 9)

It has been estimated that comprehensive liberalisation of services could raise global GDP by 4 to 6 percentage points, and raise the long-run global growth rate from 3.2 to 5 per cent (Hufbauer and Warren, 1999). Given this the United States has a powerful national economic security interest in making services negotiations a major success. But so does the rest of the world economy.

THE SEATTLE MINISTERIAL

America requires highly successful new services trade negotiations. What, however, defines success? For the service sector a successful Ministerial would:

- Give a very strong mandate to the start of comprehensive services negotiations in 2000.
- Ensure that this three-year negotiation be focussed mainly on services, agriculture and industrial products so that there is a real chance that negotiators can focus on services trade and complete an ambitious agenda of liberalisation in areas where the likelihood of liberalisation exists.
- Recognise that electronic commerce is an important new technique for trading and that it is not a new sector in and of itself. Extend the existing moratorium on duties on electronic transmissions and call on countries to refrain from adopting regulatory and other measures that would unnecessarily restrict electronic commerce. Ensure that electronic deliv-

ery of services falls within the scope of the GATS, and that there be no discrimination among foreign and domestic providers in their access to electronic networks.

- Provide that the entire new 'round' be completed by 31 December, 2002, in order to force closure on the existing agenda, reap what gains can be garnered, and begin again with a fresh agenda that could include items like investment.

AMBITIOUS US GOALS FOR SERVICES 2000

CSI believes strongly that the US should enter the new negotiations with a bold agenda, calling for sweeping commitments to liberalisation across all service sectors. We would like the American negotiators to propose broad commitments to liberalisation in areas such as the right to establish a business presence in foreign markets (commercial presence), the right to own all or a majority share of that business and the right to be treated as a local business (national treatment).

One of the areas requiring fresh, bold thinking here and abroad, is the temporary entry of foreign managerial and technical personnel. Increasingly, US consulting, accounting, legal, architectural and engineering firms need to transfer personnel at short notice to service the needs of their clients throughout the world. Delivering services via transfer of natural persons is known in GATS parlance as 'mode 4' of supply. The WTO has been unable to make any progress on achieving liberalisation of this form of supply of services. Because it is of increasing importance to US firms, and to some other countries, it should be an important element of the coming negotiations.

Foreign companies entering new markets often face formidable barriers in the form of arbitrary and non-transparent regulations and regulatory institutions. Such regulations too often deny foreign companies the opportunity to compete on an equal basis with domestic firms. They can effectively negate the benefits of trade liberalisation commitments.

Pro-competitive regulatory reforms mean abandoning forms of regulation by which governments limit the introduction of new products, restrict use of market-based pricing, and in other ways constrain competition. Transparency of regulatory processes is an important element of pro-competitive reform. This means adopting many of the procedures embodied in our more open system of government, such as the publication of existing and proposed regulations, and the right to comment and to be heard in administrative proceedings.

At the same time that we pursue an aggressive trade strategy, we must be sure that our domestic policies do not inhibit the global competitiveness of our own companies. A case in point is the active financing exception to Subpart F that expires at the end of the year. Extension of these rules permitting US-based financial services companies to reinvest earnings overseas without first being taxed by the US will be an important step in the right direction as we better coordinate our trade and tax policies to foster the ability of our companies to compete in foreign markets.

THE WTO AND SERVICES

The reduction of barriers to trade in goods began many decades ago with the 1934 reciprocal trade agreements programme of the Roosevelt era. The reduction of barriers to trade in services is in its infancy. The Uruguay Round wrote the 'constitution' or legal framework for liberalisation of trade in service: the GATS. But countries' actual commitments to liberalisation were disappointing. The actual work of liberalisation was advanced in the successful 1997 Basic Telecommunications and Financial Services negotiations. The next negotiation, services 2000, is the first real opportunity to bring to bear the lessons we have learned about the complex process of negotiating freer trade in services and to broaden binding commitments across all sectors and deepen commitments within product categories and sub categories.

The United States has a particularly big stake in a successful multilateral negotiation. We are already highly competitive in services. We can secure and enhance this comparative advantage by removing restrictions to our exports, and at the same time make a bigger and bigger dent in America's structural trade deficit. The Seattle Ministerial is a preamble to the main event, the negotiation itself. But it is essential that the Seattle Declaration gives a strong impetus to an ambitious, achievable negotiation in services. As the work of Mann (1999) demonstrates, such a result is essential to our national economic interest and to global prosperity.

REFERENCES

Mann, C.L. (1999), *Is the U.S. Trade Deficit Sustainable?*, Institute for International Economics, p. 9.
Hufbauer, G.C. and Warren, T. (1999), *The Globalization of Services, What Has Happened?*, Institute for International Economics.

APPENDIX

Examples illustrating the stake of US service industries in expanded global markets.

- Travel and tourism contributed over $25 billion to the services trade surplus in 1997. This is the largest sectoral contribution to the overall service surplus. In addition, travel and tourism are estimated to support over seven million direct jobs and generate roughly $71 billion in tax revenues for federal, state and local governments.
- Business, professional and technical services is a largely unrecognised powerhouse in American trade. In 1997, we exported more than $21 billion in these services and we had a $16 billion trade surplus. These data do not include the earnings from foreign investments and foreign affiliates, which are very substantial. Trade in business, professional and technical services – such as accounting, legal, engineering, architectural and consulting services – is especially important because it frequently paves the way for trade and investment in other service and manufacturing sectors.
- Telecommunications services are an integral component of operations of all businesses, and are essential in promoting domestic and global growth. Telecommunications services provide the necessary infrastructure for the development and continued expansion of the information society and electronic commerce. An estimated $725 billion in revenue was generated in 1997, and projections for the next five years indicate that traded telecommunications services will increase at about 20 per cent annually for outbound calls from the US to foreign markets.
- The information technology industry is also dependent on trade and trade expansion. The WTO estimates that over the next five years, sales over the Internet will double each year.
- The US asset management industry is the largest in the world. It is estimated that by 2002, 51 per cent of total asset management revenue of $160 billion will come from abroad, not the US. Today, US-domiciled investment managers manage 14 per cent of the total of non-US retirement plan assets and 5 per cent of non-US mutual fund assets.
- US law firms, when billing foreign clients, produce services exports. Overall US legal services exports approach $1.0 billion.
- Foreign students coming to American schools, net after scholarship and local assistance, spent $8.3 billion in the US, which is a US services export. We have a surplus in trade in education services of $7.0 billion.
- Although few doctors imagine themselves as US exporters, medical services rendered in the US to foreign citizens produced an export surplus of $0.5 billion.
- Air cargo transport accounts for well over a third of the value of the world trade in merchandise. However, restrictions on market access (including cabotage), ownership and control, the right of establishment, capacity, frequencies, intermodal operations in connection with air

services, wet leasing, customs, groundhandling, the environment, in particular local airport access times, all limit the ability of cargo carriers to plan their operations purely on the basis of commercial and operational considerations. A WTO framework could provide cargo carriers with clear rules addressing these problems and resulting in enhanced delivery options to the benefit of businesses, shippers and consumers worldwide.

• Energy services have received little attention in trade negotiations to date. But drastic changes in the international and domestic business climate for this industry – which in the US accounts for 1.4 million jobs and about 7 per cent of US GDP – have shown the need for global trading rules, which can provide new, common understandings on such key matters as monopoly power, anti-competitive practices and discrimination against new market entrants, including of course US companies. Thus the energy services industry looks to the coming round as a critically important opportunity to map out a blueprint for market access and free competition in energy service.

13. Developing countries and the GATS 2000 Round*

Pierre Sauvé

INTRODUCTION

It is undoubtedly an exaggeration, but only a mild one, to suggest that developing countries as a group largely gave a pass to the inaugural set of multilateral negotiations on trade in services. One of the Uruguay Round's three 'new' trade issues, alongside investment (TRIMs) and intellectual property-related matters (TRIPs), services made their way on the global trade policy agenda largely against the vocal opposition of an influential group of developing country GATT members. As was often the case in those days, Brazil and India led the resistance, arguing that services were primarily a matter of domestic regulatory conduct. Accordingly, they were seen as having little to do with international trade and were thus best left out of the trading system's purview. Sentiment was strong among developing countries that the advent of a multilateral framework of rules and disciplines for services was largely inimical to their development prospects and fledgling service sectors. Developing countries as a group did not see themselves as possessing much of a comparative advantage in the production and exchange of services. Nor, for that matter, in the crafting of hitherto non-existent multilateral disciplines in the area.[1] They also feared that a full-scale negotiation would afford developed countries (and especially the United States, the main cheerleader on both services and investment at the time) a back door way of achieving greater investment regime liberalisation than that made possible under the considerably watered-down negotiating mandate agreed for TRIMs at the Punta del Este ministerial meeting in September 1987.

Developing countries were hardly alone in their hesitancy, briefly enjoying the company even of a few OECD members. This was notably the case of members of the European Community before the latter recognised the crucial role that services trade and investment liberalisation would need to play in fulfilling the ambitions of their EC-92 Single Market programme.

* First published in the *Journal of World Trade*, April 2000, Reproduced with permission of the author and publisher.

The relative lack of engagement and defensive posturing of developing countries in the negotiation of the General Agreement on Trade in Services (GATS) minimised, with a few exceptions, their collective influence on the framework of rules produced by the Uruguay Round. It also generated a level of bound liberalisation that is widely seen as inimical to the pursuit of economically efficient policy making (Hoekman and Messerlin, 2000; Mattoo, 1999).

As it happens, being on the rule-making sidelines did not prove unduly disadvantageous to developing countries. This is so because developed countries were themselves in learning by doing mode in the area of services trade. Grappling for the first time with a complex set of behind the border issues of domestic regulatory conduct running the gamut from professional licensing to the treatment of foreign investment or immigration policies, GATT members came up with a framework of rules clearly biased at every turn towards regulatory precaution, with generally weak, à la carte, provisions on liberalisation.

CHANGING ATTITUDES TOWARDS LIBERALISATION

The paradox of the GATS, and of developing country attitudes towards it, is that the period that paralleled its development saw far-reaching changes – much of it unilaterally decreed – in developing country policies towards trade and investment in services.[2] Such changes began to surface, and became more readily apparent in a negotiating setting, in the context of the Round's 'left-over' talks in the key infrastructural areas of basic telecommunications and financial services. Because of the key role of finance and telecommunications as intermediaries into all that modern economies produce, bring to market or trade, the latter negotiations focused the attention of policy makers as never before on the economy-wide benefits to be derived from becoming a more efficient importer of services (and of capital) and of promoting greater market contestability. Both sets of negotiations also highlighted the critical importance of placing a credible floor of pro-competitive regulations under trade and investment liberalisation commitments.[3]

These latter developments suggest that the GATS 2000 round of negotiations is likely to start on a much sounder footing than the Uruguay Round did. Indeed, the coming round will take place against the backdrop of a body of rules that is by now familiar to all GATS members. The complex language and geometry of GATS rules have by now been mastered. Moreover, and partly through experience gained in negotiations on services and investment conducted at the regional level, developing countries have largely reversed their rule-making deficit in the area. In some of the outstanding areas of GATS rule-making, notably the development of emergency safeguards provisions, developing countries are in fact assuming a leadership role.

REASONS FOR OPTIMISM: INFORMATION TECHNOLOGY AND E-COMMERCE

Technology provides another source of optimism for the coming round, especially as the e-commerce revolution affords many new opportunities for the cross-border supply of services in which developing countries already possess (or could soon and relatively easily develop) a comparative advantage. The coming years will witness strong growth in the remote provision of a wide array of business and professional services, ranging from software development to engineering design, medical diagnosis, data and information processing, all of which could provide developing countries with significant new export outlets.

GATS members, developed and developing, showed considerable reluctance in opening up competition in services trade on a cross-border basis in the first round of negotiations. The mode of supply against which the greatest number of bound commitments were undertaken relates to commercial presence, so-called 'establishment-related' trade in services (see Hoekman, 1995). The GATS, at least in its first incarnation, is as much an investment agreement as one concerned with cross-border trade. In the case of developing countries, such an outcome was somewhat ironic, given their initial misgivings over the treatment of FDI under a services cover.

The greater prevalence of commitments on commercial presence over cross-border supply reflects regulatory precaution – the natural preference of domestic regulators (particularly in hitherto uncharted waters) to assert authority over economic operators conducting business in their jurisdiction. Commercial presence also brings negotiating leverage in its wake, allowing host countries to impose assorted performance requirements linked to entry by source country firms.

The relative paucity of commitments on cross-border trade in services also reflects the fact that the first set of GATS negotiations largely predated the advent of the e-commerce revolution. Harnessing the latter should be a first order priority in the next round. The implications for developing countries are two-fold. First, as concerns the supply side, they must ensure that the domestic policy environment be e-commerce-friendly, notably in terms of telecommunications infrastructure and pricing, computer literacy, access to and development of upstream distribution, transportation and marketing networks, and so on. Second, on the demand side, developing countries must see to it that genuine opportunities to service world markets not be impaired by unduly onerous regulatory requirements (for example, licensing, product standards, consumer protection, local presence requirements) in importing countries. What's more, as potential consumers of services delivered over electronic networks, developing countries stand to experience potentially important increases in consumer welfare, in effect bypassing costlier domestic sources of supply and securing access to a broader array of competitively-priced services on offer in world markets (Drake and Nicolaidis, 2000).

IMPLICATIONS FOR LABOUR MOBILITY

There is no denying that enhancing the scope for the remote supply of services over electronic networks could paradoxically shift the terms of the debate on – and ultimately lessen the need for – the cross-border mobility of service providers. That said, there remains a strong case, on both efficiency and equity grounds, to promote greater doses of labour mobility under the GATS in the coming round (see also Young, 2000). Labour movement was the mode of supply against which the fewest commercially meaningful liberalisation commitments were lodged in the first GATS round, potentially depriving developing countries of export opportunities in 'user' industries (for example, construction and engineering services) which many OECD countries had otherwise nominally opened up to foreign competition. Developing countries, particularly those in a position to supply highly skilled workers to the world market, will thus need to maintain offensive pressure in this politically charged area in the coming round. Just as developing countries should welcome greater quantities of FDI, which empirical studies have shown to be more productive than domestic investment (Borenzstein et al., 1998), so too would developed countries benefit from importing skilled labour services, such as computer programmers, in greater numbers.

The contribution of imported skilled labour to the high-technology sectors in the United States and Canada, and hence their growth performance, is now widely recognised. Much as efforts are afoot in a number of OECD capitals to 'sweeten' the deal for labour in the coming round by addressing issues relating to core labour practices, it bears recalling that the terms of that sweetening may look decidedly different when viewed from a Southern perspective. That much, if anything, is clear after the desultory outcome of the WTO's Seattle ministerial meeting. Moreover, should a decision be taken in future to launch a comprehensive set of investment negotiations at the WTO, developing countries should press for labour-mobility issues to be treated in a equivalent manner to the movement of capital under WTO law. Such conceptual equivalence was a distinguishing feature of the North American Free Trade Agreement (NAFTA), which featured separate chapters on investment, cross-border trade in services and the mobility of service providers.

CONTESTABILITY AND REGULATORY REFORM: EXPLOITING THE SIGNALLING PROPERTIES OF THE GATS

Much as the first set of GATS negotiations yielded a weak harvest of liberalisation commitments – a downpayment of sorts, the coming round affords all participants, and especially developing countries, a good opportunity to make use of the GATS to anchor ongoing policy reforms more firmly in their country schedules and to signal to incumbents, domestic and foreign, that greater market contestability lies around the corner.

Nowhere is market contestability more important than in the key enabling sectors of telecommunications (including Internet services), finance, transportation, legal and accounting services. All deserve closer attention in establishing liberalising priorities on the import side, particularly as the maintenance of high levels of nominal protection on such intermediates can result in negative rates of effective protection on the final products – goods and services – that developing countries sell in export markets.

The quickest route to promoting greater service sector efficiency is undoubtedly to soldier on with the continued unilateral dismantling of discriminatory and non-discriminatory barriers to services trade and investment. Indeed, the key determinants of success in service markets, including exports of services, are rooted in domestic regulatory reform efforts aimed *inter alia* at promoting excellence in knowledge-based activities (improving education and training), enhancing the quality of communication and transport infrastructures, and deepening financial markets.

Similarly, developing countries need to focus on the regulatory underpinnings most conducive to sustaining the liberalisation process and generating the greatest possible gains in economic efficiency. More often than not, non-discriminatory approaches to domestic rule making will be welfare maximising. Adopting international standards with a view to overcoming information asymmetries over the quality of developing country service offerings, and facilitating mutual recognition agreements, may similarly help developing countries overcome important hurdles to exporting, attract greater flows of foreign direct investment and enhance prospects for labour mobility (Nicolaidis and Trachtman, 2000; Beviglia Zampetti, 2000).

An important further challenge for developing countries going into the next GATS round is to be clearer on the economy-wide implications of the liberalisation path they voluntarily embark upon in a GATS context. The first round of negotiations saw a clear bias in commitments towards the promotion (indeed the entrenchment) of the market position of existing suppliers, domestic and foreign, rather than new entrants. The literature on regulatory reform suggests that protecting the privileged status of incumbent suppliers is not the most economically rational policy to follow. Indeed, larger welfare gains have been shown to arise from an increase in competition than from simply a change in ownership, be it from public to private hands; domestic to foreign ownership; or through a relaxation of restrictions on foreign equity participation in domestic firms (Mattoo, 1999).

The steady erosion of the natural monopoly rationale for regulation, combined with growing awareness of the enabling characteristics of key service industries and mounting empirical evidence on the benefits of competition, make it increasingly hard to justify the maintenance of restrictions on new entry into domestic service markets. By providing governments an opportunity to pre-commit to future liberalisation, and hence signal to domestic and foreign suppliers that domestic market conditions will be altered in a progressive, adjustment-promoting manner, the GATS provides a potentially important means of overcoming the considerable economic and political power that incumbents often exert on domestic policy making. Developing countries should accordingly make greater use of the signalling properties of the GATS, and where practicable, promote greater market contestability through *de novo* entry (Low and Mattoo, 2000; Hoekman and Messerlin, 2000).

REDUCING THE GAP BETWEEN APPLIED AND BOUND LIBERALIZATION

There remains, additionally, the question of the tendency of developing countries to lodge liberalisation commitments at less than the regulatory status quo. Recalling the mercantilist analogy between bound and applied rates of border protection arising in tariff negotiations, it is open to debate whether developing countries gain negotiating leverage by doing likewise in the services field given the regulatory nature of impediments to trade and investment in the sector. Binding at less than the status quo is typically viewed by foreign investors, and particularly foreign incumbents, as legitimising the scope for future regulatory backsliding. This is hardly the signal most developing countries will want to send to established foreign firms and to investors abroad (Sauvé and Wilkie, 2000).

All that can be done in the coming round to reduce the wedge between applied regulations and bound liberalisation commitments should thus be considered carefully by developing countries. Doing so will, however, likely heighten calls for developing GATS-anchored emergency safeguard measures, on which WTO members have held hitherto inconclusive talks since the end of the Uruguay Round. Much as the issue of emergency safeguards raises questions of great technical complexity in the services field, there is no denying their usefulness as insurance policy (Gauthier et al., 2000). Indeed, the main policy rationale for agreeing such measures is to impart a greater liberalisation dynamic to the GATS than would exist in their absence. The NAFTA saw recourse to an innovative safeguard-based approach to opening Mexico's previously closed financial services industry. The next round offers a good opportunity for WTO members to experiment in this area. One idea could be to pursue safeguards-based liberalisation in a sector where adjustment problems or political sensitivities about market opening are more acute – cross-border trade in financial services, for example – before contemplating its extension to all sectors subject to GATS disciplines (Sauvé and Gillespie, 1999).

CONCLUDING REMARKS

Developing countries need to establish early on where their negotiating priorities lie (both on the import and export sides) on services and in other key areas, and engage their developed country partners in a more proactive way than was the case during the Uruguay Round. The fact that the latter group of countries know how the services game is played, and better understand its rules, suggests that developing countries as a group are much better placed today to turn the negotiating dynamic in services – in which OECD countries remain strong overall *demandeurs* – to their tactical advantage. They should neither shy away from making strong demands in areas, including services, of priority export interest to them, nor hesitate to view services trade and investment liberalization – including on the import side – for what it is: a powerful means of promoting economic and social development in a transparent, fair and orderly manner.

NOTES

1. The only exception at the time being the embryonic services provisions being envisaged in the Canada–United States Free Trade Agreement.
2. In the investment field, for instance, the UNCTAD secretariat has recently reported that of the 895 policy changes made to host countries' (predominantly developing countries) investment regimes during 1991–98, fully 843 – or 94.2 per cent of measures – treated foreign direct investment more favourably than before. See UNCTAD (1999).
3. In a similar vein, and reflecting the growing awareness of governments that the information technology revolution needs to be properly marshalled, the period since the conclusion of the Round also saw considerable developing country interest – and active participation – in negotiations leading to the WTO's landmark Information Technology Agreement (ITA) (Sauvé and Fliess, 1998).

REFERENCES

Beviglia Zampetti, Americo (2000), 'Market Access through Mutual Recognition: The Promise and Limits of GATS Article VII', in Pierre Sauvé and Robert M. Stern, (eds), *GATS 2000: New Directions in Services Trade Liberalization*, Washington, DC: Brookings Institution Press, pp. 283–306.

Borenzstein, E., Grigorio, J.D. and Lee, J.W. (1998), 'How Does Foreign Direct Investment Affect Economic Growth?', IMF Working Paper, Washington, DC: International Monetary Fund.

Drake, William J. and Nicolaidis, Kalypso (2000), 'Global Electronic Commerce and GATS: The Millenium Round and Beyond', in Pierre Sauvé and Robert M. Stern (eds), *GATS 2000: New Directions in Services Trade Liberalization*, Washington, DC: Brookings Institution Press, pp. 399–437.

Gauthier, Gilles, with O'Brien, Erin and Spencer, Susan (2000), 'Déjà Vu, or New Beginning for Safeguards and Subsidies Rules in Services Trade?', in Pierre Sauvé and Robert M. Stern (eds), *GATS 2000: New Directions in Services Trade Liberalization*, Washington, DC: Brookings Institution Press, pp. 165–83.

Hoekman, Bernard (1995), 'Assessing the General Agreement on Trade in Services', in Will Martin and L. Alan Winters (eds), *The Uruguay Round and the Developing Countries,* World Bank Discussion papers No. 307, Washington, DC: The World Bank, pp. 327–80.

Hoekman, Bernard and Messerlin, Patrick (2000), 'Liberalizing Trade in Services: Reciprocal Negotiations and Regulatory Reform', in Pierre Sauvé and Robert M. Stern (eds), *GATS 2000: New Directions in Services Trade Liberalization*, Washington, DC: Brookings Institution Press, pp. 487–508.

Low, Patrick and Mattoo, Aaditya (2000), 'Is There a Better Way? Alternative Approaches to Liberalization under GATS', in Pierre Sauvé and Robert M. Stern (eds), *GATS 2000: New Directions in Services Trade Liberalization*, Washington, DC: Brookings Institution Press, pp. 449–72.

Mattoo, Aaditya (1999), 'Developing Countries in the New Round of GATS Negotiations: From a Defensive to a Pro-Active Role', Paper prepared for a WTO/World Bank Conference on 'Developing Countries in a Millenium Round', Geneva, 20–21 September.

Nicolaidis, Kalypso and Trachtman, Joel P. (2000), 'From Policed Regulation to Managed Recognition in GATS', in Pierre Sauvé and Robert M. Stern (eds), *GATS 2000: New Directions in Services Trade Liberalization*, Washington, DC: Brookings Institution Press, pp. 241–82.

Sauvé, Pierre and Fliess, Barbara (1998), 'Of Chips, Floppy Disks and Great Timing: Assessing the WTO's Information Technology Agreement', *Les Cahiers de l'IFRI*, No. 57, Paris: Institut Francais des Relations Internationales.

Sauvé, Pierre and Gillespie, James (1999), 'Financial Services and the Millennium Round', Paper prepared for 'Brookings–Wharton Papers on Financial Services: 3rd Annual Conference', Washington, DC. (28–29 October).

Sauvé, Pierre and Wilkie, Christopher (2000), 'Investment Liberalization in GATS', in Pierre Sauvé and Robert M. Stern (eds), *GATS 2000: New Directions in Services Trade Liberalization*, Washington, DC: Brookings Institution Press, pp. 331–63.

UNCTAD (1999), *World Investment Report 1999*, Geneva: UNCTAD.

Young, Allison M. (2000), 'Where Next for Labor Mobility under GATS?', in Pierre Sauvé and Robert M. Stern (eds), *GATS 2000: New Directions in Services Trade Liberalization,* Washington, DC: Brookings Institution Press, pp. 184–210.

14. A real Single Market for services?

Jean-Yves Muylle

The 1985 White Paper launching the Single Market Programme (SMP) emphasised the need to liberalise services in order to make a reality of the commitment to provide for the freedom of establishment for service providers and freedom to provide cross-border services enshrined in the Treaty of Rome. In the mid 1980s, when the SMP was launched, the European Union was characterised by a web of national regulatory restrictions that discriminated against foreign industrial producers and service providers. Sector-specific regulatory restrictions not only affected the sectors directly concerned but had knock-on effects on industries upstream or downstream, for instance in the distribution, advertising or marketing services or road freight transport. Where access to physical network was necessary to provide a service, disparities in national technical regulations further fragmented the market.

The importance of these regulatory restrictions depended on the sector. In some sectors, such as telecommunications, air transport, or audio-visual services, regulations encompassed restrictions on access to the physical network, special or exclusive rights, ownership rules or public service obligations. In other sectors, quantitative restrictions limited the scope and volume of trade. Discriminatory rules against other EU operators and administrative rules increased the cost of servicing foreign markets thereby limiting trading possibilities.

The SMP therefore proposed a package of measures aimed at:

- opening up markets to new entrants on a non-discriminatory basis, by separating out far more clearly the issues of market access from technical rules on supervision, safety, and consumer protection;
- eliminating quantitative restrictions on trade in services and barriers to the free flow of factors;
- cutting red tape and simplifying controls to reduce the costs of transactions.

Nevertheless, the initial scope of the programme was rather moderate, especially as far as services were concerned. The initial SMP focused primarily on the so-called 'traditional services' (banking, insurance, air transport). Services in 'new technologies' were included but without a detailed agenda (except for audio-visual services with the presentation of the 'TV without frontiers Green Paper' as early as 1984). As momentum picked up, the scope and depth of the legislative programme was progressively extended as witnessed in the telecommunications and transport sectors while new areas were included in the utilities sectors such as electricity, gas, post and international railway transport. More recently, the transformation of Information Services has been exerting new pressures to create the appropriate legislative framework for their development at Community level.

INTERNATIONALISATION OF THE SERVICES INDUSTRY

Even if at the time services were still mainly perceived as a non-traded activity, the launch of the SMP in the mid 1980s coincided with the rapid expansion of cross-border service transactions. In addition to the impulse given by what has been the first major exercise of regulatory reform ever undertaken at Community level, this explosion was facilitated by three interrelated factors:

1. *The rapid development of a services economy* within the EU: Services play a key role in EU economies, accounting for more than 68 per cent of total value added within the EU (up from some 60 per cent in 1985) and 67 per cent of total employment. Market services represented the lion's share, with respectively 53 per cent and 46 per cent of total value added and total employment. Their growth has exceeded overall economic performance for decades, which has resulted in the share of services in total economic activity increasing over time. The rising trend can be expected to continue or even accelerate in light of the increasing prominence of knowledge-based, service-oriented activities within the EU. Moreover, services represent the main motor of growth and job creation: over the three years of slow recovery (1994–97), services represented between 2/3 and 3/4 of GDP growth and contributed almost 1 per cent a year to job creation.
2. The *increasing interaction between manufacturing and services* which is becoming a key feature of the performance of firms. Firms have been increasingly outsourcing service inputs and activities previously performed in-house, as can be observed by the growing importance of business services. This increase may be linked to several factors and processes, including an increased tendency for firms to concentrate on core activities and the increasing demand for intangible investments such as information, skills and R&D.
3. *New modes of supply of services have materialised*: production and

consumption of services which were for long constrained to the same time and space environment, can more easily be unbundled, especially in the case of information-intensive service activities. Services, most particularly those concerned with the processing and diffusion of information (such as financial services, communication), have been directly affected by the impact of liberalisation on information and communications technologies.

INTEGRATION OF SERVICES MARKET WITHIN THE SINGLE MARKET FRAMEWORK

Any analytical work on the integration of the EU services markets, and on the services sector in general, is constrained by the lack of accurate, reliable and comparable statistical data, especially concerning the tradability of services. Many parts of the services sector are confronted with the lack of basic data for output measures. This may partly be due to the intangible nature of many services and the difficulty to define the output of key services such as banking, insurance or retailing. The volume and prices of services are therefore much harder to measure than those of goods. This may also be one of the reasons why this issue has been largely ignored by international economists until the first half of the 1980s.

Intra-EU Trade in Services

Intra-EU trade in services, as captured by balance of payment/current account statistics, has not shown any clear tendency to increase since the early 1990s relative to trade in goods and remained at a surprisingly low level, when compared with its overall economic weight. Intra-EU services trade was equivalent to some 15 per cent of GDP in 1997 and to some 20 per cent of total intra-EU trade (see Table 14.1). This relative stability in intra-EU trade in services contrasts with the sharp increase in world trade in commercial services which according to recent WTO figures grew at an implicit average annual rate of 6.4 per cent between 1990 and 1998 (slightly higher than growth in industrial products).

Nevertheless, intra-EU trade figures must be considered with caution, as some fundamental measurement problems remain. Conventional balance of payment statistics do not properly capture some large segments of the services markets, notably the most dynamic ones such as services provided via telecommunications networks.

This low level of direct cross-border provision of services is probably to be explained by a combination of factors which forced commercial producers of

Table14.1   The importance of intra-EU services trade relative to GDP

	1995	1996	1997	1998	Intra-EU trade manufacturing
Belg.-Luxbg	16.1	16.6	17.1	17.7	93.8
Denmark					40.0
Germany	4.7	4.8	5.1	5.2	25.6
Greece	8.4	8.4	9.1	9.3	17.9
Spain	7.3	7.7	8.3	8.9	27.3
France	4.7	4.7	5.1	5.2	26.8
Ireland					79.8
Italy	5.9	5.8	6.0	5.8	22.4
Netherlands	13.5	13.8	15.1	15.0	74.1
Austria	17.2	17.9	17.8	18.7	40.8
Portugal	10.2	9.5	9.6	10.4	45.4
Finland	7.9	7.8	7.5	6.7	35.1
Sweden					39.5
UK	5.1	5.1	5.0	5.2	24.6

Source: Eurostat – Current Account Statistics.

services to supply foreign markets through commercial presence. Among these factors, the proximity factor for some services, the high level of person-to-person interaction, the fact that many service providers are small firms operating on a local scale and the persistence of regulatory, administrative or cultural hurdles that restrict access to domestic markets are the most important.

Foreign Direct Investment

The factors listed partly explain why globalisation in services has increasingly taken the form of direct investment rather than trade. Deregulation, privatisation and the liberalisation of trade and investment barriers have given a strong impetus to foreign direct investment (FDI) growth and this development has been particularly noticed in the services sector (see Table 14.2). Intra-EU FDI has grown substantially over the last fifteen years. Between 1992 and 1996,[1] services attracted most FDI inflows: almost 68 per cent of all intra-EU FDI inflows went to this sector and this share has been growing substantially, from 66 per cent in 1992 to 71 per cent in 1996. Business services and financial intermediation was a prime target for FDI in the EU, absorbing more than half of all such flows between 1992 and 1996 while service sectors such as transportation, air travel, telecommunications and insurance which were subject to liberalisation fairly recently did not attract much FDI.

*Table 14.2   The share of manufacturing and services in intra-EU FDI
             inflows, 1992–96 (in %)*

	1992	1993	1994	1995	1996	1992–96
Manufacturing	33.6	30.7	28.1	28.4	21.9	28.2
Services	65.6	64.5	65.7	70.9	71.3	67.9
Electricity, gas and water	0.5	2.9	0.4	1.0	2.8	1.6
Construction	1.0	2.6	1.0	1.2	1.5	1.4
Trade and repairs	5.7	6.9	7.3	10.6	13.4	9.1
Hotels and restaurants	–1.7	0.9	1.8	2.6	–1.3	0.5
Transport, storage and communication	2.8	2.9	1.7	1.6	–4.4	0.7
Telecommunications	N.a.	N.a.	N.a.	0.7	–4.7	–0.9
Financial intermediation	35.1	27.1	27.4	23.5	16.8	25.5
Monetary intermediation	N.a.	N.a.	N.a.	5.3	3.1	1.9
Other financial intermediation	N.a.	N.a.	N.a.	17.4	9.8	6.1
Total other financial intermediation and insurance	N.a.	N.a.	N.a.	18.2	12.2	6.9
Real estate and business activities	21.5	19.9	23.8	29.5	42.8	28.2
Computer activities	N.a.	N.a.	N.a.	1.2	1.6	0.6
Total	100.0	100.0	100.0	100.0	100.0	100.0

Source: Eurostat.

Mergers and Acquisitions (M&As) in the Services Industry

The Single Market Programme is generally considered to have boosted the restructuring of the services economy: networking and cooperation in services has increasingly been formalised as external knowledge and cost-sharing are becoming more important. Cooperative agreements can be found in many services ranging from alliances in air transport and telecommunications, to buying groups, strategic alliances and franchising in retailing. Nevertheless, while internationalisation is becoming more important in sectors such as telecommunications and air transport, domestic competition remains the key driver of change in many services.

A major feature of this increasing propensity to obtain a commercial presence on a local market and so to benefit from the proximity factor while respecting the cultural traditions of customers is to merge or acquire an operation in another country. This often represented by far the best means for business operators and service providers to overcome entry barriers, challenge the anti-competitive behaviour of the incumbents and to take advantage of economies of scale offered

Table 14.3   Evolution of M&A operations – share of the total (in %)

Year	Domestic	Intra-EU	International EU-target	International EU-bidder
1987	71.6	9.6	4.4	14.5
1990	60.7	21.5	7.9	9.9
1994	62.9	15.1	12.2	9.8
1997	52.3	17.4	16.0	14.2
1998	50.1	16.5	17.1	16.3

Source: AMDATA and European Commission.

by a wider market. The recent period has been characterised by a substantial decline in the share of national operations in the total number of M&As and the increase of cross-border operations, especially international operations involving a non-EU bidder and an EU target (see Table 14.3).

M&A activity in services has been particularly intense since 1994, when the number of M&As in the services sector has been higher than in industry. After a fall in 1996, the number of operations has increased sharply in services (Figure 14.1). This pattern was certainly strongly influenced by the Single Market programme which started slowly for services but accelerated significantly in recent years. Some Single Market policies in major services sectors (financial services, transport) did not come on stream until the second half of the 1990s. Furthermore, some services previously supplied by state monopolies are becoming less and less restricted by legislative provisions, government policy and financial constraints.

This upsurge in M&As activity in services has been associated with an increase in cross-border operations in services. Even though domestic operations still count for the vast majority of the total number, cross-border mergers have become more important, both as a percentage of the total number of operations, but most importantly in value as cross-border deals quite usually involve big operations, as for instance in the banking sector. On a sectoral basis, wholesale and retail distribution and banking are the most important sectors in terms of cross-border operations. The rate of growth in wholesaling is well above average but activity in retail distribution and banking has declined since the beginning of the 1990s. Among the other important areas of M&A activity, the highest growth rates are observed in business services and recreational/cultural activities (Table 14.4).

The advent of the euro has probably been another contributing (even though more recent) factor to this surge in M&As. However, the number of operations targeting EU companies in those sectors most likely to be affected by EMU such as banking and finance has never returned to the levels achieved

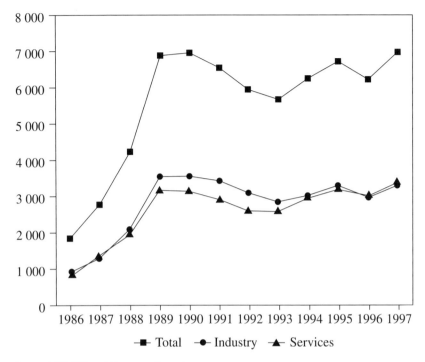

Source: AMDATA and European Commission.

Figure 14.1 *Evolution of number of mergers involving EU firms 1986–97, industry and services*

in the early and mid 1990s. As it appears from Table 14.5, national operations accounted for a very large percentage of the total number of operations in the banking and insurance sectors. This is probably to be explained by two motivating factors: the search for economies of scale by increasing market power at national level and creating the necessary conditions in terms of size for future cross-border expansion, and resistance to the entry of foreign banks into domestic markets. However, this percentage is in decline in the last two years: the pace of cross-border operations seems to have accelerated in the most recent period, particularly since the launch of EMU on 1 January 1999, if not in absolute number, at least considering the value of the transactions. Recent estimates indicated that during the first half of 1999, about 25 per cent by value of mergers and acquisitions effectively completed involved financial institutions.

Among the other services that are in the lead in terms of both total and intra-EU mergers, two deserve particular attention: business services and

Table 14.4   Intra-EU mergers and acquisitions – total number of operations

	1985	1987	1990	1994	1995	1996	1997	1998*
Total	108	267	1505	959	1 127	1 104	1 238	984
Industry	71	172	865	542	603	563	664	460
Construction	0	2	38	19	22	32	19	14
Services	37	93	602	398	502	509	555	510
Wholesale distribution	6	26	155	116	124	156	144	110
Retail distribution	5	6	70	24	40	44	51	51
Hotels/catering	2	10	33	17	12	12	23	11
Other inland transport	0	1	15	16	15	13	24	21
Air transport	1	0	2	3	2	3	6	5
Other transport services	1	4	28	10	28	15	18	17
Postal/telecomm.	0	0	2	3	9	11	17	16
Banking/finance	6	7	49	32	54	40	42	28
Insurance	4	4	23	19	26	22	26	18
Business services	7	22	142	98	108	116	135	145
Real estate	0	1	14	10	9	9	5	14
Recreational/cultural services	1	0	12	9	19	19	14	18

Note: * 1998 figures are January–1 November figures.

Source: AMDATA.

Table 14.5   Mergers and acquisitions in the banking and insurance sectors

	1985	1987	1990	1994	1995	1996	1997	1998*
Banking								
National	49	45	248	214	208	167	135	126
Community (intra-EU)	6	7	49	32	54	40	42	28
International (target EU)	16	5	17	14	20	17	31	28
International bidder EU	11	9	32	29	38	48	47	60
Total	82	66	346	289	320	272	255	242
Insurance								
National	14	18	50	49	62	66	52	38
Community (intra-EU)	4	4	23	19	26	22	26	18
International (target EU)	3	5	8	10	16	18	19	13
International bidder EU	4	3	27	14	13	20	23	23
Total	25	30	108	92	117	126	120	92

Note: * 1998 figures are January–1 November figures.

Source: AMDATA.

wholesaling. *Business services* is the lead sector in terms of number of transactions with more than 2400 operations between 1996 and September 1998 or some 14.8 per cent of the total number of M&As where the target is an EU enterprise (up from 12.3 per cent between 1994 and 1996). Even though computer services represented the largest sub-sector, large increases have been recorded in the number of M&As in the legal services sub-sector (+64 per cent). Horizontal operations involving firms from the same sub-sector have been the most important type of operations in most sub-sectors (representing up to 98 per cent of the operations in legal services). This predominance of horizontal operations does not necessarily indicate any significant weakening of competition, considering that the business sector is still characterised by a large number of enterprises. Nevertheless in some market segments, such as legal services, the recent mergers wave is likely to strongly reinforce the market power of a very limited number of firms capable of providing the sort of services required by very large companies. The same may also be true for advertising.

Activity in the *wholesale distribution* sector seems to have slightly declined since the mid 1990s but still represented some 1500 operations between 1996 and September 1998. This sector is characterised by an increased level of vertical integration where the wholesaler has been acquired by a supplier (upstream). Such operations seems to have been motivated by three main factors: the establishment of suitable distribution arrangements in a new geographic market; the cutting down of mark ups to increase the demand for the product; the exclusion of competitors by increasing the costs of setting up its own distribution system for new entrants; and the increase in relative strengths of retailers *vis-à-vis* manufacturers of (consumer) goods.

Although this intense cross-border M&A activity indicates that the barriers to capital mobility are low, it hardly gives any indication of the motives for mergers. The main motives can be summarised as follows:

- to penetrate a foreign market in the presence of high trade barriers;
- if trade barriers are low, to overcome entry barriers created by the anti-competitive behaviour of the incumbents;
- for products which require a specialised distribution network, to allow a company to enter a new market quickly, without having to construct an entirely new network;
- to allow companies to take advantage of economies of scale offered by a wider market;
- to increase market power.

While the first two motives may have prevailed in the early days of the Single Market, the last three motives nowadays appear to be behind the recent upsurge in M&A activity.

Competition and Market Structure

Within the EU, the opening up of national borders and increase in competition seems to have been less strongly perceived in the services sector than in the manufacturing sector. According to the last business survey undertaken by the Commission in the framework of its Single Market Scoreboard, only 35 per cent of firms in the services sector felt that the SMP had had a positive impact on their enterprise performance against 45 per cent in the manufacturing sector. Similarly 22 per cent of the services enterprises felt that obstacles within the Single Market had disappeared or had been significantly reduced for 43 per cent in the manufacturing industry. Another particular feature is that service companies still mainly feel an increase in competition from domestically-owned firms. The essentially local nature of increased competition in services can be explained by the fact that the need to overcome information asymmetries continues to require establishment, even after regulatory obstacles to cross-border service provision have been diluted (see below). Cross-border penetration in services has been achieved through the medium of establishment – with the acquisition of local players the preferred entry strategy, as noted above. Community service markets remain 'multi-domestic' rather than exhibiting the relatively advanced degrees of integration witnessed for manufacturing products. However, the greater national component of increased services competition also reflects the fact that the lowering of regulatory barriers to entry and competition has – at least in a first stage – been most effective in fostering competition between local players.

The impact of cross-border competition on the structure of the services sector is also heavily conditioned by the underlying market structure. In situations where competition corresponds roughly to perfect or monopolistic competition (such as road freight transport or distribution), there has been a significant increase in competition as suppliers are willing to jockey for position in partner country markets. In some cases, this can lead to significant gains in productivity. For instance, the distribution sector is increasingly characterised by growing concentration at any given stage in the chain and increased vertical integration with retailers and manufacturers encroaching on functions previously performed by wholesalers. This strategic move to cut unnecessary middlemen out of the loop was often done through the acquisition of wholesale companies by manufacturers and retailers. This trend towards increased vertical integration is also confirmed by the increasing proportion of 'private (own) labels' in total turnover, particularly in central countries (France, Germany, Belgium, UK, Netherlands), and the increasingly important role played by buying groups, that is consortia of independent retailers who combine for the purposes of enhancing their joint purchasing power. While the

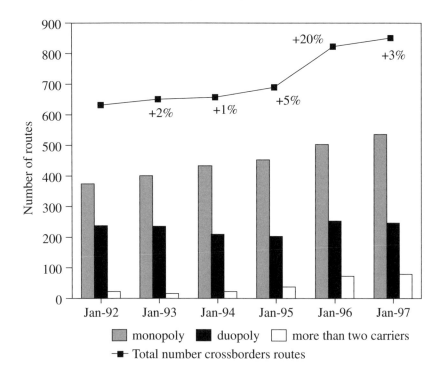

Source: European Commission.

Figure 14.2   Number of cross-border routes and breakdown per number of competitors

SMP should not be regarded as the sole driver of these changes, it is nevertheless considered as accelerating and facilitating these developments.

In the more regulated sectors where national champions were previously dominant (air transport, telecommunications), productivity and efficiency gains have been less pronounced. Strategic behaviour has probably been more important than the SMP in determining outcome. In sectors such as air transport, incumbent dominant suppliers have not yet engaged in an all-out onslaught on each other's markets. Liberalisation of the air transport sector was accompanied by a limited decrease in route concentration: the share of routes with one or two carriers continue to account for the vast majority of all routes (Figure 14.2). Companies preferred to concentrate on new products and services (for instance through an increase in the number of destinations served non-stop) and on their pricing strategy.

In general, the SMP was expected to result in considerable price convergence through a combination of arbitrage, competition and convergence of structural determinants such as income and consumer preference. In practice, a degree of price convergence has been effected for both consumer goods and market services over the period 1985–93. The standard deviation for consumer goods declined from 22.5 per cent in 1985 to 19.6 per cent in 1993, while for services the corresponding reduction was from 33.7 per cent to 28.6 per cent. However, more recent analysis showed that prices, particularly for services, continue to vary quite significantly. Price levels for services seem to be more heavily correlated with GDP than for manufactured goods. The high level of price differences persisting throughout the European Union suggests that a range of structural and behavioural factors remain which offset part of the results expected to ensue from completion of the Single Market. To this extent, price convergence and other microeconomic conditions across the EU may prove to be a longer process than was expected initially.

OVERALL PERFORMANCE IN THE SERVICES MARKET

It is difficult to assess what has been the overall impact of the Single Market Programme on services markets' performance at a macro level (growth and employment creation). As was already mentioned, the Single Market for services accelerated in the mid 1990s and therefore coincided with other developments, such as the preparation for Economic and Monetary Union, the rapid developments and the information and communication technologies as well as the liberalisation of worldwide trade. Instead of trying to isolate the direct impact of the Single Market Programme on market performance, which would be a highly risky exercise, this section rather considers the interaction between the implementation of the Single Market Programme and the contribution of services to growth and employment creation.

In almost all European countries, *growth* in the services sector has exceeded overall economic performance in the last decade, resulting in an increasing share of services in total economy in all EU countries except Ireland. The most rapidly growing sectors are finance and business services while the relative importance of the distribution sector has generally fallen (Table 14.6). This growing role for services is to be explained by a combination of different factors and the progressive removal of barriers affecting intra-EU business in services has certainly contributed to this trend.

Even though it is difficult to assess the real role played by the Single Market Programme in these developments, it is generally considered that the SMP has contributed to liberate demand and supply in the European economy in the following ways:

Table 14.6 Share of services in GDP

	Industry		Services Total		Wholesale & retail trade		Transport, storage &		Finance, insurance, real	
	1987	1997	1987	1997	1987	1997	1987	1997	1987	1997
Austria	32.6	30.4[a]	64.1	68.2[a]	17.4	17.2[a]	6.2	6.4[a]	16.7	20.6[a]
Belgium	29.5	27.6	68.6	71.3	17.3[b]	17.5[b]	7.6	8.2	6.0[c]	5.1[c]
Denmark	24.6	24.3[d]	71.6	72.1[d]	12.6	11.5[d]	6.9	7.8[d]	15.3	16.4[d]
Finland	32.5	30.2[a]	61.6	66.3[a]	11.8	9.6[a]	7.0	7.7[a]	14.0	17.3[a]
France	29.6	26.2	66.9	71.5	14.9	14.7	6.0	5.7	20.4	22.9
Germany	34.6	29.1	66.9	71.5	–	–	5.4[e]	5.0	11.3[e]	14.0[c]
Greece	25.1[f]	20.0[f]	61.1	67.9[d]	11.6	11.6[d]	7.1	6.2[d]	7.3[g]	9.5
Ireland	34.4	39.3[d]	57.0	55.6[d]	10.4	10.7[d]	5.4	5.0[d]	5.7	6.7[d]
Italy	34.1	30.5	61.9	66.9	19.1[b]	18.4[b]	5.6	6.5	22.5[h]	27.0[h]
Luxembourg	31.1	24.0[d]	66.9	75.0[d]	15.4	12.8[d]	5.3	7.5[d]	20.3[c]	18.0[c,d]
Netherlands	28.3	27.1[d]	67.8	69.8[d]	14.5	14.2[d]	6.3	6.6[d]	18.8	23.4[d]
Portugal	36.6	35.2[d]	56.1	60.9[d]	19.2	15.9[d]	6.7	5.9[d]	11.5	14.4[d]
Spain	35.3	25.6[h]	59.3	70.9[h]	20.1	22.6[h]	5.5	5.7[h]	16.7	17.6[h]
Sweden	30.7	25.7[h]	66.3	70.5[h]	10.9	9.9[h]	5.6	5.9[h]	17.4	21.4[h]
UK	32.2	27.5[d]	66.1	70.8[d]	11.7[i]	12.5	7.1	7.3[d]	18.8	22.3[d]

Note: a: 1996; b: recovery and repair included; c: real estate and business services excluded; d: 1995; e: 1991; f: restaurants and hotels excluded; g: business services excluded; community and social services included; h: 1994; i: repair services of consumer durables other than clothing included.

Source: OECD.

277

- *By creating new forms of service supply*: as for instance in the banking sector where new concepts were developed such as universal banking allowing bankers to offer a wider range of products such as 'bank-assurance'.
- *By encouraging the creation of new markets*: road transport liberalisation and elimination of border controls have fostered the growth of logistic companies improving productivity in distribution and contributing to the appearance of new businesses and business concepts such as European distribution centres, pan-European logistics services, or express and timetabled light freight transport. Growth in telecommunication services particularly mobile services is yet another successful story of the Single Market.
- *By stimulating new business and consumer demand*: road haulage and cross-border distribution are examples of sectors where the SMP has boosted business demand for services. For example, lower air fares contingent on SMP completion have fuelled a 20 per cent increase in air passenger transport, with positive knock-on effects for the tourism sector.

The combination of these Single Market effects has also resulted in large increases in *employment*. Estimates of the employment impact of the SMP range from between 0.4 and 0.8 per cent net addition to employment (up to 1.2 million jobs) over the period 1987–94. The estimated impact on employment growth in services is in excess of these figures as some job creation in services is offset by net job destruction in manufacturing. The SMP contribution to service employment has been mainly is felt in transport, construction, business and personal services. Telecommunications and financial services have experienced a slight contraction of employment because of the SMP, as rapid productivity growth and rationalisation has resulted in some job shedding (Table 14.7).

Within the EU, service employment growth was particularly buoyant in Ireland, Austria and Greece. Within services, employment growth has been strongest in community, social and personal services closely followed by finance, insurance and business services.

THE EFFECTIVENESS OF THE SINGLE MARKET PROGRAMME FOR SERVICES

The above analysis, even if very partial, suggests that the Single Market Programme has played an important role in opening formerly protected markets to international competition and fostering the performance of the services sector. Nevertheless it also demonstrated that the degree of market

Table 14.7 Share of services in total employment (% of civilian employment)

	Industry		Services Total		Wholesale & retail trade		Services — Transport, storage & communication		Finance, insurance, business services	
	1987	1997	1987	1997	1987	1997	1987	1997	1987	1997
Austria	37.7	30.3	53.7	63.8	19.8	21.4	7.1	6.6	7.0	8.9
Belgium	28.8	26	68.2	71.4	19.3	18.8	6.4	6.5	4.0	3.7
Denmark	28.2	26.8	66.0	69.5	13.0	13.4	7.0	6.9	9.7	10.2
Finland	31.2	27.5	58.4	65.5	16.3	15.9	7.3	7.7	7.7	9.5
France	30.8	25.5	62.2	69.9	17.3	17.7	5.8	5.7	9.3	11.5
Germany	40.4	36.5	55.4	60.2	–	–	6.0	5.4	2.7	3.0
Greece	28.0	22.9	45.0	56.9	–	–	–	–	–	–
Ireland	27.9	28.4	57.0	61.7	–	–	–	–	–	–
Italy	32.6	32.0	56.8	61.2	21.5	22.0	6.3	6.2	13.4	16.7
Luxembourg	33.1	25.6	62.7	71.8	22.3	21.1	5.4	7.3	7.8	8.9
Netherlands	26.8	22.2	68.3	74.1	19.1	21.3	6.8	6.6	10.6	13.8
Portugal	34.9	31.5	42.9	54.8	15.1	17.3	3.9	3.5	3.5	6.3
Spain	32.3	30.0	52.5	61.7	22.0	23.4	5.8	5.8	4.6	5.4
Sweden	29.7	26.0	66.3	71.3	13.8	14.1	6.6	6.7	7.4	8.9
UK	32.9	26.9	64.8	71.3	19.7	19.6	5.8	5.6	10.3	11.9

Source: OECD.

279

integration in many service sectors lags behind that observed for products, and that in some respects the Single Market is still operating in a sub-optimal way in the services sector. In large part, this attests to the economic characteristics of services but also that, as is explained above, the starting point was radically different – in 1985, the EU market was still an extremely fragmented market in services while it was already integrated to a certain extent for industrial goods. There are, therefore, reasons to believe that some of the key and basic principles underlying the whole philosophy of the Single Market concept are not being implemented in the most efficient way and that action must be undertaken to remedy those deficiencies that are identified below.

Regulatory failures are still generally considered as seriously limiting the scope of competition within the EU. Traditionally such regulations were introduced to deal with perceived market failures such as externalities related to investments in networks or infrastructure or asymmetric information between producers and consumers. Moreover, the 'Single Market spirit' is not yet entrenched in Member States' philosophy as most of them pursue (deliberately or not) policies that directly or indirectly restrict the access of foreign services and service suppliers to their domestic markets. The current process of economic reforms currently undertaken at the European Union level, further to the conclusions of the European Council in Cardiff (June 1998), is linked to a reassessment of these markets failures and of the capacity of governments to correct them via regulation.

In March 2000, the Lisbon European Council asked the Commission, the Council and the Member States, each in accordance with their respective powers, to set out a strategy for the removal of barriers to services by the end of 2000. The following assessment of the effectiveness of the Single Market is by no means meant to be exhaustive and does not prejudge the content of the strategy document to be adopted by the Commission. It will focus on three horizontal issues that are of particular importance for an efficient services sector:

1. The application of the two basic principles ensuring the free provision of services on a cross-border basis and the freedom of establishment.
2. The promotion and application of fair competition.
3. The access to the infrastructure.

Freedom of Establishment – Free Provision of Services

As already stressed, *freedom of establishment* has traditionally been the means through which service providers have sought to take advantage of commercial opportunities in other Member States. Much of the thrust of EU single market legislation has been designed to facilitate cross-border implantation of companies, without having to create a new legal entity from scratch in order to comply with all local administrative, legal, fiscal and other requirements. Several initiatives undertaken at EU level in the field of company law have traditionally attempted to serve this objective of facilitating establishment and cross-border merger.

At a more sectoral level, harmonisation of prudential rules in financial services has served the objective of cross-border establishment by ensuring that companies do not have to constitute separate capital bases/solvency margins and meet separate own funds requirements for every country in which they do business. The impact on cross-border establishment has been quite significant straight after the adoption of the second banking directive with a 58 per cent increase in the number of branches of banking institutions established in another EU country between 1992 and 1995. Nevertheless, this number seems to have stagnated since then. Moreover, the function of Luxembourg, Ireland and the UK as international banking centres is confirmed by overall market shares of foreign branches and subsidiaries of more than 50 per cent of total domestic assets whereas the majority of other EU countries report overall foreign market share around or below 10 per cent.

Nevertheless, freedom of establishment can still be hindered by the application of unduly restrictive administrative procedures or the need to obtain certification or licensing. This is sometimes the case for some business services. In the distribution sector, which is a crucial sector to make sure that the benefits of the Single Market materialise, establishing a commercial presence in another Member State can also involve a series of difficulties as Member States have the tendency to adopt different rules concerning the development of town centres, land planning use and shopping hours. These rules, although not necessarily discriminating against foreign firms, do entrench the position of incumbent operators.

The very low level cross-border intra-EU trade in services seems to suggest that *cross-border provision of services* is still fraught with difficulty. This is confirmed by some sectoral evidence: in business software and computer services, intra-EU exports of services were ranging between 0.5 and 5 per cent of total services in the EU countries surveyed in the Eurostat pilot study. In the banking sector, cross-border provision of services is still at an embryonic stage, as is evidenced by the limited share of bank assets and liabilities that is accounted for by cross-border business within Europe (less than 10 per cent). In the life and non-life insurance business, the share of gross premiums accounted for by non-established insurance enterprises does not exceed 1 per cent in all countries except for Luxembourg and Ireland (and Belgium in the non-life insurance business).

Nevertheless, the information revolution is likely to change the business and economics of service markets. The information needs of consumers, which were previously served by physically adjacent suppliers, can now be served equally effectively over information networks. The structural obstacles to service markets are being scaled back as physical distance is no longer an insurmountable barrier to service provision. This is particularly true in respect of services revolving around information needs (for example financial advice). The emergence of the technical means for doing business over wide geographical distances brings a number of other legal and jurisdictional issues into play. The relationship between service suppliers and consumers acting in a non-professional capacity are subject to an array of safeguards which are designed to offer a degree of confidence and security to both parties to the contract. Given that consumers are often unable to process credentials of the service supplier and the characteristics of the product offered (for example insurance where utilisation of the purchased service may be deferred in time) are difficult to assess, regulatory authorities have tended to place the emphasis on consumer protection. This has resulted in a complex web of consumer protection requirements which differ across Member States, and render the application of the *mutual recognition principle* even more difficult at the expense of an efficiently functioning single market.

The Mutual Recognition Principle

The principle of mutual recognition has a central role to play in the operation and effectiveness of the Single Market for services, as it allows free provision of services without the need for harmonisation at EU level. Under this principle a Member State may not forbid the sale on its territory of a product lawfully produced and marketed in another Member State, even if that product is produced according to different technical or quality specifications from those applied to its own products. For services, it means that an economic operator lawfully providing a service in a Member State must be able freely to provide the same service in another Member State. The Member State may oppose the lawful provision of a service by a provider established in another Member State only under extremely restrictive conditions that involve overriding reasons of public interest, such as the protection of consumers.

This mutual recognition principle is fully consistent with the overall Single Market philosophy, according to which the rules of the Member State of origin apply. It is also fully in line with the dynamic approach to the principle of subsidiarity and maintains the diversity of products and services that come onto the markets. It is therefore a powerful tool for economic integration.

It is difficult to assess the application of mutual recognition accurately, as there are no statistics about the cases where mutual recognition works within the Single Market or about cases where producers or providers decide to comply with the specifications of the country of destination or decide not to enter into cross-border operations. There is nevertheless enough evidence to stress that problems subsist in the application of the MRP, particularly in the services sector. Difficulties arise especially when Member States take steps to protect the '*general interest*', for instance in order to protect consumers. This is notably the case in financial services, commercial communications or with regulated professions.

In the *financial services* sector, national authorities have traditionally imposed detailed information requirements and conditions on the manner in which financial service suppliers can market, negotiate and conclude contracts with consumers. The relevant inter-governmental conventions (Rome and Brussels), and prevailing interpretation of the EU Treaty, result in a situation in which contractual rules will generally be enforced according to the rule of the country of the consumer. Claims will also generally be settled under the judicial system of the consumer. Hence we witness high levels of entry through acquisition or efforts to work with local intermediaries (agents or brokers) who can adapt products to local conventions and are familiar with local judicial practice in the event of litigation.

As contractual arrangements and claims settlement consideration are at the heart of most retail financial products (and insurance policies in particular), new products have to be constituted each time a service provider wishes to enter a partner country market. This is often not a viable commercial proposition. Nevertheless, if all Member States could apply the same criteria to consumer protection, financial enterprises approved in the country of origin could deal more easily with clients in other Member States without facing any further requirements on them. This is why the Commission recently announced that it will draw up in cooperation with the Member States a list of obstacles to cross-border transactions between business and consumers and analyse the conditions in which the rules for protecting the consumers of the host country should be applied.

In the field of *commercial communications*, the problems mainly stem from disparities between national regulations, for instance in advertising. The same legitimate concerns such as protection of minors have aroused widely differing responses such as total prohibition, partial ban or self regulation. The Commission has launched several infringements proceedings against national measures that restrict directly or indirectly the free provision of commercial communications. This concerned notably the ban of toy advertising on TV in Greece and the Belgian decision to allow communal taxes on antenna dishes. To avoid similar problems in the future, the Commission has proposed a new approach that would try to reconcile the objective of consumer protection and of cross-border provision of services. This approach will consist in identifying the areas where Member States are not willing to accept the principle of mutual recognition and then analysing whether the resulting restrictions are proportional to the public interest objective that is pursued.

In order to facilitate and improve the application of the principle of mutual recognition, the Commission adopted in June 1999 a communication providing for a series of actions to improve the monitoring of mutual recognition, make economic operators and the competent authorities in the Member States more aware of it, establish and improve contacts between national authorities and improve the way in which the Commission deals with individual complaints.

The Promotion and Application of Fair Competition

Respect of competition rules is essential for ensuring the effectiveness of Single Market measures promoting a high level of efficiency on EU services markets. The progressive emergence of a services economy has corresponded with the emergence of some anti-competitive practices. In particular, the liberalisation process in some sectors has been accompanied by an increasing tendency from national governments to inject money in the form of state aids in companies to help them face increased competition. On the basis of the statistics compiled by Commission services concerning notified state aids, two sectors deserve particular attention: transport (particularly air transport) and financial services (Table 14.8). Nevertheless, such statistics ignore the reality in other sectors such as audiovisual where public participation is still a dominant feature.

Access to the Infrastructure

A fully integrated and efficient Single Market needs the physical and technical means and infrastructure to allow cross-border transactions to take place as efficiently and smoothly as those within national boundaries. Nevertheless, for spatial, environmental or technical reasons, increased competition may require cooperation between rival firms to enable the interoperability of competing networks, and the enforcement of network interconnection, especially in the case where a new entrant firm is seeking interconnection with a dominant incumbent's facilities. Ensuring fair and economically viable access to physical networks for all services operators therefore requires

- the removal of physical barriers to establishment and access to existing infrastructure;
- a fair, light and transparent licensing regime;
- fair access charges set by the infrastructure provider to new entrants (air transport, telecom) or network competition when technically feasible and economically justifiable (telecom)

Table 14.8 Ad-hoc state aid in manufacturing, financial services and air transport

	1992		1993		1994		1995		1996		1997	
	Million Euros	% of total aid	Million Euros	% of total aid	Million Euros	% of total aid	Million Euros	% of total aid	Million Euros	% of total aid	Million Euros	% of total aid
Manufacturing	2 422	6	5 236	12	4 353	11	3 352	8	3 663	10	3 522	10
Treuhand aid*	5 161	13	8 774	20	10 918	26	6 623	16	4 796	13	3 602	10
Financial services			795		480		2 069		2 776		3 082	
Air transport			97		1 920		1 924		974		805	
Total	7 583		14 902		17 671		13 968		11 909		11 011	

Note: *Aid in Germany given via the Treuhandanstalt (THA) or the Bundesanstalt für vereinigungsbedingte Sonderaufgaben (BvS).

Source: European Commission.

Physical Access to the Infrastructure

This problem is of particular importance in the transport (and to some extent energy) sector. For instance, some practices currently restrict access to *port facilities* and services which still remain protected by exclusive rights and/or de jure or de facto monopoly, which sometimes has resulted in refusal of access to harbour facilities. In the same way, as many European airports are facing increased congestion, and a significant expansion in the number and capacity of airports is unlikely, the issue of *slot allocation* at peak hours is of particular concern. One point of controversy is the so-called grandfather rights which reinforce the status quo and favour incumbent operators and impede competition by restricting effectiveness of entrants. In the vast majority of congested airports, historical carriers have developed hubs. These incumbents have sometimes up to 50 per cent of the total number of slots in their respective hubs (and most peak hours slots) while the second biggest slot holder has a share between 5 and 10 per cent and the third holder has a share lower than 5 per cent. Finally, the development of a Community railways strategy and the interoperability between national networks is still hampered by differences in national standards and operating rules. In conventional rail, the major differences that remain are between electrical systems, signalling, operational rules and the qualifications of train crews.

Licensing

Liberalisation, market integration and licensing are almost inseparable topics in services sectors where entry needs to be controlled because of market failures and for public interest objectives. However, in order to encourage market forces, the restrictive nature of licensing arrangements must be minimised to what is needed to prevent market failures. Costs and delays must be low, and authorities should have the least possible discretion. This may imply recourse to a system of single Community licence, as in banking and transport, with the application of home country control, which seems to have worked well so far.

In the telecommunications sector, Community measures have recognised that licensing will continue to be predominantly a matter for each national regulatory authority, in accordance with procedures and minimum conditions harmonised at an EC level. The liberalisation of the telecommunications services and infrastructure market in Europe has promoted the rapid increase in the number of licensed operators across a range of telecommunications services. By the end of 1998, around 219 operators are authorised within the EU to *provide national public voice telephony*; around 284 operators are authorised for *international voice services*; around 90 *national mobile licenses* have been granted; around 654 operators are authorised to offer *local network services*, while 195 can offer *network services at national level* and 259 at *international level*.

The various national frameworks appear *in broad terms to function well*, even though some concerns have been expressed related to effective application mainly with regard to licence conditions imposed, a certain lack of transparency with regard to licence conditions, the level of licence fees, and time-limits for the issue of licences.

Fair Access Charges and Interconnection Rates

Interconnection between facilities and network is the key to effective competition in network services. New entrants cannot compete without interconnection on reasonable terms. The way interconnection is regulated will also be a determining factor in the fortunes of the incumbent operators. The problem is that the market for interconnection may not be fully competitive in the early years of liberalisation. Incumbent operators will retain a monopoly over many elements of the network and as new infrastructure providers enter the market they too will find themselves in control of bottleneck resources. The ability to access adequate transmission capacity, to access services at affordable price and on fair terms, and to interconnect with a competitor's network will all be fundamental to allowing businesses or service providers the opportunity to provide and/or use liberalised telecommunications services. In this context, interconnection rules ensure fair and non-discriminatory interconnection for all operators and service providers in the EU.

In the telecommunications sector, the EU interconnection framework, set out by Directive 97/33, leaves national regulatory authorities scope for discretion. Thus even if the EU directives are properly implemented, there may still be a risk of finding quite wide differences in interconnection terms and conditions beyond what could be put down to cost differences, among Member States. The Commission has therefore issued some recommendations on 'best current practice' interconnection charges for the fixed telecommunication services (Figure 14.3). Generally speaking, it is considered that interconnection charges in several Member States have dropped substantially.

All this combined with the legacy of monopoly control, the existence of potential bottlenecks, the need for prudential controls against systemic risks and the necessity for network interconnection are all arguments in favour of some degree of regulatory oversight in the different stages towards full liberalisation. Regulatory systems vary within the EU. Variety is not a problem as long as governance structures in place have in common the ability to restrain arbitrary actions, especially to promote national interests. In network industries, national regulatory authorities (NRAs) may be asked to intervene to solve three types of conflict (which are nevertheless intertwined): conflicts in

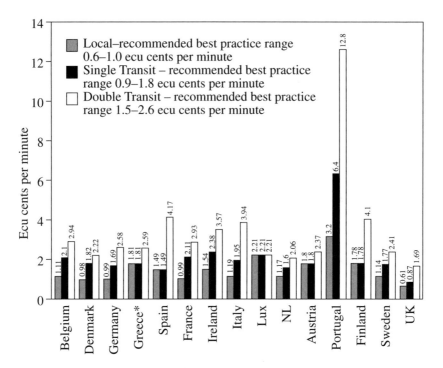

Note: * Greek data refers to mobile-to-fixed interconnection.

Source: Fourth Report on the Implementation of the Telecommunications Regulatory Package COM(98)594.

Figure 14.3   Interconnection rate for call termination in the EU15 (Sept 1998)

the market place between incumbents and new entrants; conflicts between national objectives and Community objectives; conflicts between the regulatory and the competition policy objectives. Concerns are still expressed not only about the efficiency of these regulatory institutions, but even sometimes about their independence, with staff occasionally being seconded from the operators to the NRA or from the Ministry representing the State's shareholding.

CONCLUSIONS

The building up of a Single Market and of the single currency have been the main driving forces for the construction of Europe as an economic and political entity. Europe is nowadays considered as a highly integrated economy.

Trade and investments among EU Member States and with the rest of the world has increased substantially, and competition has intensified, resulting in lower prices and greater choice of products and services. Unfortunately, this movement towards integration has coincided in time with a persistent deterioration of the employment performance in Europe. Community policies to foster economic integration do not appear to have been sufficiently effective in curbing the high and persistent unemployment rates that Europe has recorded since the 1970s.

Conditions in labour markets, weaknesses in human capital formation and other structural problems affecting labour markets must certainly account for a very significant part of current unemployment levels in Europe. But they are not the only causes explaining the present situation in labour markets. Weak competition in some product and services markets and inappropriate regulations interact with labour market regulations and institutions to affect the functioning of the labour market in important ways. The importance of tackling these structural weaknesses has been fully recognised at the highest political level. In particular, the Cardiff European Council launched a new process to foster economic reforms among Member States and expand the traditional process of economic policy coordination into microeconomic policy making, thereby maximising the growth and employment potential brought about by EMU.

Nevertheless this process of review of the individual situation in Member States and the identification of relevant policy priorities at the national level needs to be completed by a continuous review of the priorities to get the Single Market to work. In November 1999, the Commission adopted its strategy for the Internal Market which is intended to provide a coherent framework for Internal Market policy over the next five years. This combines a shared vision of its longer-term (five-year) aims with agreed short-term operational targets.

So far, the Community's efforts have been geared to constructing the legal framework necessary for the integration of national markets; in the future we will need to ensure that this framework functions optimally, so that it creates the conditions in which business can flourish and that it generates growth, employment and other benefits for Europe's citizens. The policy mix is changing accordingly – although there will inevitably be some new legislation, much more time and resources will be devoted to non-legislative activity which seeks to ensure that the existing rules are applied in practice and which constantly reviews the impact of those rules on the market. Action at Community level must be accompanied by structural change at national level.

Four strategic objectives will set the broad policy direction for the Internal Market over the next five years.

- To improve the quality of life of citizens
- To enhance the efficiency of Community product and capital markets

- To improve the business environment
- To exploit the achievements of the Internal Market in a changing world

This proposed new strategy also clearly identifies the services sector as a sector where little progress has been made so far and where further efforts are necessary to eradicate any remaining obstacles to cross-border trade and the emergence of new barriers. These include problems already identified in this chapter such as the application of the mutual recognition principle, inadequate access to public procurement markets, misuse of national rules protecting the public good. In the same way, further Community action will be necessary to ensure that the benefits of electronic commerce are not offset by divergences between national rules. This approach has been later confirmed by the Lisbon European Council which called for urgent attention to the completion of the Internal Market, especially in the services sector, to augment the EU's economic outlook as part of an overall strategy of structural reform.

NOTE

1. Most recent year for which sectoral data are available.

Index

absolute advantage theories 35
accountability
accountancy sector 199–205
accounting rates 222–3, 249
acquisitions, *see* mergers and acquisitions
Actor-Network Theory (ANT) 177
adaptation 146–8
added value 42
advertising services 34, 41, 128, 146–7,
    283
    agencies 29
    campaigns 6
    on-line 32
    regulation 223
AEG 183
agriculture 61, 237–8
air and water pollution 207
air transport 226–7, 243, 265, 275
    cargo 255–6
    state aid 284–5
air transport review 249
airline catering 227
airports 286
Alexander, N. 155, 156, 170
alliances 50, 157, 160, 165, 176
Amin, A. 3
AMP (advertising-related services) 128
Anderson, E. and Gatignon, H. 159
Annan, Kofi 213
antenna dishes 283
Application Service Providers 223
applied liberalisation 262
arbitrage 276
Arbos, J. 170
Asia 91
ASME (American Society of Mechanical
    Engineers) 181, 183
asset management industry 255
assets 48
asylum seekers 218
audio-visual services 223, 266
Australian service sector 5

Austria 278
Axford, B. 2

Bailly, A. et al. 46
balance of payments (BOP) 31, 116–17,
    267
Baltic States 167
banking services 8, 32, 37, 39–40, 154,
    173, 242, 265, 270, 278, 281
Baumol, W. J. 31
BBC 185
Bedaux, Charles Eugene 185
Belgium 5, 283
Bell Laboratories 186
best practice manuals 176
Bethlehem Steel Works 181, 184
BITs (bilateral investment treaties) 216
Bloomfield, B. P. and Best, A. 177
bonds 5
Bosch 183
bound liberalisation 262
BPTS (business, professional and techni-
    cal services) 122–4, 126–9
branch plants/offices 138, 140
brand loyalty 156
Brandeis, Louis D. 184
brands 36, 42–3, 47–50, 52, 156, 165
Brazil 257
broad reciprocity 216
broadcasting 223
brokerage 146–7
bureaucracy 169
bureaucratisation 159
business media 176, 188
business services 5–6, 28–9, 30, 81, 87,
    89, 94, 97–100, 232
    advanced 28, 32, 33
    EU 122–4, 126–9
    globalisation 39–41
    Haute-Garonne companies survey
    134–48
    internationalisation indicators 102–4

business services (*cont.*):
  M & A activities 270, 271, 273
  R & D 31
  United States 255
buying groups 274

Cable and Wireless Plc 37
cabotage 227, 255
Callon, M. 177
Canada 5, 81, 195
Cardiff European Council 289
Central Europe 167
child morality 228
China 91, 175
chroncyclograph 182
civil aviation 207, 226–7, 243, 256, 275
claims settlements 283
cleaning services 6
client-supplier relationship 34
client trust 42
coercive isomorphism 178
Coffey, W. J. and Polèse, M. 46
commercial intelligence services 146–7
commercial services 151–72
commodities, *see* goods
communication services 10, 28, 47, 89, 92, 94, 99–100, 102–4, 232
communications 37
  improvements in 1, 4
  problems constraining internationalisation 169
  used by service providers 142
comparative advantage 35, 68, 136–7
competition
  external economic 4
  laws 219
  liberalisation of service markets 10, 20–2
  maritime transport 227
  pro-competitive reforms 20
  Single Market programme 274–6, 284
  telecommunications 223
competitive advantage 154–6, 179
competitiveness 19, 31, 35, 136–7
computer literacy 259
computer services 6, 29, 32, 33, 41, 87, 92, 146–7, 232, 269, 281
consortia 274
construction services 223–4, 232, 240, 260, 269, 272

consultancy services 45
  environmental issues 224
  human resources 146–7
  on-line 32
  technical 146–7, *see also* management consultancy
consumer goods 276
consumer protection 281, 283
consumers 42, 241
  behaviour patterns 52
  Engel's law 75
  freedom of choice 209–10
  global production system 63–4
  market liberalisation benefits 193
  regulated professions and 220
  utilisation 68
consumption patterns 52
container trade 227
contestability 261
continuous improvement 176, 185–7
contractual rules 283
corporate leadership 168
corruption 159
cost internationalisation 35
courier firms 222
creativity, service-inspired 19
cross-border trade 44, 140–2, 259, 260, 263
  competition 274–5
  distribution services 248
  EU 267–8
  financial services 242
  freedom of establishment 280–1
  infrastructure access 284–6
  mergers and acquisitions 270–1, 273, 274
  Single Market programme 266
Crozier, General William 184
CSI (Coalition of Service Industries) 251–6
CTS (Council for Trade in Services) 215
cultural diversity 34
cultural problems 169
cultural services 226, 232
currency control 169
currency exchanges 5
customers 49–50, 141–2, *see also* consumers
Czech Republic 167

Daniels, P. W. 36
Dawson, J. A. 151, 169
de-industrialisation 7, 29–30
delivery modes 140–5, 146–8, 165
delocalisation 31, 67–8
demand related services 35
Deming, W. E. 176, 186–7
Denmark 5, 161, 165, 167
deregulation 153, 155, 198, 226
design services 33
developed-non-developed trading 46
developing countries 7, 21, 198
   financial services restrictions 242
   GATS 240
   GATS 2000 257–63
   importance of services in 231
   service providers 244
   telecoms 223
   WTO 211
Dicken, P. 156, 157
DiMaggio, P. J. and Powell, W. W. 178
discrimination 233, 241–2, 261
dispute settlement 201, 208, 212, 287–8
distance reduction 28
distribution services 5, 39–40, 63, 92, 224, 232, 240, 270, 272
   freedom of establishment 281
   mergers and acquistions 273
   SMP boost for services 278
   vertigal integration 274
distributors' brands 48–9
diversity 10, 34
division of labour 37
domestic markets 37
domestic regulation 217, 236, 241, 245–6
driving licences 196
Dunning, J. H. 35, 38, 154, 156, 158

e-commerce services 5, 228, 248, 252–3, 259, 290
e-commerce work programme 249
Eastern Europe 165, 167
Eastern Rate Case 184
economic geography 31, 176, 188
economic integration 288–9
economic theory 58, 63, 70, 72, 74, 75
economics 151, 210
economies of scale 37, 74, 159, 163, 239, 270, 271

economies of scope 156, 159
education
   developing countries 261
   production of professional expertise 178
   regulated professions 221
education services 195, 196, 197, 232
Edvardsson, B. et al. 154, 157
efficiency 180, 184, 185–7
electic paradigm 154–5
electronic commerce, *see* e-commerce services
electronics industry 32
Emergency Safeguard Measures 218–19
employees 1, 10–11, 38, 44, 113, 253, 260, 261
employment 1–3, 5, 30, 278–9
EMU 270, 271
encryption 228
'end of geography' myth 2, 3
energy services 232, 240, 256
Engel's law 75
engineering services 32, 33, 223–4, 260
entrepreneurial risk 66
ENTs (Economic Needs Tests) 218
environmental protection 207
environmental services 224, 232, 240
equilibrium price system 64–5, 70, 75–6
equity 210, 212
establishment brands 52
ethics 210–11, 221
EU (European Union) 9
   balance of payments 116, 117
   compared with US service globalisation 90–3
   FDI 83
   foreign subsidiaries in financial sector 242
   franchises 51
   international trade 82, 86–7
   internationalisation service index 100–4
   maritime trade 243
   mutual recognition of equivalence 209
   natural persons temporary movement 244
   public services policy 247–8
   regulated professions 221

EU (European Union) (*cont.*):
  services 85, 86–8, 111–14, 119–29,
    231, 232, 266
  Single Market Programme 265–88
  trade 38
euro currency 270
European Commission 289
  GATS 2000 237, 238–9
  interconnection charges 287
  mutual recognition principle 283–4
European Court of Justice 212
European Economy (2000) 46
expertise 179
exports 82, 85, 86, 91
  EU services 111–14, 118–29, 119–29
  markets 261
  Scandinavian 161–2, 167
  stage approach 36–7
extra-EU trade 38

fair access charges 287
FDI (Foreign Direct Investment) 9, 38,
    42, 44–6, 80, 82–5, 87–8, 90
  developing countries 259
  EU-US comparison 91–2
  European services 101–4
  globalisation in services 268
  mergers and acquisitions 46–7
  Scandinavia 161
Fernández, T. 46
financial capital 168
financial services 63, 87, 89, 92, 94,
    99–100, 254, 263, 269
  cross-border activities 281
  GATS 224–5, 239, 242–3
  internationalisation indicators 102–4
  mutual recognition principle 283
  SMP 278
  state aid 284–5
Financial Services Directive 126
Financial Stability Forum 225
finished manufactured products 161
Finland 161
fish 161
Fladmoe-Lindquist, K. 51
Fogel, Professor Robert W. 58–9
Fontagné, L. 45
Fordism 176, 179, 180, 181, 188
foreign affiliates 9, 19, 46, 51, 80–1,
    141, 208, 216, 255

foreign exchange rates 169
Fourastié, J. 30
France
  business-to-business service interna-
    tionalisation survey 134–48
  GATS 195
  service sector 5
  service trade and investment 95–100
  Taylorism 185
franchises 19, 51–2, 143, 145, 157, 165
fraud 159, 165
freedom of establishment 280–2

Gantt, Henry Lawrence 182, 183
GATS (General Agreement on Trade in
    Services) 8, 9, 20–1, 44, 134,
    139–40
  coverage of 232–4
  governmental services 193–201
  impact on major sectors 220–8
  international law 206–9
  legitimacy issues 209–13
  provenance of principles and rules
    214–19
  standard and specific obligations for
    WTO members 233–4
  unfinished horizontal rules 235–7
GATS (General Agreement on Trade in
    Services) 2000
  developing countries 257–63
  domestic regulation 245–6
  e-commerce 248
  important service sectors covered by
    240–3
  preparation for 237–40
  public services 246–8
  reasons for new round of negotiations
    234–7
  temporary movement of service
    providers 244–5, 253
GATT (General Agreement on Tariffs
    and Trade) 20, 21, 68–9, 212, 214,
    215, 216, 258
GDP (Gross Domestic Product) 4, 119
  distribution services sector 241
  intra-EU services trade 268
  liberalisation of services and 252
  services in EU 231, 277
General Equilibrium Theory 64
geography 2, 3, 10, 160

economic 31, 176, 188
Scientific Management 180
Germany
changing structure of economy 62, 63
foreign affiliates 81
Scientific Management 183
service trade and investment 95–100
services boosting manufacturing 29
Gilbreth, Frank Bunker 182, 183
Gilbreth, Lillian 182
globalisation 4–6, 28–41, 79–85, 100–4,
see also internationalisation
glocalistion 3
Goldman Sachs 29
goods 86–7, 116–17, 276
governments
civil aviation 226
domestic regulation 245–6
entry terms 218
environmental consultancy 224
GATS 193–4, 195–8, 211
guaranteed formal work 72–3
health care 225
insurability 66–7
multilateral trade negotiations 209–10
procurement 236–7
regulated professions 221
grandfather rights 286
Greece 278, 283
greenfield FDI 44, 45, 46, 80, 90
ground handling 227
growth paradox 29–30
guaranteed formal work 72–3

H-O-S model 36
Haber, S. 184
Harvard Business School 187
Harvey, David 2
Haute-Garonne business-to-business
service internationalisation survey
134–48
health and safety 223
health care services 195, 196, 197–8,
225–6, 232
health issues 207
Hein, Pete 60
Held, D. 3
high speed steel work 181, 183
higher education 247, 255
Hirsch, S. 45

Hollander, S. C. 157
hospitals 197, 247
hotel services 39–40, 48, 49, 51, 81, 87,
89, 92, 94, 102–4, 226, 269, 272
human resources 34, 36, 165, 168
consultancy 146–7
flows of 42
management 188
human rights 207
hypermarkerts 224

IATA Traffic Conferences 226
ICT (information and computer technology) 111, 113, 169, 255, 259
idea flows 42
IKEA 166, 167
ILO 207
IMF (International Monetary Fund) 4, 7,
207, 225
immigration 218, 224
imports 82, 85, 86, 91, 112, 167
Incandela, D. et al. 154
incentive schemes 180
indentity and control 171
India 257
industrial espionage 175
Industrial Revolution 7, 61, 65, 68, 71,
72, 74
information services 87
information technololgy, *see* ICT
infrastructure access 284–6
Institute for International Economics
252
Institute of Mechanical Engineers 183
insurability, notion of 66–7
insurance 37, 39–40, 65, 242, 265,
272
inter-firm trade 46
interconnection rates 287
Internal Market 289–90
internalisation advantages 156–7
international calls 222
international law 206–9, 212
international organisations 207
International Road Federation 226
International Road Union 226
international standards 218, 224
international trade 6, 9–10, 19, 42, 82,
86–7, 207
International Union of Railways 226

internationalisation
  delivery modes 140–8, 165
  effect on services 33–8
  European service index of 100–4
  factors that promote or deter 167–9
  IMF definition of 4
  increasing complexity of 1–2
  motivation 38, 138, 157, 163–4, 167,
    170
  organisational strategies 164–5
  Scandinavian commercial services
    study 163–71
  services promotion of 28–33
Internet 1, 4, 6, 8, 31–3, 169, 228
Internet Service Providers 223
interpreting services 146–7
Interstate Commerce Commission 184
intra-EU services trade 38, 267–8, 272,
  281
intra-firm trade 34, 46–7
intuitive learning 185–6
investment-orientated services 42
investment-trade study 95
investments 7, 38, 45–6, 68, 161, 216,
  257, *see also* FDI
IPF (international flows of productive
  factors) 44
Ireland 82, 167, 278, 281
isomorphism 178–9
Italy 95–100
Itochu 37
ITU (International Telegraph Union)
  222
Iwata, Yoshiki 185

Japan 91, 185–6
  EU exports to 120, 122, 123, 125
  foreign affiliates 81
  service trade and investment 95–100
job security 195
joint ventures 143, 144, 157, 165
Joynson, Sid 185–6
justice 246

Kacker, M. 170
kaizan 185–7
Karsenty, G. 70
Knight, Frank 65
knowledge services 36, 175–87
Kobrin, S. J. 157
Krupp 183

labour 212
  costs 7
  division of 37
  mobility 10–11, 38, 44, 113, 253,
    260, 261
  recruitment 33
  skilled 35
LAMP (legal and related services) 128
land transport 243
language construction 179
language problems 169
Laujalainen, R. 170
law 206–9, 212
lawyers 6
lean production 186
learning economy/region 157
leasing 65
legal services 40–1, 128, 255
leisure services 10, 32
Leo, P-Y., and Phillipe, J. 42
Li, J. and Guisinger, S. 38
liberalisation 35, 38, 90, 153, 211, 239,
  286
  developing countries 258, 261–3
  distribution services 224
  multilateral 227
  progressive 217
  service markets 10, 20–2
  telecommunications 254
  trade unions 227, *see also* GATS
licensing 165, 203–4, 286–7
limits and boundaries 59–61
Lindahl, D. P. and Beyers, W. B. 137
linguistic services 10, 28
Lisbon European Council 280, 290
Littler, C. R. 182
loans 5
localisation 10, 35, 36
location-specific advantages 154,
  158–9
locational advantages 166–7
logistics sector 136, 278
Long, Olivier 211
Lowe 183
Lucretius 59–60
Luxembourg 5, 281

macroeconomics 20, 74, 136
maintenance 63
Mallampally, P. and Zimny, Z. 84, 85

management consultancy 19, 28, 31, 34, 40, 43, 135, 175–87
  neo-Taylorism 185
  sociology of knowledge 177–9
  world market for 175
management gurus 180, 184, 185
managers, local 38
mandated agenda 237
Mann, Catherine L. 252, 254
manufacturing industries 7, 8, 9, 29, 37, 87, 90
  developing international markets 138
  economic theory and 74
  internationalisation indicators 101, 102, 103–4
  intra-EU FDI flows 269
  services and 266
  state aid 285
  strategic management 36
  variation 186
maritime transport 227, 243
market
  asymmetries 30–1
  contestability 261
  creation 278
  integration 286, 288–9
  performance 276–8
  saturation 137, 155, 164, 169–70
  segmentation 165
  structure 46, 113, 274–6
market access
  commitments 234, 240
  domestic regulation 236
  e-commerce 248
  GATS Article on 215–16
  negotiations 238
market research 6, 29, 41
marketing 29
Marrakech's Annex on 'Movement of Natural Persons' 244
Marshall, Alfred 60
media
  advertisement regulation 223
  business 176, 188
  comment on GATS 193
  created fashion 180
  platform for Taylor's views 184
medical services 255
mergers and acquisitions (M & A) 4, 9, 19, 20, 29, 38, 80, 84, 88–9, 90

EU-US comparison 91–2, 94
European services 101–4
existing brands 49–50
FDI 44–7
Scandinavia 162, 164
Single Market policies and 269–73
UK and German legal firms 128–9
Mexico 263
MFN (Most-Favoured Nation) principle 195, 197, 214, 215, 216, 217, 233, 239, 243, 249
Midvale Steel Company 184
migrant workers 218, 224
mimetic isomorphism 178
Mitsui & Co. 37
mobile services 222, 286
monopolies 21, 196, 221–2, 287
MRAs (mutual recognition agreements) 221
multi-cultural learning 158
multilateral agreements 4
multilingual employees 1
multinational companies 7, 9, 134, 187
mutual recognition principle 282–4, 290

Nadworny, M. J. 182
NAFTA (North American Free Trade Agreement) 260, 263
National Health Service 197
national treatment 214, 234, 236, 248
nationalisation 42
'natural persons,' *see* workers
natural sciences 75
Nelson, D. 182
Netherlands 5, 95–100
networks 19, 20, 29, 43, 50–2, 143–5, 157, 160, 165
New Corporation 37
New Economy 5, 8, 19, 31–3, *see also* Internet
niche markets 155, 159, 163
Nicolaidis, K. 42
Nilsson, J.-E. 154
Nissho Iwai 37
non-discrimination principles 211, 214, 217, 261, 287
non-macroeconomic variables 35
non-monetized and non-monetarized activities 59
normative isomorphism 178–9

Norsk Hydro's gasoline station network
    165
Nortel Networks 37
Norway 161, 167, 168, 170–1
Noyelle, T. J. and Dutka, A. 45
NRAs (national regulatory authorities)
    287
NTBs (non-tariff barriers) 215
Nusbaumer, J. 35
Nyström, H. 156

OECD (Organisation for Economic
    Cooperation and Development) 4,
    5, 34, 81, 257, 260
Ohno, Taiichi 186
OLI model 35, 154–9
on-line consultancy 32
output measuring 58, 70
outsourcing 30, 90, 176
    environmental services 224
    health care 225
ownership advantages 154–6

part-time work 73
participatory democracy 213
partnerships 45, 144
patents 175
performance 58–9, 64
    indicators 144
    market 276–8
    quality 69–71
personnel 34, 164–5, 171
    foreign construction workers 224
    GATS on temporary movement of
        244–5, 253, 260
    working abroad 216
petroleum companies 167
petroleum products 162
piece-rate system 181
PMI (Process Management International)
    187
Poland 167
police services 196
pollution 224
population 119
port facilities 243, 286
Post-Fordism 179
postal services 221–2, 232, 272
prestige 36

price
    convergence 275–6
    equilibrium 64–5, 70, 75–6
    reductions 5
prison services 225
privacy issues 228
private express courier firms 222
private patients 197–8
private security companies 196
privatisation 67, 196–7
    environmental services 224
    postal services 221–2
    public services 225–6
    transport 227, 228
proactive motivation 138, 157, 164
problematisation 177–8, 183–4
producers 209, 241
product cycle theory 97
product differentiation 42
production
    costs 61–2, 63, 136
    factor inputs 74
    pre-planning 182
    service 43
productivity 29–30, 31, 69–71, 71–2,
    274–5
professional associations 176, 178, 180,
    220
professional qualifications 199–200,
    204–5
professional services 220–1, 232, 255
professionalism 178
progressive liberalisation 217
property 35
prosumers 63, 68, 72
protectionism 7, 31, 76, 201
'prudential carve-out' 225
public morality 208, 223
public-private partnerships 246–7
public services 5, 21, 194, 195,
    246–8
Punta del Este Ministerial meeting
    (September 1987) 257

QRs (Quantitive Restrictions) 215
qualifications 217
quality
    assurance 36
    control 20, 34, 42, 143, 148, 186
    management 176

performance and 69–71
   standards 50
quotas 215, 218

R & D (research and development) 9,
   31, 63, 92
railways 184, 226, 228, 243, 286
rationality 66, 76
reactive motivation 38, 138, 157
real estate 33, 87, 92, 269, 272
reciprocity 211, 216
recreational services 232, 270, 272
recycling 63
refugees 218
regulation 113, 253
   developing countries 259
   different national 34
   domestic 217, 236, 241, 245–6
   EU 280
   fair access charges 287–8
   financial services 242–3
   freedom of establishment 281
   government services 198–201
   product 6
   reform 261–2
   telecommunications 223
religion 223
relocation 7, 29, 37
reputation 36, 42–3, 179
'request and offer' process 216
research 63
restaurant services 39–40, 51, 81, 87,
   89, 92, 94, 102–4, 226, 269, 272
retail services 153–4, 156, 157, 158,
   161–2, 167, 170, 171, 224, 270,
   272, 274
Ricupero, Rubens 211
risk management 59, 65–7, 157
Roberts, J. 35, 37, 42
Rover Car Group 185, 187
royalties 82, 159, 165
Rubalcaba-Bermejo, L. and Gago, D. 35

safeguard clauses 236, 263
Salmon, W. J. and Tordjman, A. 171
saturation hypothesis 137, 155, 164,
   169–70
Scandinavia 5, 163–71
Schindler (manufacturer) 63
science 75–6

Scientific Management 176, 179–85
Seagram Company 37
seaports 227
Seattle Ministerial WTO Conference
   (1999) 134, 237, 249, 252–3, 260
securities 242
security services 6, 246
self-employment 216
self-service 71–2
selling 63
service providers 244
services 2
   brands 47–50
   commercial 151–72
   customisation 42
   differentiation 35
   employment 278–9
   GATS impact on 219–8
   globalisation 4–6, 28–41, 79–85,
      100–4
   growth of trading in 86–90
   Haute-Garonne companies survey
      136–48
   insurability 64–7
   international transactions 44–7, 120
   mergers and acquisitions 269–73
   networks 50–2
   orientation perspective analysis 42
   as part of manufacturing process 62
   performance and quality 69–71
   production system and 63–4
   public 194, 195
   recent trends in world trade 114–19
   Seattle Ministerial WTO Conference
      237–8
   Single Market programme 265–88
   standardisation 51–2
   trade and investment link 45–6
   value 74–5
   WTO members incomplete sector
      commitment to 235
servicisation 84, 87
Shewhart, Walter 186
shop floor management 181, 183
Siemens 183
Silicon Valley 33
skilled workers 260
SMEs (small and medium-sized enterprises) 34, 81
   Haute-Garonne survey 136–48

Smith, Adam 58, 61, 74, 75
SMP (Single Market Programme) 113,
    126, 265–88
social policy objectives 197
social sciences 75, 76
social services 73, 195, 225–6, 232
sociology of translation 177, 178
software 259, 281
sovereignty 206, 213, 247
specialisation processes 29
specialised activities 145–6
'specific' liberalisation commitments
    234
sporting services 232
staff recruitment 171
staff training 146–7
stage approach 36–7
standardisation 35, 36, 50, 140, 148
state aid 284–5
Stibble Simont Monahan Duhot (law
    firm) 209
strategic planning 6, 145, 154–5, 157,
    176
subsidiaries 138, 140, 143, 144, 164,
    218, 242, 244–5
subsidies 196, 198, 219, 236
Sumimoto 37
supply and demand 64, 70, 72
supply chains 29
supply related services 35
Sweden 161

takeovers 4, 9, 19, 20, 29, 38
tariffs 9, 34, 214–15
tarriffs 38
taxation 254
Taylor, F. W. 176, 179–85
Taylor Society 183
technical assistance 146–7
technical engineering 135–6
technical services 255
technological
    developments 8, 61, 181
    revolution 32–3
    transfers 51, 156
telecommunications 6, 32, 39–40,
    141–2, 147, 193, 201
    accounting rates 222–3, 249
    developing countries 258, 259
    GATS 232, 239, 240–1, 254

interconnection rates 287
    intra-EU FDI inflows 269
    licensing 286
    mergers and acquisitions 272
    Single Market programme 266, 278
    United States 255
Telefónica S. A. 37
television 266, 283
terminology 179
tertiarisation 7, 9, 29–30, 50
third generation licences auction 222
Thomson Corporation 37
time-and-motion studies 180, 182, 184
time-space compression 2
TNCs (transnational companies) 2–3, 4,
    7, 28–9, 35, 37–8, 90, 91, 92
Toffler, Alvin 63–4
Tokyo Round (GATT) 68
total factor productivity 8, 9
Toulouse Chamber of Trade and Industry
    134
tour guides 226
tourism 10, 39–40, 44, 45, 48, 50, 97–8,
    100, 224, 226, 232, 255
Toyoda, Kiichiro 186
Toyota 186
trade 42, 44–7, 79–80, 82, 86–7
trade and repairs 269
trade associations 180
trade fairs 6, 10, 29, 33, 41, 50, 146–7
trade liberalisation, *see* liberalisation
trade unions 183, 184, 195, 225, 227
trademarks 47
trading routes 7, 275
training 19, 34, 144, 221, 261
transactions, international 42, 43, 44–7,
    120
translation, sociology of 177, 178,
    183–4
translation services 146–7
transparency 202–3, 215, 217, 225,
    236
transport 4, 10, 39–40, 82, 87, 89, 92,
    94, 99–100, 125, 146–7
    access to infrastructure 286
    balance of payments data 116–17
    costs 28, 38
    distance reduction 28
    GATS 226–8, 232, 240, 243
    GATS 2000 negotiations 243

insufficient WTO members
  commitment 235
internationalisation indicators 102–4
intra-EU FDI inflows 269
mergers and acquisitions 272
networks 8
Single Market programme 266, 275
state aids 284–5
travel services 48, 117, 125, 226, 232,
  255
Treadgold, A. D. 171
Treadgold, A. D. and Davies, R. L. 155
TRIPs (intellectual property-related
  issues) 257

UK (United Kingdom) 281
  exclusion of government services
    from GATS 197
  PMI 187
  retailers 170
  Scientific Management 183, 185
  service sector 5
  service trade and investment 95–100
UN International Civil Aviation
  Organisation 226
UN (United Nations) 4, 37, 206, 207,
  213
uncertainty 76
uncontrolled variation 186
unemployment 183
UNEP 207
UNESCO 207
United States
  compared with EU service globalisa-
    tion 90–3
  CSI statement on service trade negoti-
    ations 251–4
  Eastern Rate Case 184
  EU exports to 120, 122, 123, 125
  FDI 83–4
  foreign affiliates 81
  growth differentials between Europe
    and 31–2
  international trade 82
  management consultancy 175
  New Economy 31–2, 33
  Ordinance Department 184
  services 5, 9, 85, 95–100, 254–6
  Taylor's impact on capitalism in
    180

Universal Postal Union 221
universal service obligation 223
universities 178
Uruguay Round (1994) 68–9, 196, 199,
  215, 227, 232, 234–5, 243, 246,
  258, 262, *see also* GATS
utilisation systems 63, 64, 68
utilities 266, 269

value 5, 58, 70–1, 74–5
Vandermere, S. and Chadwick, M. 42,
  100
variation, manufacturing 186
Vernon, R. 97
vertical integration 274
visas 218
vulnerability control 66–7

waste management 63
wealth promotion 61
Welch, L. S. 157
wholesale distribution 153, 156, 158,
  161–2, 167, 170, 224, 270, 272,
  273, 274
Williams, D. E. 170
WIPO 207
women workers 73
work permits 218
workers 73, 218, 244, 253
World Bank 207, 225
world power companies 171
world trade 4, 231–2
WTO (World Trade Organisation) 68–9,
  79, 153, 193, 194, 195, 199, 201,
  207, 210, 211
  classification of services 232
  financial services 225
  gaps in commitments 235
  GATS 208–9
  ITU and 222
  legitimacy of 212–13
  non-discrimination 214
  preparations for GATS 2000 237
  Seattle Ministerial Conference 134,
    237, 249, 252–3, 254, 260
  services negotiations 233, 234
  standard and specific obligations
    233–4
  transfer of natural persons 253, *see
    also* GATS; GATT